Researching race and racism

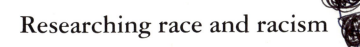

Race and racism have become huge areas of study in the social sciences over the past two decades. However, whilst this has been reflected in the growing body of theoretical and empirically based work, surprisingly little has been published exploring the methodological and practical issues involved in researching race. In *Researching Race and Racism* Martin Bulmer and John Solomos have brought together contributions from some of the leading researchers in the field, using the benefit of their experience to explore the practical and ethical issues involved in doing research in this sometimes controversial, often heavily politicised, field. This book will provide students and researchers – both new to the field and experienced alike – with an invaluable tool to help them find their way.

Martin Bulmer is Professor of Sociology at the University of Surrey and **John Solomos** is Professor of Sociology at City University, London.

Researching race and racism

Edited and introduced by
Martin Bulmer and
John Solomos

Routledge
Taylor & Francis Group

LONDON AND NEW YORK

First published 2004
by Routledge
11 New Fetter Lane, London EC4P 4EE

Simultaneously published in the USA and Canada
by Routledge
29 West 35th Street, New York, NY 10001

Routledge is an imprint of the Taylor & Francis Group

Typeset in Garamond by Taylor & Francis Books Ltd
Printed and bound in Great Britain by TJ International Ltd,
Padstow, Cornwall

British Library Cataloguing in Publication Data
A catalogue record for this book is available from the British Library

Library of Congress Cataloging in Publication Data
A catalog record for this book has been requested

ISBN 0–415–30089–4 (hbk)
ISBN 0–415–30090–8 (pbk)

Contents

Contributors

Claire Alexander is Lecturer in Sociology at the London School of Economics. Her research interests are in the area of race, masculinity and youth identities. She is author of *The Art of Being Black* (Oxford University Press 1996), *The Asian Gang* (Berg 2000) and co-editor (with Caroline Knowles) of *Race, Identity and Difference: Dialogues across Race and Gender* (Palgrave Macmillan, forthcoming).

Les Back is Professor of Sociology at Goldsmiths College, London. His main interests are the sociology of urban life, youth, racism and right-wing extremism, music and popular culture, and the sociology of sport. His recent books include *Theories of Race and Racism* (co-edited with John Solomos, Routledge 2000), *Out of Whiteness: Color, Politics, and Culture* (with Vron Ware, University of Chicago Press 2002) and *The Changing Face of Football: Racism and Multiculture in the English Game* (with Tim Crabbe and John Solomos, Berg 2001).

Chetan Bhatt is Reader in the Department of Sociology, Goldsmiths College, London. He is author of *Hindu Nationalism: Origins, Ideologies and Modern Myths* (Berg 2001) and *Liberation and Purity: Race, New Religious Movements and the Ethics of Postmodernity* (UCL/Taylor & Francis 1997), and various articles on nationalism, racism, ethnicity and social theory.

Sophie Body-Gendrot is Professor of Political Science and American Studies at the Université Paris IV and a CNRS researcher. Her research focuses on comparative public policy, urban unrest, ethnic and racial issues and citizen participation. Among her recent books in English are *The Urban Moment* (co-edited with R. Beauregard, Sage 1999), *The Social Control of Cities? A Comparative Perspective* (Blackwell 2000), *Minorities in European Cities* (co-edited with M. Martiniello, Macmillan 2000) and *Social Capital and Social Citizenship* (co-edited with M. Gittell, Lexington 2003). Her current research focuses on the impact of September 11th on New York and Paris, and on new forms of violence and discrimination.

Mitchell Duneier is Professor of Sociology at Princeton University and the Graduate Center, City University of New York. He is the author of

Sidewalk, (Farrar, Straus and Groux, 1999) winner of the 2000 C. Wright Mills Award, and *Slim's Table*, (University of Chicago Press, 1992) winner of the American Sociological Association's 1994 Distinguished Publication Award. He was previously Professor of Sociology at the University of Wisconsin-Madison and the University of California, Santa Barbara.

Philomena Essed is Senior Researcher at the University of Amsterdam, Amsterdam Institute for Global Issues and Development Studies, and Visiting Professor at the University of California, Irvine, Women's Studies and African American Studies. She also serves as an adviser to NGOs, to governmental bodies and to international organizations on issues concerning gender, ethnicity, racism and leadership development. She is author of the monographs *Everyday Racism* (Hunter House 1990), *Understanding Everyday Racism* (Sage Publication 1991) and *Diversity: Gender, Color and Culture* (University of Massachusetts Press 1996), and is co-editor of *Race Critical Theories* (Blackwell 2001), *Refugees and the Transformation of Societies* (Berghan Books 2004) and *A Companion to Gender Studies* (2004)

Joe R. Feagin is currently Graduate Professor of Sociology at the University of Florida. His research interests concern the development and structure of racial and gender prejudice, stereotyping and discrimination. Among his forty-five books in this and related areas are *The First R: How Children Learn Race and Racism*, with Debra Van Ausdale (Rowman & Littlefield 2001), *Double Burden: Black Women and Everyday Racism*, with Yanick St Jean (M.E. Sharpe 1998), *Racial and Ethnic Relations*, with Clairece Feagin (seventh edn, Prentice-Hall 2003), *Racist America* (Routledge 2000), *White Racism*, with Hernán Vera and Pinar Batur (Routledge 2001) and *The Many Costs of Racism* (Rowman & Littlefield 2003). His books have won numerous national and professional association prizes, including a nomination for the Pulitzer Prize. He is also author of more than 160 articles on racial, gender and urban issues. He was the 1999–2000 President of the American Sociological Association.

Ruth Frankenberg is Professor of American Studies at the University of California, Davis. She has researched aspects of whiteness and racial identities, and has published widely in this area, including *White Women, Race Matters: The Social Construction of Whiteness* (Routledge 1993). Her most recent book, *Living Spirit, Living Practice: Poetics, Politics, Epistemology*, will be published in 2004 by Duke University Press.

Michèle Lamont recently joined the Sociology Department of Harvard University after serving on the faculty of Princeton University for the past 15 years. She is the author of *The Dignity of Working Men: Morality and the Boundaries of Race, Class, and Immigration*, which won the 2000 C. Wright Mills Prize and the 2000 Mattei Dogan Award for the Best Comparative Book. She has published broadly in the fields of cultural sociology, inequality, race and immigration, sociological theory and the sociology of knowledge. She is completing a book on definitions of excellence used by funding panels in the social sciences and the humanities. She is co-director of the research programme on 'Successful Societies' of the Canadian Institute for Advanced Studies. In this context, she will be working on equality and equalization, and in particular on anti-racist strategies used by subjugated groups, including African Americans.

Ann Phoenix is Professor of Social and Developmental Psychology at the Open University. Her research interests centre on social identities and the ways in which psychological experiences and social processes are inextricably interlinked. Her research includes work on gendered, racialized social class and national identities, as well as on motherhood. Her current funded research is on young people and the identities associated with consumption. Her publications include: *Young Mothers?* (Polity Press 1991), *Black, White or Mixed Race? Race and Racism in the Lives of Young People of Mixed Parentage* (with Barbara Tizard, Routledge 2001) and *Young Masculinities: Understanding Boys in Contemporary Society* (with Stephen Frosh and Rob Pattman, Palgrave 2002).

Stephen Small is Associate Professor in the Department of African American Studies at the University of California, Berkeley. He previously taught at the University of Massachusetts, Amherst and in the University of Leicester, England. His most recent book is *Representations of Slavery. Race and Ideology in Southern Plantation Museums* (co-written with Jennifer Eichstedt), published by Smithsonian Institution Press in 2002. He does work on people of mixed racial origins in the USA, the Caribbean and England, and on museum exhibits on slavery.

Miri Song is Senior Lecturer in Sociology at the University of Kent. She is the author of *Helping Out: Children's Labor in Ethnic Businesses* (Temple University Press 1999) and *Choosing Ethnic Identity* (Polity 2003). Her research interests include ethnic identity, racisms, racial hierarchy immigration and the 'second generation', 'mixed race', family economy and intercountry adoption. She is currently researching the 'ethnic options' of 'mixed race' people in Britain

Hernán Vera was born and grew up in Santiago, Chile, where he practised law until, at the age of 31, he came to the USA to teach political institutions of Latin America at the University of Notre Dame. In 1974 he obtained a Ph.D. in Sociology from the University of Kansas and joined the faculty at the University of Florida where he is now Professor of Sociology. He has also taught at the State University of Utrecht, in the Netherlands, and at the Universidad de Chile, in Santiago. He is author of six dozen articles and seven books, among which are *Screen Saviors: Hollywood Fictions of Whiteness* (with Andrew Gordon, Lanham ; Oxford : Rowman & Littlefield Publishers, 2003), *White Racism: The Basics* and

Liberation Sociology (both with Joe R. Feagin, Routledge 2001), and *The Agony of Education: Black Students at Predominantly White Universities* (with Joe Feagin and Nikitah Imani, Routledge 1996). He teaches sociology of knowledge, sociological theory and courses in race relations. His current projects are the creation of an interdisciplinary minor in social justice in his college, and a book on the theory and methods to study the good life.

Michel Wieviorka is Professor at the Ecole des Hautes Etudes en Sciences Sociales, and director of Centre d'Analyse et d'Intervention Sociologiques. His last book was *La Difference* (Balland 2001). He is currently researching violence, on the one hand, and contemporary anti-Semitism, on the other. He is a member of the Executive Committee of the International Sociological Association.

Alford A. Young, Jr is Associate Professor in the Department of Sociology and the Center for Afro-American and African Studies at the University of Michigan. He is the author of *The Minds of Marginalized Black Men: Making Sense of Mobility, Opportunity, and Future Life Chances* (Princeton University Press 2004). He divides his time between writing about the experiences and world views of urban-based, low-income African American men; how Americans of various class levels think about and try to engage socio-economic mobility; and how African American scholars define the social utility of their research and their political and intellectual objectives as members of the academy.

Acknowledgements

One aspect of editing volumes such as this one is that it inevitably involves the accumulation of numerous debts along the way. The most important acknowledgement is to all the authors of the papers that make up this volume, for keeping to their deadlines and making this book possible, and for writing their chapters in keeping with the objectives of the volume as a whole. We hope that, now that they see the final product as a whole, they share our belief that the effort involved in putting this volume together has been worthwhile. We are also grateful to Mari Shullaw and James McNally, who initially took on this project at Routledge and helped to get it going. In the end it has come to fruition under the guidance of our new editors Gerhard Boomgaarden and Lizzie Catford, and we are equally grateful to them for still believing in the project. Along the way we have also benefited from the advice and suggestions of a number of colleagues: Claire Alexander, Gargi Bhattacharyya, Clive Harris, Michael Keith, Karim Murji, Liza Schuster and Howard Winant. Jointly editing the journal *Ethnic and Racial Studies* brings us into contact with a wide range of scholars working in this field, and we are indebted to them in many different ways. It is for our readers of course to judge how successful we have been in meeting our main objectives and in stimulating more reflection and debate about the methodological aspects of researching race and racism. We do hope, however, that in this period of innovation and change in research agendas in this field, that the publication of *Researching Race and Racism* will encourage more self-reflection and debate.

Martin Bulmer
University of Surrey
John Solomos
City University, London

Introduction

Researching race and racism

Martin Bulmer and John Solomos

Race and racism have become foci of interest in the social sciences. In the past two decades there has been a noticeable expansion in scholarship and research about race and racism in contemporary societies. This has been reflected in a growing body of theoretical and empirically based work on various facets of race and racism in both contemporary societies and historical periods. Although much of this research has historically been located within the discipline of sociology, a notable feature of recent trends has been the growth of research in disciplines such as anthropology, politics, geography, media and cultural studies, law and the humanities (Bulmer and Solomos 1999b; Goldberg and Solomos 2002). In addition to this rapid transformation of scholarly research we have seen a notable growth in the teaching of courses about race relations, racism and ethnicity and nationalism at both undergraduate and postgraduate levels. This has created a demand for student-focused texts on questions about race and racism, and this demand has led to a growing body of scholarship and research-based monographs on both historical and contemporary patterns of racism and ethnic relations. What is also clear, however, is that there is still a dearth of texts that explore the methodological aspects raised by research in this field. This absence has only partly been remedied by the appearance of a number of studies in recent years that focus on this dimension (Stanfield 1993; Twine and Warren 2000; Ratcliffe 2001; Gunaratnam 2003). In this environment there has been a relative dearth of reflection and debate on the range of methodological problems and dilemmas that confront those engaged in research in relation to the history and contemporary forms of racism and racial relations.

It is with this situation in mind that we set about bringing together a number of both established and up-and-coming scholars who have carried out research in this field to reflect on various aspects of the methodologies they have used and the dilemmas they have faced in developing their research. *Researching Race and Racism* is the outcome of this endeavour and is held together by a series of narratives based on researcher's everyday experiences and a smaller number of papers that reflect on broader methodological and research dilemmas. We asked all the authors we invited to contribute to this volume to reflect specifically on their own experiences in embarking on particular research projects, and in this sense, the main concern that we had in putting this collection together was to produce a volume that was both reflective of actual research situations and suggestive of the kinds of issues that researchers in this broad field are likely to confront at an everyday level.

What is striking in looking at the range of arguments that run through this volume as a whole is that there is a wealth of experience from which both other scholars and students can learn a great deal. The various chapters cover a range of empirical questions, national and local situations, ethnic and racial groups, and policy arenas. In doing so they by no means agree on either the questions that should shape research or the methodologies to be used. But they do suggest that, alongside the on-going theoretical debates about the nature of race and racism, we have much to learn by exploring in greater detail the methodological dimensions of research in this field. Before moving on to the substantive arguments to be found in the fourteen chapters that follow, we want to use the opportunity offered us in writing this Introduction, to reflect on some of the core themes and arguments about methodological aspects of research in this field, in order to situate this volume in relation to current debates in race and ethnic studies.

The contributors to this volume are themselves from a variety of racial and ethnic backgrounds. We mention this because two trends are discernible in the academic study of race and ethnicity in Western Europe and North America. On the one hand, a more racially and ethnically diverse group of scholars has become involved in the field, in marked contrast to the situation a generation ago. Although black sociologists were earlier prominent – for example W.E.B. Du Bois, Charles S. Johnson, Franklin Frazier and Ralph Bunche in the USA, at a later period W. Arthur Lewis, M.G. Smith and Stuart Hall in the UK – the great majority of early scholars conducting social science research about race and racism were white. This is no longer the case, and this diversity is reflected in this collection, as well as being directly addressed in Al Young Jr's chapter. On the other hand, the base from which race and ethnicity are studied has broadened, both in terms of discipline and department. The range of disciplines interested in these issues is no longer confined to sociology and anthropology, and in the USA in particular the range of departments from which the subject is pursued is much greater than formerly.

Conceptual and methodological dilemmas

There is by now a relatively long history of research in sociology and other disciplines about both what has come to be called race relations, and more specifically on racial discrimination, racism and forms of racial thinking of one kind or another. If we start from the early work of W.E.B. Du Bois, Robert Park and other early pioneers in the USA, we can trace the history of research on aspects of race and racism back to the beginning of the twentieth century. Throughout this history, however, there has been intense debate about what the focus of such research should be and on the appropriateness of conceptual and methodological tools for analysing the changing and evolving patterns of race and ethnic relations in contemporary societies.

Researching race and racism, as any other topic, forces all researchers, implicitly or explicitly, to pose questions about the nature of the reality that is being examined. That is to say, no matter how much sociologists or other social researchers may disagree with each other about the nature of their craft and its theoretical foundations, there are fundamental questions that they must agree are worth asking before there can be any dialogue concerning concrete sociological work. In the case of research on race and racism it has proven particularly difficult to agree on what the phenomenon to be studied is and on the boundaries of this sub-field in relation to other social phenomena. From the earliest stages of scholarly research in sociology about race, there has been some tension about what the focus should be. Should the core concern be to study the relations between racial and ethnic groups in specific social environments? Or should the focus be on the impact of processes of discrimination and exclusion, and their impact on minority communities?

More generally, it has been an area of research that has been closely linked to wider policy and political debates in societies such as the USA and UK among others. It is interesting to note in this regard that W.E.B. Du Bois, a pioneer in early empirical research on race and ethnicity in the USA, acknowledged that the impetus for the study *The Philadelphia Negro* was the need for the white decision-makers of the city to have some data on the significant and largely corrupt Seventh Ward in order to plan a campaign of reforms (Du Bois 1996 [1899]; see also Bulmer 1991 and Katz and Sugrue 1998). Such linkages to everyday political and policy considerations have been an important feature of race research over the past century and more. If anything the period of expansion in the field has emphasised the inherently politicised and often controversial nature of research on race and racism.

Precisely because of the historical and contemporary forms of the subject matter of research on race and racism, it has proven notoriously difficult to pin down the fundamental questions that researchers should be asking. Part of the reason for this lies in the diverse range of theoretical perspectives and methodologies that have emerged over the past two decades or so. There has been a proliferation of theoretical and empirically focused accounts of the history and contemporary realities of race and racism, and this very expansion of research has meant that little attention has been given to the need to develop some agreement about the broad parameters of the questions on which research should be focused. As a consequence we have seen the emergence of agendas that often speak to particular academic and policy communities and not to others, and which encourage little dialogue about the methodologies to be used in developing research in this field.

While there has been an explosion of writings on theoretical debates there has been surprisingly little research-based discussion of the methodological and practical issues involved in carrying out particular projects. To some extent this is surprising, given the controversial and heavily politicised nature of this research over recent times. It is also the case, however, as Les Back emphasises in his contribution to this volume, that many researchers in this field have engaged in little critical self-reflection about what work in this field is supposed to achieve and the practical and methodological dilemmas that they have confronted in developing their projects and in carrying them out in practice.

Despite the relative paucity of discussion of the methodological aspects of research on race and racism, we have seen important developments in research agendas. Ever since the 1960s, there has been intense debate about what the focus of such research should be. These debates came to the fore in the USA during the 1960s, in the aftermath of the intellectual and political turmoil of the civil rights movement and Black Power. In the period since the 1980s, however, there has been an on-going debate about the shifting boundaries of research in this field and on the balance between theoretical reflection and empirical research (Centre for Contemporary Cultural Studies 1982; Banton 1973, 1976 and 1991; Ballard 1992).

A recurring area of concern since the 1960s has been the increasingly politicised nature of research on race and racism. Social scientists of race and racism in the USA during the 1960s found that the norms of pure disinterested scientific investigation were not necessarily adequate. The subjects had changed from passive objects to active critics of the research process. Increasingly, the social scientist began to look in the 1960s like another agent of the power structure, like the policeman, teacher, welfare worker: an outsider who entered ghettoes and barrios to advance personal and institutional goals that were determined outside the community of study. This led to calls for a new dialogue between social scientists and the racially oppressed. Accordingly, many researchers set themselves the goal of sympathetically understanding why blacks, as a collectivity, are located where they are today in relationship to whites – in terms of power, wealth, status and development.

The experience of research during the period since the 1960s has brought to the fore questions about the funding of research on race and racism, who does the funding: who carries out the research: what the key findings are; who is responsible for the dissemination of findings; and how they are used in public policy debates and in the mass media. A particular area of concern from the 1960s onwards, in both the USA and the UK to take just two examples, related to the depiction of blacks in terms of 'social problems' of deviancy and marginality. This was seen as partly the result of government policy agendas and the availability of research funding. Money was available to study racial and ethnic minorities as social problems or culturally deprived communities, but not as cultures with their own normative values, behavioural patterns and institutions.

An important facet of work in this field is that in practice researchers have been pulled in a variety of directions, by both political and academic pressures. Given the politicised nature of this field, this is not surprising, but the consequences for research and scholarship have been negative. This is an argument that others working in this area have recognised for some time. Take for example John Rex, one of the leading British researchers in race and ethnic relations for the past five decades. Writing in 1979, and drawing on his long experience, he argued perceptively that anyone embarking on research in race relations was pulled in a number of alternative directions:

> First, there was the demand that research should be put to the service of policy, as though there was a consensus about ends, and the only questions which need to be researched were about means;
>
> Second, there was the pull for a retreat into academic theorising, in which the research questions asked are not seen as necessarily related to the issues that made race relations a public issue;
>
> Third, there was the option of rejecting academic research in this field as a whole, in favour of political activism or action oriented work.

Rex himself rejected all of these options, and called for an approach to race relations research that was both theoretically informed and politically relevant, but essentially concerned with a longer-term structural view of race relations. What Rex called 'a perspective on race relations based on a serious political sociology' (Rex 1979a: 17).

In hindsight, Rex's typology of different approaches captured some of the recurrent problems that social researchers working in this field have had to come to terms with. It helps to make clear why they have found it hard to (1) establish a rounded research agenda that included all facets of race and racism in British society and (2) have been pulled in different directions by contrasting political and academic pressures.

In the years after Rex published his typology, there have been tremendous changes in both the theoretical and the empirical focus of much of the literature on race and racism. There has been a pronounced broadening of research paradigms and a plethora of theoretical perspectives have come to the fore, particularly from a range of radical schools of thought. A proliferation of new theoretical texts, journals and edited collections has explored various aspects of both race and ethnicity, and provided a basis for new areas of scholarship to develop, as with issues such as 'new ethnicities' and 'whiteness' (Bulmer and Solomos 1999a and 1999b; Bhattacharyya *et al.* 2002; Goldberg and Solomos 2002). But one of the ironies of recent trends in the analysis of racism is that we have seen a move away from research on social action and on institutions and a fixation with theoretical abstraction and textual and cultural analysis. Whatever the merits of some of the recent theoretical debates, there have been few sustained attempts to link them to research on institutions and processes of social change. In this environment there has been, if anything, a retreat by researchers into abstracted theoretical debates and discourses.

A different trend is apparent in some quarters in US sociology, where race and ethnicity are approached in terms of quantitative research that can create an obstacle between researcher and audience through the technical nature and complexity of the analyses being undertaken. Such research addresses key theoretical issues, but not in a way that is immediately accessible. Examples include comparative analysis of the position of black and white immigrants in the USA (Lieberson 1980) and Lieberson's methodological reflections (1985) upon the complexity of causal analysis in this area; the use of census data to throw light on US experience (e.g. Lieberson and Waters 1988); the study of racialisation and racism in US politics (cf. Sears *et al*. 2000); and the study of the immigrant second generation (Portes and Rumbaut 2001). Such studies are testimony to the continuing liveliness of the fields of racial and ethnic studies, but also to barriers that methodology can sometimes erect in communicating the results of sociological research. They also reflect different technical standards between US and some parts of European social science (cf. Goldthorpe 2000).

The consequences of these shifts have still to be thought through and digested. At the beginning of the twenty-first century, it is important to provide a basis for more dialogue between these often important scholarly debates and the social actors who are part of the subject matter of research. This is a theme that is discussed in a number of the contributions to this volume, and this seems to highlight that the question of the relevance of research on race and racism remains a live issue in current research agendas.

Political and ideological context

A part of the context for the transformation of research agendas that we have seen in recent years has been the growing evidence of diversity in the experiences of ethnic minority and immigrant groups. The differentiation in economic position, gender, migration history, political participation and perceptions of social citizenship are significant among minority ethnic groups, and they are becoming increasingly evident.

Differentiation of socio-economic and political position has coincided with a rise in what has been called 'identity politics'. Such developments have been reflected in the emergence of new areas of scholarly debate and research in relation to the study of race and racism, particularly focusing on the cultural politics of difference or the politics of recognition, carrying with it calls for a new pluralism, radical democracy and empowerment.

Debates about the ontological status of race, the object of investigation and the agenda for research in this field are partly the result of these transformations. It is perhaps because analytical debates necessarily involve a growing degree of uncertainty about what the focus of research should be that no one theoretical perspective is dominant at the present time. Banton may well be right in his contention that different theoretical paradigms may be able to contribute their own distinctive accounts of the processes that involve the attribution of specific meanings to racial situations (Banton 1991). However, the point that Banton misses is that the various paradigms adopted within this area of research contain an implicit or explicit political position *vis-à-vis* the politics of knowledge production (Back and Solomos 1993; Back *et al.* 2001). In this case, it is not a matter of choosing appropriate analytical tools from some diverse theoretical bag, but rather it is necessary to situate these paradigms in relation to each other and political debates over what could or should be the focus of analysis.

Stuart Hall's work on new ethnicities and the scholarly debate it has helped to stimulate over the past decade and more is a case in point. Hall's interventions in this context started from the need to recognise the complex identities that all individuals in modern societies occupy. His work on the construction of 'new ethnicities' articulates a view of contemporary racial and ethnic relations as composed of multiple identities, complexly constructed through time and place, often resulting in the emergence of new forms of identity in complex urban environments (Hall 1991). He has been highly critical of this way of thinking of cultural identity, arguing instead for a definition that recognises that there are critical points of deep and significant difference that constitute 'what we really are'. Hall argues that the ruptures and discontinuities in shaping racial and ethnic identities must be acknowledged, since they are not something that already exists, transcending place, time and history. Rather, cultural and ethnic identities come from somewhere, have histories, and they undergo transformation. Far from being fixed in some essentialist past, they are subject to the continuous play of history, culture and power. Far from being grounded in a mere 'recovery' of the past, which is waiting to be found, and which, when found, will secure our sense of ourselves into eternity, identities are the names we give to the different ways we are positioned by, and opposition ourselves within, the narratives of the past.

It is partly on the basis of these interventions that we have seen in recent years a refocusing of research on race and racism to address questions about culture and identity in a fuller manner. The notion of a sovereign subject who possesses unparalleled powers of clairvoyance affording direct apprehension of internal and external reality has been supplanted by a conception of the self as an unstable constellation of unconscious desires, fears, phobias and conflicting linguistic, social and political forces. From this perspective, questions about cultural production and change must be integrated within a contemporary conceptualisation of racism. What seems to characterise the contemporary period is, on the one hand, a complex spectrum of racisms, and, on the other, the fragmentation of the definition of blackness as a political identity in favour of a resurgence of ethnic, cultural and religious differentiation. At the same time, and perhaps paradoxically, new cultures and ethnicities are emerging in the context of dialogue and producing a kaleidoscope of cultural syncretisms. There may well be contradictory trends emerging, but neither an emphasis on race relations nor on racism can adequately deal with the contemporary situation.

The historical and conceptual questions outlined above raise a number of questions about the nature of research on race and racism in the contemporary environment. The political struggles that underscored the debates are constantly shifting and raise important dilemmas that have to be faced by researchers working in this field. We would suggest, then, that the following are among those basic questions: What is the nature of race and racism in contemporary societies? How do we research race and racism within specific societies or institutions?

The question of how to conceptualise racism is not purely an academic matter, it is connected with a wider political culture in any given historical conjuncture. Contemporary racisms have evolved and adapted to new circumstances. The crucial property of these elaborations is that we have seen in the past two decades or so a whole range of new debates emerge about the nature of racism as well as the forms of identity that racist movements and ideologies espouse. As the papers by Wieviorka and by Vera and Feagin in this collection make clear, the political articulation of racism today takes a variety of forms that cannot be reduced to the kinds of ideologies that were perhaps dominant 50–100 years ago. For example, the new racisms within the past two decades are coded within a cultural logic. As a result, the champions of these racisms can claim that they are protecting their way of life and that the issue of colour or phenotype is irrelevant. In this context, unitary or simplistic definitions of racism become hard to sustain. However, it seems clear that contemporary racisms share some central features. They attempt to fix human social groups in terms of natural properties of belonging within particular political and geographical contexts. The assertion that racialised subjects do not belong within – say British society – is then associated with social and cultural characteristics designated to them within the logic of particular racisms.

It follows from the above argument that racist discourses need to be contextualised against the background of the wider social relations and political cultures that shape them and allow them to develop. This means that racisms need to be situated within specific social and cultural environments. The effect of a particular racist discourse needs to be placed in the conditions surrounding the moment of its enunciation. This means irrevocably crossing the analysis of racism with other social relations surrounding gender and sexuality or the culture of institutional politics. In this context, the meanings of race and racism need to be located within particular fields of discourse and articulated to the social relations found within that context. It is then necessary to see what kinds of racialised identities are being formed within these contexts. With regard to the ontological status of these classifications, we view them as political constructions of identity that need to be situated within specific social and discursive contexts. We in no way accept that these identifications relate to natural communities, or that one notion is more politically legitimate than others. Rather, they constitute moments where community and identity is defined: manifestations of racial and ethnic closure. We are suggesting a position that builds into any analysis a rigorous scrutiny of racialised definitions, whether they are operated by the local state or the range of political mobilisations occurring around racial and ethnic identities within black communities.

This approach seeks to decipher the meanings of racialised identities without attempting to prioritise one classification as more legitimate than another. We are suggesting a model for conceptualising racisms that is sensitive to the diversity of racist discourse and to the often messy manifestations of racist ideas in specific institutional and social environments. As yet, the theoretical work on racism has produced accounts of racism that derive contemporary forms of racism from public political discourse. This evidence is then used to generalise about broader political and ideological trends.

We are suggesting that there is a need to situate the meanings attached to ideas about race within particular social relations, although it is also the case that, from a sociological perspective, we need to develop more general accounts of their wider significance. If racism is to be understood in its totality it cannot be reduced to class relations, but neither can it be seen as completely autonomous from wider social relations such as gender and sexuality.

Developing new research agendas

During the past decade and more, however, it is fair to say that we have seen a more critical awareness of the ethical and methodological dilemmas that have to be addressed by researchers working in this field. Alongside these trends, however, it is also evident that there has been a growing preoccupation among many scholars with the need to develop ever more sophisticated theorisations of key concepts and ideas. Taking their cue from wider postmodernist and poststructuralist discourses in the social sciences, scholars of race and racism have followed the 'postmodern turn' and moved in the direction of focusing their scholarly interests on (1) theoretical exegesis and debate about the conceptual status of race as a notion in the social and human sciences and (2) the analysis of ideas about race and cultural practices. Such research has been influential in a number of particular fields of study, including cultural and literary theory, social theory and media studies. It has also helped to open the boundaries of race and ethnic studies as a field of scholarly research and teaching.

This re-envisioning of research agendas has in some respects broadened the agendas of researchers studying various facets of race and racism in both contemporary societies and from a historical perspective. What also seems evident, however, is that it has encouraged a type of research agenda that seems overtly textual and theory-driven in focus. If anything, we have seen a retreat from research that is focused on empirical research methods and even a denigration of the role of ethnographic and fieldwork styles of research. The conflation of the world and text is particularly evident when the theme of racism is considered. Although it is clear that in contemporary societies there are a variety of forms of racism and racist expression, it is important that research addresses the impact of racism in real-life situations. Racial harassment, direct/indirect discrimination, racist violence and victimisation are not fictions or figurations that admit of the free play of signification. The victim's account of these experiences is not simply an arbitrary imposition of a purely fictive meaning on an otherwise meaningless reality. A victim's knowledge of the event may not be exhaustive; indeed, the victim may be oblivious to the fact of premeditation, may not comprehend the motive for the assault, may not know the identity of the assailant. But it would be premature to conclude from the incompleteness of the victim's account that all other accounts are equally valid or that there are no objective grounds on which to distinguish between truth and falsity in divergent interpretations. There is a modicum of permanence within the fluidity of the life-world: traditions, practices, relationships, institutions and structures persist and can have profound consequences for individual life prospects, constraining opportunities for growth and development, resisting reconstitution, frustrating efforts towards direction and control.

It is precisely around the need for a more detailed analysis of the life-world of contemporary racisms that we need to think about research agendas that allow us to explore social relations and institutions more deeply. The various accounts of research experiences collected together in this volume provide important insights into the ways in which the emergent research agendas on race and racism need to be rethought in the context of the current political and social environment.

Themes and arguments

In thinking about putting this edited collection together, we wanted to allow space for a wide range of theoretical perspectives and methodologies. In addition, we asked contributors to reflect on their actual experience of carrying out research on issues concerned with race and racism, and on the conceptual dilemmas and limitations of existing theoretical perspectives. Most of the chapters have an empirical flavour about them, but we have also consciously sought to give some space for papers that take on board current conceptual and epistemological concerns. We have hopefully been successful in both of these objectives and certainly the substantive papers as a whole provide a good starting point for scholars and students who want to engage with the underlying methodological and conceptual dilemmas involved in carrying out research on various facets of race, racism and ethnic relations in contemporary societies. In order to place the main arguments within a broader intellectual and theoretical framework, we want to move on now to touch upon the main arguments that are contained in each of the chapters and the themes that tie them together.

In order to overcome the limitations of current debates, we have sought in this volume to bring together contributions that:

- reflect the experience of social researchers with first-hand knowledge in this complex area;
- address questions about various aspects of carrying out research on race and racism;
- reflect on the political and ethical dilemmas that confront researchers;
- look forward to the emergence of new research agendas in the coming period.

All the papers in this collection intentionally draw on the experiences of both established as well as up-and-coming scholars and researchers. In particular, they seek to give voice to the often messy and complex sets of issues that confront researchers in the field rather than remain at a general abstract analytical level.

We begin the book through Chetan Bhatt's masterful overview of recent debates about race thinking and 'raciology' within the social sciences. Bhatt's reflective piece highlights the need to question some of the core assumptions about how the notions of race and racism are utilised and refor-mulated in contemporary academic discourses. More importantly, he suggests that, in a number of ways, current preoccupations with identity and hybridity in research on race and ethnicity may lead research in direc-tions that close up important avenues of scholarship, rather than provide a basis for critical analysis to emerge and develop in fruitful directions. He places particular emphasis on the limitations of current theoretical preoccu-pations and fashions, and in doing so, he brings to the fore the need to analyse the historically specific and often contingent processes that shape what he calls 'race thinking' in contemporary societies.

The conceptual and ethical dilemmas raised by Bhatt provide a starting point for engaging with some of the more empirically focused concerns of most of the chapters that follow. A recurring theme in a number of these chapters is the need to explore the shifting boundaries of race and ethnicity in contemporary societies. A case in point is the exploration in Ann Phoenix's chapter of the complex ways in which young people talk about issues of race and identity in their everyday environments. Phoenix draws on recent scholarship about the role of language in the construction of the meanings attached to race. In doing so, she focuses specifically on recent research concerned with the ways in which young people from a range of ethnic groups talk about their experiences of race and racism in their everyday lives. Taking her cue from interviews carried out with young

Londoners aged 14–18, Phoenix provides an analysis that is focused both on the shifting terms of discourse as used by the young people themselves and the issue of whether the arguments they articulate can be made sense of by reference to psychoanalytic concepts and methods. In addition, she uses this discussion to reflect more broadly on the linkages between qualitative and quantitative approaches to research on race and racism.

Phoenix's account is followed by two chapters that reflect the challenges faced in different national and cultural environments when the phenomenon of racism. Michel Wieviorka's account draws on his experiences during the late 1980s and early 1990s of researching the emergence of political forms of racism and ethno-nationalism in France. Wieviorka situates his theoretical concerns within the framework of *sociological intervention* articulated in the work of Alain Touraine; and he focuses much of his discussion on the ways in which he sought to utilise this approach as a tool in the empirical analysis of racism in France. He suggests that researchers need to avoid the easy use of labels in carrying out research on the everyday forms of mobilisation and organisation that utilise ideas about race and difference; and he highlights in particular the need to explore the class and cultural dynamics that lie at the heart of the social transformations that racist social movements seek to exploit and manipulate for their particular objectives. This line of argument links up to the research described in the chapter by Hernán Vera and Joe R. Feagin, which is centered on the study of white racism in the USA. Highlighting the relative absence of methodological discussion on the problems faced in carrying out research on racist events, Vera and Feagin suggest that there is a need for a more systematic understanding of what actually happens in racist events and how actors perceive them. Taken together, these two chapters suggest that, in studying racism, we need to develop appropriate tools to tell us something both about underlying social processes and about the values of the individuals that are drawn into forms of racist mobilisation and action.

The following chapter by Stephen Small draws us in a somewhat different direction. Small uses his own experiences of researching 'mixed race' as a social and historical category in the USA to reflect on the problems raised by the use of historical and archival sources. The use of such sources as essential tools in this research has become more widespread in recent years, although; as Small argues, there is often little reflection on the problems of using archival sources to reflect on sociological questions and issues. Perhaps what is most challenging about Small's meticulous discussion of the use of archives in research on 'mixed race' is the need to be aware of the danger of merely reading the archives through the language and the concepts of previous generations of scholars, without asking questions about the theoretical and historical limitations of how this issue has been conceptualised.

Mitchell Duneier's chapter turns our attention to the ethical and practical dilemmas of carrying out longer-term ethnographic work in this field. Duneier focuses on the research he carried out in writing his classic study of

New York street vendors, *Sidewalk*. He discusses in an evocative manner his own feelings of unease in embarking on the study and the ways in which issues of race, class and education shaped key facets of his relationship with the street vendors who became central to his research. A particular focus in Duneier's account is the complex relationship he developed during the course of his research with Hakim Hasan, one of the street vendors who proved to be an important source throughout the course of his research. In discussing these issues, he is highlighting dilemmas that lie at the heart of ethnographic research among minority communities, both at an ethical and a practical level (from different angles, see also Liebow 1967; Alexander 2000; May 2001; Bourgois 2003).

The following two chapters take up issues that have received much attention in recent years and which raise important ethical and political dilemmas for researchers. Ruth Frankenberg's chapter traces the changing terms of her own experience in researching whiteness over the past decade or so. Arguing that the study of whiteness emerges out of a constellation of debates about the meanings of 'white privilege' and relations of power in contemporary societies that are riven by racial inequalities and racism, Frankenberg engages both with what the study of whiteness has come to mean and with what her own role in this field of research has been. Drawing extensively on critical reflections of her own earlier work, she evokes both the underlying concerns that drew her into this area of scholarship and the impact of research on whiteness on the broader field of scholarship into race and racism. This analysis is followed by Philomena Essed's chapter about her experiences of attempting to put issues of racism, or more specifically everyday racism, onto the academic agenda in the Netherlands. She suggests that scholarship in this field has been controversial from the start precisely because of the ways it touched on issues of power and privilege. In discussing these issues, Essed draws both on her own experiences of research and on the dynamics of research on racism in Dutch society more generally.

The everyday realities that researchers have to try to capture are highlighted in Claire Alexander's evocative account of her work among young Bangladeshi men in South London in the late 1990s. Alexander's study is located firmly within a tradition of ethnography, and she focuses much of her discussion on the shifting dynamics of ethnographic research on race and ethnicity. In doing so, she links up with the concerns articulated by Duneier earlier in the volume, though she is in many ways more ambiguous about the role of the 'native' ethnographer and her own role as a researcher focusing on young black and Asian men.

As research on race and racism has blossomed in recent years, it has also put the question of the problems raised by carrying out research across national boundaries more squarely on the social science agenda. The chapters by Sophie Body-Gendrot and Michèle Lamont focus precisely on aspects of this question. Body-Gendrot draws on her experience in the USA and France to discuss the difficulties that arise in conducting research on racism in the

French political and cultural environment. Michèle Lamont's account of her comparative work among US and French working-class men living in the suburbs of New York and Paris (see also Lamont 1999) touches on issues that link up with the concerns expressed by Body-Gendrot, and by Michel Wieviorka earlier in the book.

Many scholars and researchers in this area have acknowledged the heavily politicised and controversial nature of scholarship on race and racism. It is perhaps no surprise in this regard that such research is often categorised under the generic heading of research on 'sensitive issues'. What does this positioning of research in this field mean in practice? This is the question tackled by Miri Song in her critical account of current debates about racial hierarchies in the USA and Britain. Song's analysis is framed by a concern to argue that research on race and ethnic relations needs to be more sensitive to the need to explore forms of internal variation and the interweaving of class, gender and race inequalities.

In the penultimate chapter, Alford A. Young Jr focuses on the on-going debate about the role of 'insider' and 'outsider' research on race and ethnicity. The starting point of Young's analysis is his own critical reflection on his experiences of carrying out qualitative research among African American communities. Based on this experience, he seeks to outline the impact of 'insider–outsider' status in conducting research in this field. What is particularly interesting about Young's analysis is that he refuses to simplify the often contradictory positions occupied by researchers working on questions of race and ethnicity in US society (Alcoff 1991/2; Stanfield 1993; Stanfield and Dennis 1993).

The concluding chapter by Les Back is framed around a broader set of concerns. Writing from the standpoint of someone who has done research on various aspects of race and racism in British society, and more recently on whiteness, he suggests that we need to think seriously about the craft of writing up research, which in his eyes always involves researchers 'writing in and against time'.

In a book of this kind there are bound to be a range of different voices and perspectives about both the theory and the practice of research on race and racism. Indeed, as editors we wanted very much to bring together authors whose work crossed a range of disciplinary boundaries as well as national and theoretical traditions. When we take all the contributions to this volume together it seems clear, however, that they share at least some preoccupations and methodological concerns.

Where do we go from here?

To conclude, we hope that the contributions offered here will help to encourage further debate and reflection on the practice of doing research on race and racism. The history of social scientific research on race and racism can be traced back over a century now. Over that period, we have seen the emergence and decline of a wide range of different approaches both from a theoretical and methodological perspective. The recent expansion of research and scholarship in this field has, however, highlighted the need for a reflective and critical approach to the methods and tools that we use to study various facets of contemporary racial situations, racist ideas and practices and policy agendas. The experiences of the various researchers included in *Researching Race and Racism* are of course specific in a fashion, but we feel that they touch on dilemmas and issues that are more general and that need to be discussed more fully, if we are to reach a stage where we are able to look forward to a better understanding of the changing research agendas and shifting paradigms concerned.

It remains of concern, however, that, apart from a few recent examples, many of the problems and dilemmas covered in this volume are not fully discussed among researchers and practitioners in the field. Part of the cost of the move towards theory in recent times has been the relative neglect of debate about method and the practicalities of carrying out research in key arenas where race and racism are lived and experienced. In editing this collection, we have become even more aware of the need for social researchers working in race and ethnic studies to address, more fully than they have done in the recent past, questions about method. By this we mean not only the need to think about the concepts that we work with and the way that we seek to develop research strategies to analyse specific aspects of racial relations, racism and patterns of racialised exclusion.

We hope that, as we see a growth of both scholarly and policy-related research on race and racism over the coming period, that researchers will address more fully the methodological problems and dilemmas involved. *Researching Race and Racism* has brought together a wide range of 'tales from the field' that are interesting in their own right from the perspective of the work that they discuss, but perhaps more importantly for the questions that they raise about what it is that we do when we research these social phenomena.

1 Contemporary geopolitics and 'alterity' research

Chetan Bhatt

One can resist only in terms of the identity that is under attack.

Hannah Arendt

[The] problem of the twentieth-century is the problem of the colour line.

W.E.B. Du Bois

[Once the] name has been spoken, all the language that has led up to it, or that has been crossed in order to reach it, is reabsorbed into it and disappears.

Michel Foucault

Conceptions of the social as equivalent to the frolic of signification, and of politics as based wholly on modes of agonistic subjectivisation, appear to have settled as key axes for many academic questions, methodological assumptions and research agendas concerned with racism, religion, culture, identity, subjectivity and the like, these claim at another level the actual referents of minority communities, their political, social, economic and cultural conditions and identities in the UK and USA. In part, this is related to the valorisation of the linguistic-cultural turn in social theory (a cantian imperative) and the liberation of the domains of language and power from their embeddedness in institutional processes, social structures and histories. The dislocation of language and power from actual structures and institutions, especially states and economies, can allow for the proliferation of gargantuan 'sociological imaginations' arising from assessments of the marginal and liminal. This is a methodology of the abridgement of the social, political and economic to the calculus of signifiers. The *hegemon* being criticised is characteristically not an actual structure of power, oppression or exploitation, but other cultural or academic interpretations and interpreters (Gates 1994: 208). The fantasy, a self-conscious one, is that social or imperialist injustice is being remedied through the manufacture of neologisms, new language games and 'fields of discursivity' – academic critique of venial indiscretions, academic labour as manifesto, academic fields as *agora*. The dislocation of the ethical from the political is significant, as is the demotion of politics to the veracity or density of any particular portrait of representation and mirror of recognition. An orphic compulsion drives the academic labour that will disclose hitherto concealed structures of supremacy and domination, or transgressions of the latter, entrenched in the lattices of cultural production or theory. From another direction, the quadrangle of transatlantic slavery, the Holocaust, Orientalism and a dehistoricised colonialism provide the grids of intelligibility for how dissimilitude and modernity are to be theoretically reckoned. There is a range of in-between ventures, especially in that interface between sociology and cultural theory, which are preoccupied with the phraseology of identity, subjectivity, essentialism, alterity, hybridity and other allied concepts (the politics of pronouns) that are put to use in analysing and excavating race, gender and diaspora. These various areas are heteromorphic and relate to a wide range of projects. They have nevertheless become academically intertwined and present a productive set of semantics and rudimentary oppositions that define much of their field of study, its 'empirical', theoretical and methodological concerns.

If culturalist sociology, despite its overwhelming emphasis on 'globalisation', has made only fleeting references towards actual contemporary geopolitics, global political economy, and international corporate economic and political institutions, this also announces ethical problems of significant density. The sharp disjuncture between the concerns of race research in the UK or USA and the magnitude and scale of the global economic and political discrepancy between Western nations and those of the 'Third World' raises a variety of issues, not least, as Spivak (1999) puts it, that the interests of minorities in the West and the subaltern of the Third World are not simply delinked but may be opposed. From this vantage point, racism, whether manifesting as an analytic or as an evaluation, is less the mystification that races exist, than it is a mechanism for eliding the absolute differences in dispensation, status and power between, and the different order of scale and magnitude that apply to, minorities in the West and non-elite populations in the 'Third World'.[1] (The alleged contradiction between domestic liberal democracy and military and economic tyranny abroad is less important here than the apparently seamless organisation of both through new configurations of Euro-American nationalisms, nation-states and supranational institutions through which bare national interest and purportedly postnational legal and economic instruments co-exist.)

If race organises both the discrimination and incorporation of migrants in the West, it can also provide resources for its subjects (and some of its academic representatives) to perform their relations with and differences from subaltern populations in the 'Third World' in a variety of over-determined ways. One of these is the possibility that a racial or religious victimology of innocence in the West might be inextricably linked to an expression of tangible and manifest power by sections of minorities in the West over absolutely less powerful subaltern groups in the 'Third World'. This is a complex process whose political and ethical import is neutralised by the over-explanatory use of the term 'racialisation' (or 'racial formation') to describe any hegemonic representation or description of minority groups, regardless of the glaring taxonomic incommensurabilities that result – for example, in equating minority religious-political assertion with the politics of racial discrimination. Of additional importance for sociology is an ethical and moral distanciation between research on racism, anti-racism, whiteness, minority religious and cultural identity, varieties of syncretism and hybridity and the like, and the provenance of these ideas as academic exports resultant upon US and European hegemony.

The naturalised semantics of identity, subjectivity, difference and anti-essentialism, the analytical matrix of race, gender, sexuality and class, and various permutations and combinations of both, also announce a range of reductionisms. The languages of 'interweaving', 'intersection', 'connection', 'relationship', 'link' or 'multiplication' (of race, gender, sexuality and class) curiously associate motoring with *matheme*. The noun suffix mitigates the labour of political action – gender*ing* race, class*ing* sex, rac*ing* research. The reduction travels from complex social and political processes to abstracted communitarian identity and then to the theoretical phenomenology of an encounter between abstract subjects. This is a caricature of some strands of social and cultural theory no doubt, but one that will be familiar. These analytics are incapable of addressing wider geopolitical and global economic disparities, unless the latter are illegitimately reduced to reflect the partial concerns of Euro-American theory and its black, white, in-between and *en passant* varieties.

The sociology of the sociology of race, racism, ethnicity and religion is also of consequence. The self-marginalising discourses of diaspora academics who have witnessed or experienced the racism of institutional academia can share much with the political spaces of official multicultural Britain that provide a niche from which to expound an 'anti-Western' victimology based on racial or religious 'essentialism' while claiming to do otherwise, claiming even to decentre the West through projects of home-grown multicultur-alism. The canonisation of a sociological field focused on racism, minority/majority community identities, and sustained as a canon through an iterative performance of marginalisation, can highlight a parochial, protected space that both delimits its fields of intellectual inquiry to Euro-American concerns and, in its evasiveness of contemporary global geopolitics and political economy, can reproduce 'Western' narcissism, even as what is conceived as 'the West' is regularly berated. There is a different sociological issue about the investment in alterity thinking in academia that is about the disclosure and excavation of what are considered to be important instances of discrimination, or previously marginalised manifestations of identity. It is not the argument here that these are unimportant or inessential projects. However, it seems important to register a productive regime of truth and power that defines a particular intellectual and lexical universe in which certain tropes of race, alterity, difference and identity are naturalised as *doxa* under the fundamentally less dangerous, even if still unevenly precarious conditions, that racial and ethnic minorities face in contemporary Euro-America. This chapter[2] is a critical reflection on these and related areas, and draws out some of the theoretical, methodological and ethical consequences of such work.

The vagaries of race in a geopolitical context

There has been a recent and welcome re-emergence of critiques of race thinking and 'raciology' (Memmi 2000: 191; Gilroy 2000). These can advocate an anti-racism that is understood in its formative (mid-1930s) characterisation as a strict anti-race-ism, rather than as a naturalised aggrandisement or reification of black identities (which seems to be the contemporary normativity of 'anti-racism'). In Gilroy's formulations, which are more complex than their reduction here allows, race thinking and the 'end of the colour line' are also counterposed to the necessity of developing an ethics founded on 'planetary humanism', though one can be less convinced about the meaning and relevance of the latter, even if conceived in utopian terms. Planetary humanism would, for example, seem to be an extraneous cipher for practitioners and advocates of 'development' and anti-poverty projects outside the West. Furthermore, such a humanism founded as a counter to (the history and persistence of) 'race thinking' already situates the latter as *the* key problem facing the twentieth-century world and this claim is by no means unproblematic. Du Bois's assertion that the problem of the twentieth century was the problem of the colour line is only warranted if one concurs with the reduction of colonialism and imperialism to dermatochromatic racism. There are, of course, many who would seek to situate race as the presentist adhesive that inextricably binds Enlightenment, industrial modernity, slavery, imperialism, (neo-)colonialism, the contemporary north–south divide and the position of minorities in the West (just as there are those whose presentist vision is fixated on Hulagu, the Crusades, the Ottoman caliphs or the gates of Vienna).

Similarly, claims that transatlantic slavery, the Holocaust and Orientalism characterise either or both the normativity of modernity or its destructive pathology require problematisation. This is not because other modern, even colonial, empirical instances can be found for which these characterisations may only be partially relevant. In some cases, transatlantic slavery and the Holocaust can be privileged markers for modernity, metonymic memorialisations and academic stigmata for contemporary anti-black and anti-Jewish racism. But they can also displace other horrors for which prodigious and monumental tombstones can be found, and can elide a range of other historic or contemporary victimisations.[3] However, of interest is how totalising claims about the structure and historicity of Western modernity are announced through these efforts in a way that can rehearse a claim, from the margins as it were, that confirms the declarations of magnitude, enormity, immensity, historicity, universality and totalisation made by the classical sociological champions of modernist thinking. The 'West–Rest' dichotomy (Hall 1992) and the adjacent proliferation of languages of alterity ('the West and its others') are both causes and symptoms of this dehistoricisation that reconfirm, in a presentist language and on a grand scale, the claims about historicity within the modernist imaginations that are being criticised without, however, being able to convincingly propose an alternative non-Western intellectual universe, except in the most nominal ways (see Spivak 1999 on this point). A related theme concerns the way that, in the name of anti-essentialism, dehistoricised and superficial abstractions of an 'essentialist' kind provide the schemata for understanding contemporary geopolitics. Elementary tropes of alterity and difference become the nominal, dehistoricised lexical map for understanding non-Western or global conflicts – the colour line, 'Islamophobia', the 'clash of civilisations', of 'the twentieth-century problem of difference' being dominant examples of grand right and left Manichaean understandings of global history and contemporary geopolitics.

This is as relevant to presentist understandings of colonial history. Consider, for example, how race abstraction, undertaken as anti-racist critique, works in the example of colonial India. James Mill's *History of British India* (1817) is described thus:

> Mill attacked the 'hideous state' of 'Hindu and Muslim civilization' that prevailed in India. Like the Chinese, Indians were 'found to be tainted with the vices of insincerity, dissembling, treacherous…disposed to excessive exaggeration…cowardly and unfeeling…in the highest degree conceited…and full of affected contempt for others. Both are, in the physical sense, disgustingly unclean, in their persons and houses.' Indians and Chinese, in short, were found completely lacking in morality. This state of affairs Mill ascribed to underlying political causes, namely, the shortcomings of 'oriental despotism'.
>
> (Goldberg 1993: 34–5)

This is a faithful and accurate rendition of Mill's view of colonised Indians, and its purpose is to show the predominance of paternalist racism in colonial modernity and hence the legitimation of imperial government. Much more could be elaborated about Mill's racial, civilising, modernising, anti-romantic rationalism. An intricate and credible argument could be made about the imbrication of racism in Mill's Utilitarianism, theory of right, population control and representative government. A nimble philosophical argument could even be proposed about the embeddedness of the racial-civilising mission in Mill's theory of property and the labour theory of value, and a pointed conclusion could be drawn about race as a core impulse in what is otherwise conceived as an abstract rational economics that characterises modernity.

However, the importance and impact of Mill for India relates to his phantasmatic historicity of India as one primarily determined by *religious* (not racial) periodisations – crudely, the Ancient-Hindu, the Medieval-Muslim and the Modern-British[4] (Thapar 1989). His temporality was not only consequential for secular tendencies of the national movement, sections of which appropriated it for the purposes of nationalism and nation-building, but also for religious tendencies that wished to create their own Hindu or Muslim theocracies. Its contemporary resonance, monumental in scope, is also precisely religious and is the foundation for dominant religious fascisms that wish to institute a Hindu nation-state and whose Bharatya Janata Party representatives have brought South Asia to nuclear brinkmanship in recent years. These tendencies have had no trouble in denouncing Mill's racism. The key issue here is how assessments of the history of the colonial period can reflect the racialising concerns of academia in the West to the elision of actual and consequential histories, social formations, political trajectories and geopolitics.

This is exemplified further in arguments that speak of the organisation of planetary politics in terms of 'a racist world order' or which claim:

> Race in all its forms continues to preoccupy us, to surprise us, to shape our world....While perhaps more properly defined as 'ethnic', ferocious conflicts taking place at the fringes of the 'developed' world, from South and South-East Asia to the Middle East, from Burundi to Burma, from Azerbaijan to Bosnia, exhibit at least 'protoracial' features. Arguably, the world today is a vast racial battlefield.
>
> (Winant 1994: 266)

To pluck just one regional example here: how are National League for Democracy protests, communist or Buddhist insurgencies, Karen or 'God's Army' revolts against the Burmese military dictatorship, or even Buddhist–Muslim violence, *racial* conflicts? Such ventures that couple anti-racism with a universal racialisation suggest a different sociologic, partially related to the Euro-American export of a racial theory of everything.

The starkest manifestation is perhaps the extrapolative gesture of raci-ology that creates a semblance between the confessional mode of the phenomenology of individual racial experience in the USA or UK and the racial structuring of other polities, nations and civil societies:

> Although Brazilians are materially and symbolically marginalized on account of their ancestry phenotype, Brazilians of salient African descent do not typically possess a different political standpoint from whites when questioned about definitions of racism and racial disparities....My experience suggests that some Brazilians of color do not necessarily feel more comfortable discussing the topic of race and racism with those who resemble them racially. Rather, this particular topic generates discomfort regardless of the racial origins or phenotype of the inter-viewer....We see, then, that the utility of racial matching [in interview situations] is contingent on the subordinate person having acquired a

particular subjectivity. It is premised on racial subalterns considering their skin folk their kin folk and being more distrustful of the racially dominant group. In my experience, US scholars typically interpret this as an inevitable by-product of racism. That is, they presume that different ideological positions are attached to one's location in racial hierarchies. It should be evident, however, that when racial subalterns do not possess a developed critique of racism or idealize the racially privileged group, race matching may not be an efficacious methodological strategy.

(Twine 2000: 15–16)

Leaving aside the methodological implications (Brecht comes to mind), what is significant is how race provides the unwarranted legitimacy in transplanting the racial phenomenology of the researcher from the USA to research subjects in Brazil, who are then found wanting. The fantasy of Brazilian nationalism as one of a harmonious 'racial democracy' has been the focus of political struggle, as are indigenous peoples' rights. However, this kind of racialised sentiment seems somewhat abstracted from postwar social, economic and political conditions, including a two-decade military dictatorship, state and political repression, the absence of full democratic rights (until very recently), and processes of economic and social stratification and spaces for expanding political liberty within which 'race' may well have independent salience. To argue this is not to evade race in favour of class or politics, but to interrogate how phenomenological understandings of race derived from the US academic experience can provide the only legitimate grid of intelligibility for mapping and understanding racial stratification elsewhere. In this kind of diminution of the space of politics to the possession of an appropriate phenomenology of racial encounter, or in speaking solely of racial rights or cultural rights, which other research questions of political economy, democracy, exploitation and social justice are being elided?

It is similarly conceivable that such chromatic logic, both ostensibly anti-racist and wilfully promoting racial conceptions, would find in India a racially stratified, racial or racist social formation in which much of the (especially Northern, urban) populace would be found to valorise 'white supremacist' thinking. Certainly, there are some dalit political tendencies that have created transnational intellectual and political alliances with both US and UK Afrocentrists, grounded in a common belief in a transcendental, world-historic white supremacism and the oppression of 'Negroid people' (their term), and animated by an anti-Aryanist venture that is a mirror image of Gobineau and Chamberlain. Other dalit campaigns have sought to get international recognition of caste oppression, segregation, exclusion and injustice as a form of racism and apartheid (most notably at the World Conference against Racism, Racial Intolerance, Xenophobia and Related Intolerances, held in Durban, September 2001). The ethical position may be to support such moves against the Indian government's unyielding opposition, and in the face of the persistence and entrenchment of untouchability, manual scavenging, institutional exclusion and systematic violence against dalits. However, it is still unclear whether racial extrapolations of the kind addressed earlier would have much to say about the political sociology of the Indian social formation, the murderous xenologies and heterophobias of caste, religion, ethnicity or region that may animate it, or their historical associations with the colonial and postcolonial state.

An ontological fascination, by both left and right, with the detail of the spectra of light reflected by the body's epidermal layer[5] can take us to odd places. There is no warranted reason for assuming that US imperialism, anti-racism, Western black nationalism, and the legitimation of ethnocidal tyranny are incompatible. The Libero-American elite, primarily descendants of liberated US black slaves who had been given free passage by the variously charitable and variously racist American Colonization Society to Liberia, monopolised political and economic power in the state after 1847 (initially organised as the True Whig Party). In the post-Second World War period and until the early 1980s, Liberia was governed by the dictatorial and corrupt regime of William Tubman, and then his successor William Tolbert; it was one of the USA's closest Cold War allies in Africa. If the resonance of the US civil rights movement, and US guilt about slavery and racial segregation, prevented criticism of the Libero-American dictatorship and its exploitation of other ethnic groups in Liberia, it was also the case that a current of US black nationalist opinion would not harbour denigration of an ex-slave state, nor, later, an ethnocidal tyranny (Berkeley 2001; Ellis 2001). Samuel Doe's (and the Armed Forces of Liberia's) coup in 1980 led to a brutal military tyranny that exploited the ethnicities of Liberian peoples based on the politicisation of Krahn against Gio and Mano ethnicities (and periodic bloodletting against the latter). The Doe tyranny was strongly financially sustained by the USA under Reaganite foreign policy, but received no criticism from influential African American political lobby and pressure groups that had emerged to fight US collusion with South African apartheid. The conflagration initiated in late 1989 and early 1990 by the Libero-American, Charles Taylor, against the Doe regime plunged the country into anarchic bloodletting and destruction, directed against Krahn ethnic groups, often led by child militias equipped by Taylor. Some 150,000 Liberians were killed between 1989 and 1997, and tens of thousands of women and girls raped. Inevitably, the US and European media portrayed the violence as a manifestation of primordial African tribal conflict, though the kind of ethnic conflict seen had not been a feature of Liberian society until the early 1980s. However, of significance in the postwar history of Liberia was the active collusion of racist and anti-racist, Cold War and black nationalist, left and right tendencies in the USA, what Michael Chege, writing about general orientations to African states, characterised as the 'specious dichotomy' between right and left in the USA (Berkeley 2001:

90). A key aspect of this related to the equivalence created between the integrity, self-esteem and moral standing of the African American population in the USA and the alleged consequences *for it* of the successes or failures of independent African nation-states (Berkeley 2001: 89–91). If, for some, anti-racism and the colour line meant an unethical defence of politicised and tyrannical ethnocide, the recent example of Liberia (and Sierra Leone), by no means exceptional, illustrates how the interests of minorities in the West may not only be opposed to populations outside the West, but may also take precedence.

The empirical, political and ethical limits to theoretical obsessions with cultural 'flows', consumption, icons, and their relation to minority diaspora cultures – all movements consequent upon globalisation – are illustrated by the recent and bloody history of Sierra Leone, itself related to the Taylor regime in Liberia. The example of the conflict in Sierra Leone can similarly pose an alternative, and sharp, ethical challenge to the empirical content of sociologies concerned with 'cultural flows', the global traffic in commodities, the semiologies of cultural products, and the relations of the latter to minority diasporic cultural formations. Foday Sankoh and his Revolutionary United Front (RUF) returned to Sierra Leone through Liberia in the early 1990s (Sankoh had previously initiated a coup in Sierra Leone in the early 1970s but had left the country in the late 1980s; Sankoh was also close to Liberia's Charles Taylor, an important source of support and regional protection for the RUF in Liberia.) The so-called civil war in Sierra Leone escalated from 1991 as the RUF attempted to gain control of important diamond-mining regions in the country. The RUF method of terror was based on abduction of both children and adults as forced combatant recruits, killings, systematic sexual violence, mutilation and limb-amputation of adult and child civilians, and forced adult and child labour in diamond mines. In 1997, the Armed Forces Revolutionary Council (AFRC) took power in Sierra Leone and, in alliance with the RUF, unleashed state terror on the civilian population. The AFRC was ousted in elections held the following year, but, with the RUF, continued a campaign of increasing terror and brutality against civilians. Several thousand adults and children were abducted, forced into fighting for the RUF/AFRC, mutilated, raped or killed, or became sexual slaves or slave labourers in diamond mines. The terror unleashed on the population of Freetown in 1999 was unprecedented in its brutality and involved the deliberate and systematic mutilation, amputation of limbs, and gang rapes of adults and children (Human Rights Watch 1998). Two million refugees were displaced internally or into neighbouring countries (Guinea and Liberia) where atrocities continued.

The murders, mutilations and slave labour in Sierra Leone were inextricably linked to the merchandising of love and romance in the jewel districts of Antwerp, London's Hatton Garden, Tel Aviv, Johannesburg, Kiev and New York. Blood diamonds were also central to the purchase of arms from Eastern Europe (mainly Bulgaria), which fuelled the conflict in Sierra Leone,

Liberia and elsewhere. These are the diamonds that decorated the fingers and the teeth of modish urban youngsters in London, Los Angeles and New York. The Millennium Star, which was the target of a dramatic but failed robbery at the Millennium Dome in London in November 2000, was also alleged to have emerged from the trade in African blood diamonds. (*Guardian*, 9 November 2000). Liberia, which became a key West African hub for the export of illegal diamonds from Sierra Leone, reported a dramatic increase in diamond exports in the late 1990s though it has relatively poor natural diamond resources of its own. It was allegedly from the diamond 'trade' in Sierra Leone and Liberia during 2000 and 2001 that Al Qaeda partially funded its attack of 11 September 2001 or through which it made arrangements to secrete its funds in the aftermath of the attack. Liberia was also alleged to have harboured Al Qaeda operatives following the New York attack (*Washington Post*, 1 November 2001; the *Observer*, 20 October 2002; *Washington Post*, 30 December 2002). The human rights atrocities in Sierra Leone and Liberia from the mid- to late 1990s are at the core of a range of sociological associations between diamond merchants and jewellers in Europe, the USA and Russia with arms dealers from Eastern Europe, dictators and child militias in West Africa with matrimonial couples in the West, Islamist terrorists with diamond-cutting centres in Antwerp, Israel and India, and the historic domination of diamond cartels in the apartheid era with the affectations of urban black youth culture in London.

The West–Rest abstract machine

The prominence of the grand 'West–Rest' map and the embedded, if frequently disingenuous, critique of 'the West' in much sociological and cultural theory illustrates further related themes. In much *mainstream* social and cultural theory, with few exceptions, 'the West' functions as stenographical ruse that both elides the empirical, historical world beyond Euro-America, and ethically fails to account for that elision (in seemingly particularising through a demarcation as 'Western' what is otherwise self-consciously intended to function as a universal, the responsibility for ethical judgement or empirical engagement is evaded).

Of additional importance is how the West–Rest 'abstract machine' (Deleuze 1988), and its associated motifs of transatlantic slavery, Orientalism and racial colonialism, can function in social and cultural theory in a presentist, dehistoricised and foundationalist manner. This suggests less a concern with history than with the necessity to analogise the contemporary phenomenology of racial and religious migrants and the descendants of slaves. The West–Rest trope is providential, and its emergence from within cultural studies is significant since it is not thematically or empirically bounded. It analogises a wide range of conducive oppositions, such as Self–Other, Modernity or Enlightenment and Otherness. It admits a declension from the 'primordial' colonial encounter of the fifteenth century to the personal phenomenology of contemporary racial and cultural engagements and the ahistorical logic of frontier reasoning. The spatial and temporal diagram that the West–Rest trope provides is significantly global in scope and productively temporally motile. A temporal indeterminacy, enabled through a transcendental conception of race, allows the West–Rest trope to be over burdened with explaining an extraordinarily wide range of phenomena, from domestic racial discrimination, the possibilities of and limits to multiculturalism, the recent British fascination with 'Asian cultures', to 'Islamophobia', the North–South divide or the 'war against terrorism'.

The West–Islam dichotomy is another productive rendition of 'the new cultural politics of difference' predicated on the 'West–Rest' abstract machine. It relies on an active evasion of the role of US foreign policy ('the West') and historic US allies in both creating and sustaining Islamist movements in the midst, and especially towards the latter part of the Cold War (Halliday 1996). This is not to say that the movements that the USA, Saudi Arabia and Pakistan fostered could not also be viscerally ideologically and politically opposed to them, or (could) have remained under their political or military control. The USA has also, indeed, fought two hot wars during the 1990s in military defence of Muslims (in the former Yugoslavia, and against the Iraqi invasion of Kuwait) and by proxy in Afghanistan against the Soviet-backed communist regime, during which the USA spent up to $5 billion up to 1992 in financial aid to the anti-Najibullah *'mujahideen'* military forces,[6] the most dominant of which were animated by varieties of Islamism. The Saudi Arabian oiligarchy, one of the two closest allies of the USA and UK ('the West') in the Middle East, has been the most effectual sponsor of Islamism in the world (Roy 1994), or at least the versions of Islamism consonant with sectarian Wahhabism, its particular renditions of *salafiyya* 'doctrines' and its novel interpretations of *sharia* as an instrumental code (Ayubi 1991; Al-Azmeh 1993). This has been exemplified in its direct and indirect financial and political support for various nationally based branches of the Muslim Brotherhood movement (Roy 1994: 116–19) and the Pakistani Jamaati-i-Islami (Nasr 1994: 60), movements which are otherwise proscribed in Saudi Arabia itself, as well as other Islamist movements (some of whose activities or offshoots have had reverberations for the Saudi regime itself.) It also included active Saudi Arabian support for the Taliban regime (Rashid 2000: 201–2). Equally of importance has been US foreign policy that has closely sustained dictatorships in Pakistan, including the Jamaati-influenced Zia dictatorship, and materially supported the activities of the Pakistani Inter Services Intelligence Directorate (ISI), itself significantly Islamist in its higher echelons and preoccupied with furthering Islamist currents and networks in South Asia, including Kashmir. Crudely, the 'balance of powers' in South Asia prior to the collapse of the Soviet Union linked the USA, Pakistan and China against India, the Soviet Union and (varyingly) Bangladesh. In Afghanistan, both prior to and during the Taliban regime, the configuration of transnational powers (which included the involvement of Iran, India, the Central Asian republics, Turkey and Russia) was more complex, but the USA–Pakistan and USA–Saudi axis was decisive. The Taliban movement and regime was also initially supported by the USA for a variety of reasons (see Mackenzie 1998; Rashid 2000: 180) until Bin Laden's financial aid to the Taliban became evident, and because Taliban violation of human rights and repression of women and girls led to both international and domestic pressure on the US government.

The reason for highlighting US foreign policy in furthering Islamist projects in the Middle East, South and Southeast Asia and parts of Northeastern and West Africa is not to point out, post-11 September 2001, the vagaries of US political expediency and the contradictions and reversals in US foreign policy, but to question the tropic languages and assumptions that infect many sociological understandings preoccupied with sustaining an ahistorical division between 'the West' and 'its Others', or 'the West' and 'Islam'. In this imagined Manichaeism, the different order and scale of US military involvement in Korea, Vietnam and Cambodia or a comparative focus in relation to El Salvador, Cuba, Chile and Nicaragua during the 1970s and into the 1990s can be elided (Halliday 1996). The 'paradox' of Islamism is not its emergence in late modernity as a premodern or counter-modern threat to Western Enlightenment, but its embeddedness in Western, regional and national geopolitical interests, the politics of state power, the emergence of political elites, the reorganisation of civil societies and their personal and gender laws and codes, and the consolidation of a complex variety of political, economic and ethnic interests (Ayubi 1991; Halliday 1996). This does not imply that those movements are remotely completed by US associations, nor that visceral political hatred of the USA or Britain (or Europe or communism) is not a primary factor in their ideologies or motivations. It does however mean that theoretical and methodological understandings based on 'the West' versus 'Islam' are interestedly abstract, deliberately ahistorical and can represent a mendacious political interest that can elide the recent provenance of Islamism, as well as the role of US geopolitical, military and economic interests in fostering Islamist obsessions with the logics of personal and territorial 'purity' rather than with democracy, women's and human rights. Academically, they represent a conflation of sociological abstractions with the political ideology of Islamists (which some may want to render as another emic–etic conflation), and a consequent suspension of analytical and critical judgement.

A naturalised West–Rest trope is also equally productive for some diaspora apologists for authoritarian Islamism, such as Bobbie Sayyid (2000). This enables a marginal site of otherness from which to decentre or destabilise whatever is meant by 'the West', methodologically using only the recent grimoires of the West, but unable to advance a non-Western intellectual paradigm or undertake an intellectually significant or ethical assessment of socio-political formations and histories emanating from outside the West. The proclamation of anti-foundationalist anti-essentialism masks what is a familiar philosophical matrix – a confluence of teleological ethics, convenance and selective nihilism that characteristically disguises a preferential identitarianism. If prevarication defines its methodological style, its own methodological approach is one in which 'the West' and 'Islamism' (or 'Islam' or 'umma') are the nominal patronymics that announce a transcendental conflict between contending and exceptionally rendered graphemes. The ethical and intellectual obligation to excavate the actual West or Islamism, their histories, philosophies and social and political formations, is elided through the methodological sovereignty of insubstantial discursive abstractions. If empiricism intrudes, it is to project a characteristically moralising language of formal and venial misdemeanours (ibid.: 260–2). Indeed, it is unable to advance a substantive, historical or politically effective critique of the actual West, since its methodology reduces the latter to a cipher (it does have hopes for the possibility of a new, non-Western language game, though – ibid.: 269). It is similarly unconcerned with the actuality of especially the non-Muslim 'Third World'. Hence, the moralising choice is not only rendered as one between 'the West' or 'Islamism', but is reductively posed as simply one of subjective prejudice arising from tradition (ibid.: 266). Unless prejudices are constitutionally natural and cultures and traditions immutable (even relatively so), why choose Islamist fascism over another anti-Western fascism, such as Hindutva?

An academic ruse is at work here, not that dissimilar to that used by more politically effective fundamentalists,[7] in which 'the West' is relativised, reduced to whatever is abstractly meant by its culture, polity and power, and expanded as the *imperium* that embraces everything from contemporary US imperialism, liberalism, socialism, democracy, nationalism, fascism, communism and capitalism to Muslim secularism, feminism, humanism or rationalism. Culturally and ethically relativist resources made available in some strands of poststructuralism and deconstructionism are employed to make the ambidextrous claim that 'Enlightenment' or 'Western' philosophical, juridical and political products (such as human rights, democracy, secularism, rationalism and the like) are matters of faith, and hence equivalent to ideologies founded on beliefs in the preternatural, the celestial, the truth of the cosmic sacred in print. This is an epistemic subreption – the embracing of both Western postmodernism and religious infallibility to reprimand those, Muslims or otherwise, who are secular. The alleged epistemic equivalence between secular modernity and religious foundationalism is also a strategically important heuristic in various fundamentalist movements, and was explicated most forcefully by Abul A'la Maududi, later founder of the Jamaati-i-Islami, during the 1920s.

Sayyid's subreptive mode, as well as the absence of engagement with substantive intellectual themes and arguments (both of which appear to be a methodological *manqué*),[8] are central to his attack on Aziz Al-Azmeh's *Islams and Modernities* (1993) – though most of the attack is on the Author and is not a substantial critique of his Text. It is claimed that Al-Azmeh is undertaking a selective critique of Islamist essentialism that disguises his own essentialist identification of universalism with the West, one ultimately based on valorising the culture of the latter. This is because Al-Azmeh writes of political, economic and intellectual dominance by the West since the early nineteenth century that led to the formative impact of European ideas in the genesis of Islamism during the twentieth century. Sayyid argues that this is another attempt to universalise the West through the claim that Islamism owes, in essence, to the West. It is not simply the misconception of the actual history (which is not, as he claims, equivalent to its historiography) of nineteenth-century colonial modernity that is palpable. Of significance here is a prevalent identitarian narcissism that cannot accept that ideas from Europe – nationalism, the state, populace, revolution, modernist enumeration, governmentality, social Darwinism, fascism and Nazism, eugenicism, vitalism, palingenesis, communism, Marxism, liberalism, nobility, democracy, liberty, equality and freedom, among many others – had a manifest impact globally, during various historical periods (of which the early decades of the nineteenth century, after the mid-1800s, and the interwar period were particularly important). Whether one today disagrees with or rejects these ideas is a separate issue from their historical influence.[9] One implicit consequence of this kind of nativist argument is a rendition of imperialism and colonialism as ineffectual, colonial subjects as passively naturalised and colonial history as effectively inert. It also furnishes a political alibi for whatever atrocities some 'Third World' nation-states or elites wish to inflict on their populations in the name of nativist, anti-Western theology. In similarly evading the significance, substance and complexity of the vast range of Muslim democratic, secular, feminist, humanist intellectual efforts and debates (and in not addressing older currents of Muslim reformism and rationalism), it demonstrates an *amour propre* characteristic of Western diaspora advocates of *Unanimisme*, in this case by announcing 'Islamism' as a welcome alternative entelechy.

This is a consequence of some strands in recent political theory that combine: deconstructionist (and psychoanalytic) undecidability at (or as) the limit point, ineffability or constitutive outside of rationality, philosophical foundation and cognomen; poststructuralist conceptions of the political as the production of both abstract universal subjecthood and particularist subjectivities; Foucauldian approaches applicable to *liberal* governmentality; an iterative conception of authoritative nomination undertaken (performatively) between the spaces (division of) the illocutionary and perlocutionary; a critique of the essentialism of (only) left social movements and their politics of identity; and a selective appropriation of (some of) Carl Schmitt's legal, constitutional and political writings that announce the political through a basal vitalism (contrasted by him with romantic stasis) and an iniquitous distinction between friend and adversary. Variants of this scheme are accepted as a true theory of what the political is.

There is a different range of debates about 'the West and the Rest', emergent from several directions in economic and social history over the last decade, but exemplified in recent years in Frank's work (Abu-Lughod 1991; Frank 1998; Pomeranz 2001). These can propose a non-reductionist historicity of 'the world system', and the place of European economic and industrial expansion within it, which manifestly do 'decentre' Europe. They have a range of consequences, including judgements about the relative economic importance of both transatlantic and plantation slavery, and their relation to US and European industrialisation, the critical role of the Far East, as well as South Asia and the Ottoman empire within which European expansion was much later imbricated, and the differential entry of North America and South America into a global economic system of trade and industrialisation. If determinism may seem to be its alleged fallacy, one pointed consequence of some of this work is a thoroughgoing displacement of the economic and historicist claims of classical European sociology, falling not that short of rejecting entirely the traditional sociological and economics canon, but without wishing to institute nativist or civilisational chauvinisms. By implication, this critique travels through to the claims of late modern sociology (whether concerning a runaway world, risk society or globalisation itself). Of central methodological importance is a foundational distinction between the actual history of modernity, the *epistemes* of historicity within Western modernity, and the historical claims arising from within Western modernist enterprises. It is not only that such distinctions are necessarily elided in some of the 'West–Rest' efforts addressed earlier; the latter becomes a contemporary euhemerism that re-establishes the historical mythology of the West.

Identity and methodological narcissism

The two quotations by W.E.B. Du Bois and Hannah Arendt at the beginning of this chapter can be seen to form the parameters for another intellectual field of conception and production for certain fairly embedded trajectories in US and UK theoretical work and empirical research about race, racism and minority communities. At their most trivial, they result in dissertations and essays about the distinctive and different identities of minority (South Asian, Caribbean, Chinese, Muslim, African or other) communities and subjects, the role of racism or religious discrimination in shaping these, and a critique of popular cultural iconographies (representations of burden). This is trivial at one level, but also indicative of what some sections of the next generation of sociologists and cultural theorists are thinking about, and the disciplinary matrices of corrigibility that are made available to them in situating questions of racial and ethnic minorityhood.

It is significant that, as the most vicious forms of racism of the 1970s and 1980s have receded, the literature on race, racism and minority identities has flourished both in the USA and UK and across a variety of disciplines. Varieties of alterity thinking are, however, *doxa*, performed by those who would characteristically reject a biological – or even a social or cultural – realism regarding race. If one can speak of the academe of race as its own self-propelling, self-prophesying Foucauldian 'field of discursivity', this is now rendered through a poststructuralist mimesis: an academic field of discursivity organised in and through race that announces race as 'a historically and socially specific discursivity'. However, if a nominal cluster comprising the subject, identity, race, gender, sexuality, class and sometimes religion constitute the *a priori* of alterity thinking, these can be figurative abstractions, rather than dense, historicised formulations. Their status as, variously, empirical or social variables, theoretical tropes, social structures, discursive or ideological constructs, 'transcendental analytics' or substitutions for groups and communities is importantly indeterminate, and hence generative.

The current academic focus on alterity and difference requires a much deeper discussion than can be provided here of its lineages in both eighteenth- and nineteenth-century xenological thinking, as well as in nineteenth- and early twentieth-century European philosophies founded on the ontology of partition and the necessity of representation; the trinity of monism, dualism and plurality; transcendental ineffability; hylomorphism; and an indeterminate temporal closure. However, in the contemporary epistemic embeddedness of alterity, a common humanity is regularly enunciated (though humanism is historically predicated on the speciation of part-humans (Spivak 1999) or infrahumanity (Gilroy 2000)). This seeming contradiction is a productive diocracy, at once concerned with a detailed excavation of racial difference while at the same time and in the same move addressing an architecture of a common humanity under which racial difference is a contingent, historical, social absurdity that has little epistemic or analytical purchase. In the analytic of race, neither difference nor sameness can be sequestered, since both manifest, convey and inhabit each other. The vigilance that Gilroy calls for, alive to the histories of race, and which requires an open, necessarily undecidable analytics of race in order to contest and subvert its authority, is certainly preferable to those positions that seek to brusquely reify a racial ontology, nestle within paradigms of over-integrated ethnicity, or seek to find the real determinations that race has mystified. However, these problems indicate a range of general issues: a focus on alterity, even the need for its recognition or respect, through which a broader provisional universality (a species-becoming) is announced. The theoretical compulsion to both reify and transcend the reification is less a predicament than an exemplary productive apparatus for contemporary academia, suggestive of several older traditions of European (and non-European) philosophy.

An important instance of the more sophisticated versions of these efforts is to transcend entirely and dispose of the glossary of alterity. This is especially relevant to whiteness studies, which seek to disinter their object, ascertain its enduring power and effectivity, excavate its empty normativity, and call for transcending its status, nomenclature and content altogether, even as they reproduce and fill it – perhaps best caricatured here as a move from the invention of the white race to the abolition of whiteness. The challenge and importance of these efforts is not being disregarded here. The issue is how they mirror a similar epistemic structure that has figured race – the analytical over intergration of a master trope as the key to understanding its under-determination, which arises from its pure sociality and discursivity.[10]

The excavation of alterity in order to announce its transcendence also analogises a social dissolutionist paradigm that founded the classical sociological tradition, and which crossed Comte, Saint-Simon, Marx, Weber, Durkheim and Simmel. The classical Marxist paradigm is the exemplar in manifesting a field of discursivity regarding the archaeology of capital and capitalism, and prophesying their future evaporation even as their essences are necessary requirements for, and must inhabit or destabilise, any proposed future closure (Berman 1982). The contemporary fixation on identity is somewhat similar: a dense focus on the boundaries and limits of identity, its consequent destabilisation, the proclamation of its provisionality, and the subsequent bifurcation into a self-consciously strategic essentialism[11] while grasping a future horizon of undecidability, ineffability, limit and abyss – and concluding with a repetitive return to an ahistorical alterity and subjectivity. This is like a Comtean conception of a far futurity that cannot be legislated but which cannot exactly be conceived non-teleologically either. Less abstractly, if most writers on hybridity, syncretism and the like were required to abandon the paraphernalia of blackness, race, ethnicity, identity, alterity or subjectivity, they would not be able to do so. There is a similar inability to creatively describe what a non-essentialist identity or futurity might be like without recourse to provisional universals and essences.

Academic hybridity talk, and postmodern ruminations about fractured, multiple identities, are part of this same trajectory. As much as these celebrate the fragmentation of identities, they cannot manage with the dissolution of identity itself, relinquish the language of identity, and sacrifice a clandestine political imaginary of resolution based on some kind of transcendental wholeness or integrity. (To be sure, some versions utilise a morphology of the social and subjectivity that is a syncretism of Spinoza and Hume, extensionalism and classical empiricism, in which wholeness or monism is rendered as the abstract vitalism of something akin to 'nature' – something like a Deleuzian theory of nature's magic.) That this wholeness can take affective forms is of interest, such as the love between the *hegemon* and the subaltern that Spivak describes (1999: 383).

The reduction of multiculturalism to the necessity of recognition is relevant to some of these areas, though there are other reasons to disagree with Taylor's (1992) somewhat tidy coupling of Hegel and Rousseau. However, if a movement from questions of redistribution to issues of recognition under

broader rubrics of multicultural citizenship has become important for char-
acterising black and ethnic minority social and political aspirations within a
liberal *habitus* (Parekh 2000), then it can also follow that academic identity
projects of both the left and the right can be compulsions to narcissistic
recognition. Within some of these identity projects, there is a dense reduction of the social field to the phenomenology of a fragile, precious and
embattled selfhood of the kind Sennett (1993) discussed as emblematic of
metropolitan modernity. This selfhood oscillates perpetually between articu-
lating its fragility (in the language of a survivalist problematic), and
therefore the need for its revitalisation, but also its strength, resilience and
survival in the face of the magnitude of oppressions it faces. This undulation
between potency and frailty, vitalism and victimology, is significantly
productive.

There is a nostalgia here for a fictive, wholesome selfhood of the future. A
nostalgia for the future is precisely that Hegelian formulation of primordial
separation, dissolution and return that infects much classical sociology. This
tension between the threat to identity and therefore fear of its dissolution –
the fear of the literal occultation of identity – and its other side, the need for
its renewal, is reflected in a variety of ways. Indeed focus on the fragmentation of identity, even the critique of whatever is meant by 'essentialism',
while seemingly presenting a corrective to left or right forms of identity
politics, actually only confirms them at another level of the political imaginary, indeed cannot actually escape them entirely. It is here that the
distinction between 'identity politics' and 'the politics of identity' itself
evaporates through the various reifications that the latter is compelled to
utilise.

There was during the 1970s much official social policy and academic
apprehension about Asian and black youth subject to the vagaries of adjustment to British society and the incommensurability of their lives with those
of their parents. Hence a 'between two cultures' paradigm came to dominate
official ruminations on these youth (Community Relations Commission
1976; Watson 1977). These approaches were fiercely criticised by black and
anti-racist academics in the 1980s, both for pathologising those youth and
as concrete manifestations of liberal academics and social policy stakeholders
fragmenting those communities generationally (Centre for Contemporary
Cultural Studies 1982). Even though the political motivations are usually
different, it can be those same black and anti-racist academics today who
celebrate the hybrid, syncretic cultures of urban black youth as a positive
characteristic – a culture neither one nor the other but something else
besides, in-between (Bhabha 1994).

This return of the excluded middle can be as problematic now as it was in
the 1970s. Certainly, in-betweenness acts as an academic counterposition to
various nativisms and fundamentalisms that also announce the syncretism of
cultures (or civilisations) as the key problem for their abhorrent projects of
purity. However, academic focus on the often trivial artefacts of youth

cultural production – marginalia as the key analytic for understanding dominant modes of consumption, signification as the key analytic of culture and society – implicitly proposes syncretism as the avant-garde cultural manifestation that minority cultures must aspire to in their quest for Western liberal cosmopolitan status. It has also produced a new academic endeavour preoccupied with the often banal, scholarly rummage for indications of hybridity and syncretism, splitting and doubling, hypostatisation and rupture, limit and abyss. This may be politically necessary in the face of real and manifest authoritarian claims to authenticity (though this is not usually the impetus for such projects.) However, even in their own terms, the critiques of essentialism, now a couple of decades old, have been unable to advance a political strategy in the face of those white and black nativists and patriarchs who would happily and unhesitatingly concur with their critics that they are essentialist. The epistemic objects (and spatial-temporal political limits) of much theoretical production are also significant – the archives of racial-colonial discourse and the fleeting fancies of contemporary Western popular culture: assessment of neither seems to muster critical projects of social, political or economic transformation. The spatial and temporal landscape these old and new cultural texts provide is appreciably distant from and incongruent with the topography of contemporary geopolitics and their temporal landscapes (Appadurai 1996).

It seems puzzling that the overwhelming academic obsession with the diasporic, racial, ethnic, mixed, hybrid, syncretic, passing self and all its variegated possibilities is occurring during a period of impersonal, brutalising geopolitics and the greatest relative and absolute impoverishment of large sections of the non-Western world. However, a fundamental thematic aspect of much of this work is about the exceptional and inimitable nature, capacities, capabilities discovered only in black or diaspora subjectivities – whether this is the privileged angle of vision that black women have, the double consciousness of Western modernity of the black subject, that unique third space of hybridity that blacks inhabit, or the distinctive deconstructionist locus of the subaltern in which it cannot not want the gifts of Western modernity, yet must persistently criticise that modernity, and that is the only (im)possible imperative. Other versions present something like a moral or ethical necessity that only the black subject possesses in which it is compelled to simultaneously face a multitude of directions in a comprehensive 'politics of criticism', critical race feminism or the like. An analogy of the chosen people, and of the implicit moral and ethical rectitude of the diaspora[12] or hybrid subject, seems to permeate many of these theoretical efforts, distant as they might seem from the lived, empirical, mundane or brash cultures, or the moralities, political formations and stratifications in the minority communities of the West.

Notes

1 The contemporary relevance of centre, semi-periphery and periphery, or the language of 'First' and 'Third' worlds, has been questioned from a number of directions (see, for example, Appadurai 1996), as has the transhistorical imaginary that situates 'neo-colonialism', or a contemporary 'Empire', as somewhat like a new mode of production, distribution and information that re-establishes a topographical continuity with the maps of old European imperialism and colonialism, though one in which the USA has been definitively inserted. This requires more discussion than can be provided here, but for these limited purposes the 'Third World' appellation is useful.

2 I would like to thank Stephen Cross, Jane Hindley, John Solomos and Les Back for comments.

3 See Banerjea 2002 on this point. The issue here is not about diminishing the scale or historical and socio-political distinctiveness of either the Holocaust or the transatlantic slavery of Africans from the fifteenth to the nineteenth century, grossly sacralising competing genocides, or instituting a non-Atlantic diagram of modernity. Instead it is important to interrogate the academic, historical and ethical limits that are preserved. What kind of chronographies and topographies of modernity, and therefore geohistorical sociologies, also become possible in seriously considering, for example, Cambodia from 1975–9, Rwanda in 1993–4, Bengal in 1769–70 or 1943–4, or the USSR from the late 1920s to the mid-1940s? What ethical and political associations become possible in expanding from transatlantic slavery to contemporary institutions of slavery and an international traffic in humans, not primarily determined by the transactions of 'chattel' (though forms of chattel slavery are entrenched in a few nations), but which currently permanently ensnares at least 27 million adults and children globally in lifelong bondage, servitude, punishment and institutional violence. The creation of new forms of slavery, serfdom and feudalism in late modernity is less important for empirically contravening the teleological conceits of classical sociology than it is in being entirely ignored by the disciplinary inheritors of that tradition. Much contemporary slavery (institutional slavery, not hyper-exploited but legally free serfdom) is inextricably linked to new technologies and economies of globalisation that deliver the commodities whose branding and semiology is a source of much analytical fascination for some. Similarly, which ethical imperatives become necessary in expanding from an ethical critique of colonial discourse to one focused on postcolonial states and elites?

4 This particular temporal matrix, especially where the authentic archaic is claimed to have been superseded by an irreducibly alien medieval period, informs a considerable number of contemporary nationalist, ethnic and religious chauvinisms.

5 Though the fascination with melanocytes exhibited by some Afrocentrist tendencies, which are characteristically combined with a contemporary theory of bodily humours and somatic energy fields, illustrates a penetration beyond skin.

6 Rashid (2000: 18) states that the Afghan '*mujahideen*' received over $10 billion from the USA, Europe and Muslim countries. See also Mackenzie 1998: 94.

7 A characteristic Jamaati-i-Islami rendition of 'the West and the Rest' can be found in al-Ahsan (1992).

8 In an attempt at deconstruction, Al-Azmeh is implicitly charged with alignment with apartheid, racism and US neo-Nazis – a manifestation of a fertile, creative and empyreal sociological imagination that does not seek to unduly trouble itself with the burden of academic veracity or integrity.

9 The ethical-historical burdens here are dense and imperceptible in bare forms. The rendering of histories as limited to histories of the present, equivalent to the methodology of writing histories, equivalent to the histories of historiography, or fully imbricated in hegemonic interests or regimes of truth and power raises a range of difficult issues that requires a dialogic marshalling of the whole critical, intellectual, interdisciplinary project. These disciplinary difficulties, and dialogic and interpretive necessities, are erased by happy presentist abstractions.

10 When sociality (and discursivity itself) is then invoked as the primary essentialising gesture, and when there is no essence to essentialism, we have naturally reached a productive theoretical impasse, one outside historicity, politics, context. See Fuss (1990).

11 Spivak's invocation of strategic essentialism has been far more complex than its various popular academic renditions suggest. Nevertheless, the 'strategy' of strategic essentialism indeterminately signifies a calculus of essentialism and an evaluation of ethico-political conditions of possibility. Which subject-actor of strategic essentialism is this capable cogito? See Cross (2001).

12 The non-absolutist and proto-cosmopolitan affinities elaborated in Gilroy's compounded diaspora require preserving. I am less certain though of their application for self-consciously diasporic absolutists, both within and outside the West, fixated on the importance of territory, blood, metaphysical identity or hierarchy for their projects of a specifically diasporic consciousnesses, ones integrated with a foundational universal humanity and which need not necessarily depend on homeland. I am also thinking here of the spatial scale and topography implied in Gilroy's diaspora and its application for a variety of diasporic formations entrenched outside their national homelands in African and South Asian countries; empirical examples are legion and can controvert the kinds of dispositions and sensibilities implied both in the secular, non-nationalist Askenazi cosmopolitanism of mid-nineteenth- to early twentieth-century Europe, and in what is understood as the cosmopolitanism of populist varieties of syncretic black diaspora modernism in Euro-America. There is a differently positioned range of debates regarding cosmopolitanism, migration and diaspora, postcolonial nationalism and authenticity outside Euro-America that complicates these areas considerably, not least through the assertion that the phenomenology of diaspora has historically been more important for creating modes and structures of confessional nativism outside the modern national homeland than it has for cultivating a cosmopolitan consciousness.

2 Extolling eclecticism

Language, psychoanalysis and demographic analyses in the study of 'race' and racism

Ann Phoenix

Research on 'race' and racism has proliferated in the human sciences over the last few years so that, although there are lacunae in some disciplines, some areas and in the work of some researchers, there is an excellent corpus of research scholarship in this field. Indeed, research in this field has been published for more than eighty years demonstrating the sustained (although changing) importance of these issues in some societies. As would be expected when there is a burgeoning of research in any area, the stories told in the literature are far from unitary. At the very least, the questions that preoccupy researchers shift over time. It is not surprising, for example, that in the post-Second World War years that research on 'race' and racism tried to understand how ordinary people could be complicit in genocide. Classic studies such as *The Authoritarian Personality* (Adorno *et al.* 1939), the Minimal Group Paradigm (Tajfel *et al.* 1971) and *Obedience to Authority* (Milgram 1974) or segregation among US miners (Minard 1952) were all attempts to throw light on such issues. As classic studies, all have been reinterpreted from the vantage of later theoretical and epistemological understandings (e.g. Billig 2002; Milner 1983; Wetherell and Potter 1992).

As the wealth of work available has accumulated, the theoretical, epistemological and methodological approaches taken have also proliferated. Recent research on 'race' and racism has focused mostly on everyday instances of racism, rather than gross examples of genocide. Qualitative research has gained legitimacy in many disciplines and much of this work pays close attention to what people say and write on the understanding that, since meanings are constructed in language, this should be the primary site for understanding social interactions (Potter and Wetherell 1987). This 'turn to language' has influenced all forms of qualitative methodology and generated many debates about epistemology. The resulting methods have produced much insightful and exciting work. However, the application of these methods to research on racism raises a number of tricky issues. For example, are there, as Stephen Frosh *et al.* (2001) and Hollway and Jefferson (2000) argue, important 'things that can't be said' because the emotions they arouse lead them to be pushed into the unconscious? If so, what are the implications for our understanding of accounts that confirm or deny experiences of racism.

In addition, how can large-scale demographic data (much favoured by policy-makers) contribute to qualitative analyses?

The first part of the chapter discusses the contribution to the understanding of racism of qualitative analyses that focus on language. The second part of the chapter uses data from two studies of young people from a range of ethnic groups to examine examples where young people report that they cannot remember incidents of racism, as well as examples where young people report conflicts over whether or not culture is racialised. It considers whether psychoanalysis can make a particular contribution to analyses of what the young people say. The final part of the chapter uses the example of two studies to address the question of whether quantitative analyses of large-scale data sets are necessarily antithetical to qualitative analyses. The chapter concludes that an eclectic approach can help to provide richer understandings of 'race' and racism, provided that a consistent epistemological approach is adopted.

The contribution of the 'turn to language' to research on 'race' and racism

Over the last twenty years research methodologies that take language as their prime analytic site have flourished (e.g. discourse analysis, narrative analysis and conversation analysis). Within this genre, there are now some classic studies of 'race' and racism. Undoubtedly, the 'turn to language' has stimulated understanding that contemporary racism has taken on a 'new' form that is now rarely associated with ideas of superiority and inferiority, but is constructed on notions of 'natural difference' and incompatibility (Barker 1981). In addition, it is much more subtle than blatant racism and has been argued to be predicated upon liberal notions of individualism that construct racialised disadvantage as the result of personal, individual shortcomings, rather than socio-economic structural disadvantage (Augoustinos et al. 1999).

Moreover, a focus on rhetoric, argumentation, 'common sense' and thinking as cultural products has enabled insights into the widespread 'norm against prejudice' (Billig 1991) and how it functions in everyday interaction. Focusing on the common construction 'I'm not prejudiced/racist, but...' Billig argues that taboos against prejudice are evident when people use such phrases because they feel compelled to justify language that could be interpreted as prejudiced. In anticipation of potential criticism of such views, the speaker or writer has to defend him or herself in advance by denying that they are prejudiced. In keeping with Barker's conclusions about 'new racism', there is thus a recasting of prejudiced ideologies in non-racial terms or a deracialisation of discourse. Such a short phrase indicates the complexities and dilemmas involved for many people in everyday talk about 'race' and racism. These include ambivalence, the construction of the self as reasonable and the projection of unreasonableness, irrationality and extremism onto others. In analysing the same phrase looking at the relations between cognition and action, van Dijk (1993a) further elucidates the broader societal and political functions of disclaimers and other denials of racism. Such discourses use a double strategy of positive self-presentation and maintenance of liberal discourses on the one hand and negative Other presentation on the other.

In keeping with Barker's, Billig's and van Dijk's work, Wetherell and Potter's (1992) study of the discourses of Pakeha (white) New Zealanders also indicates how everyday discourses serve to legitimate racist and exploitative social relations while maintaining liberal discourses of advocating respect and tolerance for cultural difference. Such discourses seem more benign and are less likely to raise objections. They suggest that racism is a collective discursive practice with ideological effects:

> Racist discourse is discourse which has the effect of categorizing, allocating and discriminating between certain groups and, in the context of New Zealand, it is discourse which justifies, sustains and legitimates those practices which maintain the power and dominance of Pakeha New Zealanders.
>
> (Wetherell and Potter 1992: 70)

Wetherell and Potter's findings are echoed by those from more recent studies. For example, Augustinos et al. (1999) found that non-Aboriginal Australian university students routinely drew on themes that exculpated colonialism and justified Aborigines' 'plight' in ways that made them responsible for their situation. In a detailed study of 'racial politics in Birmingham', Solomos and Back found that white politicians used discourses of 'culture which pre-empts accusations of racism' (1995: 129).

One of the strong messages from research focusing on discourses, rhetoric or conversation is that people do not have singular, unitary identities, but instead have multiple, potentially contradictory identities. Not surprisingly, then, they often behave in inconsistent ways. For that reason, language-based approaches argue that a focus on *people* as racist is not helpful to the understanding of racism. Instead, a focus on racist discourses and practices is more illuminating of the contradictory processes involved. Billig *et al.* provide a powerful example of this:

> Immediately after the interview, conducted at school, this young supporter of a racist party, and of compelling all of 'them' to leave 'our country', was to be seen walking arm in arm with a young Asian girl, chatting and laughing in easy friendship.
>
> (1988: 106)

This contradiction is repeatedly found to characterise people's discourses and what they do. For example, in a study of how US university students

account for informal segregation on campus, Buttny (1999) found differences between black and white students and within these groups in how
they accounted for lack of contact between different racialised groups.
Buttny argues however that:

> Perhaps the most interesting finding is that some participants hold
> seemingly conflicting accounts; they are ambivalent about self-segrega-
> tion....Some students spoke of separation as problematic, but when
> challenged by interlocutors, claimed that it was understandable. Or,
> some participants voiced the desire to have more interracial contact,
> while at the same time, they seemed unable to know how to achieve it.
> These conflicting accounts fit Billig and colleagues' (1988) notion of
> 'ideological dilemmas,' the notion that various and even opposing
> accounts can be avowed by participants to make sense of their circum-
> stances.
>
> (1999: 263).

Such paradoxes allow contradictory possibilities in relation to racism and
interactions across racialised boundaries. For example, it is well established
that 'insulting routines' are a marked feature of young people's (particularly
boys') interactions (e.g. Back 1996; Eder *et al.* 1995; Nayak and Kehily
1996). These enable shared (pleasurable) interactions but also serve to fore-
ground racism in ways that limit communication by reinforcing boundaries
(Tannock 1999). A research focus on language thus enables understandings
of the richness and complexity of everyday interactions.

The limits of language?

Despite the undoubted richness of the contributions made by a range of
language-based approaches, other research approaches have helped (and
continue to help) to elucidate our understandings of 'race' and racism. A
clear example of this is provided by research (from a variety of disciplines)
on the social geographies of 'race' and racism. For example, geographers have
used combinations of demography, cultural and political readings with analyses of spatial location to produce understandings of racialised segregation
and the complexity of spatial location (e.g. Smith 1989; McDowell 1999).
They have also analysed the geographies associated with racialised identities
and racism (e.g. Bonnett 1999). A non-linguistically based geography has
allowed us to see how, in what Doreen Massey (1994) calls 'the power geom-
etry of time-space compression', different social groups have different
relationships to mobility with some being more in charge of it and some
being more at the receiving end.

Back *et al.* (1999) used a variety of methods – including a 'fashion
parade'; getting young people to photograph their neighbourhoods; a video
walkabout; audio diaries; guided fantasy; family genograms and place

mapping – to demonstrate the complex strategies young people use in mapping and negotiating their 'ethnoscapes'. For some of the young people, there was a clear binary between 'safe' and 'unsafe' spaces; belonging and not belonging. Back *et al.* are able to show that young people use much more complex strategies than viewing some neighbourhoods as safe and others as dangerous. Instead, their strategies could be typified as: (1) safe world/dangerous spots; (2) Safe world/dangerous belts or clusters and (3) dangerous worlds/islands of safety. This study and the related Hamburg study (Räthzel 2002) both show that there is an articulation between the subjective experience and everyday practices of racialisation in neighbourhoods and gender. Similarly, in a study of racialised segregation on post-apartheid South African beaches, Dixon and Durrheim (in press) did an observational mapping of people on the beach as well as interviewing 'white' South Africans about racialised relations on South African beaches. This combination of methodology allowed them to conclude that there were three types of racialised segregation on the beach. First, the observation of umbrella use demonstrated that almost everybody used umbrellas in racially segregated ways. Second, 'black' people tended to sit or lie in a few regions of the beach, while white people used large areas of the beach. Third, on the two holiday days when black people came to the beach in larger than usual numbers, white people tended to avoid the beach.

Clearly then research on 'race' and racism has profited from using a range of methods. However, questions also arise about whether language itself can tell us all we need to know about the processes through which people have identities and how they make social meanings. A major debate in the human sciences concerns the 'things that can't be said' because they are not open to conscious scrutiny:

> It seems to me that while the 'turn to language' has been enormously valuable in attending to the production of (particularly) conscious meanings, there is a danger...of *reducing* meaning to what which can be narrated, that which can be clearly said....My view on this is that psychoanalysis show very clearly that there is a point where discourse fails, where language is characterised by its insufficiency rather than its expressive capacity, where what is known in and by a person lies quite simply outside symbolisation.
>
> (Frosh 2002: 134–5)

Similarly, Davies and Harre (1990) argue that people are not always conscious of the subject positions they set up and/or take up for themselves and others.

An increasing number of researchers have turned to psychoanalysis in order to account for what 'can't be said' (e.g. Frosh *et al.* 2003; Rattansi 1994; Walkerdine *et al.* 2001). Hollway (1984, 1989) and Hollway and Jefferson (2000) drew on the ideas of the psychoanalyst Melanie Klein in their research that we are all meaning-making and 'defended', i.e. we have anxiety-driven emotional investments in the meanings we produce and with which we align ourselves. The same thing may, therefore, have different meanings to different people. In addition, people may not know why they experience certain things as they do and they may have unconscious motivations to disguise certain meanings. An 'individual's history of positioning in discourses and consequent production of subjectivity '(Hollway 1984: 251) result in an investment in using power in ways that protect them from vulnerability. Hall (1996) also draws on psychoanalytic ideas to explain how people take up particular identity positions by investing in them. Althusser's notion of interpellation – the process by which we come to be 'hailed' ('interpellated') – has been used by various researchers to explain the unconscious process by which we are recruited into particular ways of understanding the world and ourselves as subjects (Blackman and Walkerdine 2001; Brah 1999).

The increasing appeal of psychoanalytic ideas is, however, contested. Wetherell (1998) has argued that it is unnecessary to appeal to psychoanalysis to explain social meanings in that the unconscious is produced in discourse and it is in discourse that 'troubled subject positions' are produced and resolved. She argues that analyses informed by psychoanalysis move behind language to explain psychological processes such as splitting and projection in ways that leave the actual psychology involved mysterious and ambiguous, almost beyond empirical investigation and asocial (Wetherell 2003). By way of contrast, Wetherell argues, a focus on discourse shows that the boundaries between the social and the psychic may be more porous than a Kleinian framework presupposes. The discourses people use show complexity and ambivalence, but whereas in psychoanalysis this is interpreted as unconsciously produced, Wetherell argues that people also routinely draw on genres of 'educated discourse' that may be more 'sociological' or in documentary style. The analysis of these help to unpack the ways in which people take up subject positions. Furthermore, she uses Edwards (1997) to argue that 'emotion discourse' can be considered to be 'an integral feature of talk about events' rather than unconsciously produced.

So is it possible, empirically, to decide between these apparently opposed theoretical positions on analysis from the analysis of talk on 'race' and racism? Consider the following examples from an interview study of the social identities (including racialised identities) of 248 14–18-year-old Londoners studied by Barbara Tizard and myself:

Q : So have you ever been called names?
A : I remember an occasion when I was walking down the street and these three guys who I didn't know from Adam started calling me names. I was a bit gutted about that actually at the time.
Q : What sort of things were they calling you and how old were you?

A : I was coming to this school. I think I was lower down the school actually, maybe about 2nd or 3rd year. I can't remember the incident clearly
– remember what they actually called me. It was sort of one of those
incidents where you sort of remember but only sort of half remember –
can't exactly remember what was said but remember that it cut you up
at the time. I don't know whether it is because it is a chapter that I
would rather not remember, so on purpose I've blocked it out or whatever [young black woman].

The following young woman started this particular account by going into
detail about the names she has been called in the past at school:

A : ...I can't remember it now, but I had an ordeal at school once to do
with colour.
Q : You had a what?
A : Ordeal, at school, about my colour. Can't remember what it was now.
Q : Junior school this was?
A : Yeah. Can't remember....
Q : When you say an ordeal, it must have been something pretty bad?
A : Yeah, I'm just trying to remember what it was. School, school, school,
school. Ah no. You just have something – it's just blanked out of my
brain. I'll come back to it [young black woman].

A few young black people in the study explicitly used 'emotion categories' and psychoanalytic explanations to account for the impact of their
racialised positioning on their recollection of racist events. The two young
women reported above appeared to be aware that they did not wish to
remember specific incidents. They showed this by invoking psychoanalytic
explanations of psychically defensive reasons for forgetting the detail of
stressful incidents. One way of analysing these (un)recollected experiences is
viewing them as demonstrating the ways in which some young black people
(construct how they) deal with the contradiction of not wanting to be
affected by racism while being hurt by it. Their accounts indicate that they
repress the detail while being meta-analytic about the fact that they are
doing so. According to this analysis, the accounts of these two young women
also illustrate how discourses of the past are always emotionally marked
discourses of current self-presentation. Their identities are as people who
recognise the existence of racism, have experienced bad manifestations of it,
but do not dwell on these. At the same time, they are articulately reflexive
about them.

However, it is also possible to reject psychoanalytic analyses in interpreting the above two accounts. For, clearly, psychoanalysis forms part of
these two young women's discourses. In Wetherell's (2003) terms, the
'educated discourse' they are drawing on is an individualistic psychoanalytic
one. This is hardly surprising since psychoanalytic discourse has become

commonplace in late capitalist societies (Phillips 1999). In both cases the appeal to psychoanalytic notions of repression occurred when they were asked for a specific example of a general claim they were making. As the interviewer I can be seen to have constructed what Wetherell (1998) calls a 'troubled subject position' for these young women by possibly challenging their implicit claims to veracity by asking them to substantiate what they have said. Alternatively, the potential trouble may result from not wanting to discuss something so painful, and potentially controversial, with an unknown interviewer. A response in terms of repression is a culturally acceptable way of extricating themselves from these troubled subject positions. Could it be then that such ideas are readily drawn upon at points when speakers cannot produce an example that would be expected? If so, talk about repression can be seen as a rhetorical device – a readily available discursive strategy. Indeed, we might expect that repressed material would not be sufficiently open to consciousness for speakers to know that they were psychically defending themselves in this way. Billig, however, suggests that people use rhetorical devices as the means by which to repress unwelcome thoughts so that it is language that forms repression:

> What is customarily said may also routinely create the unsaid, and, thus, may provide ways for accomplishing repression...we can move dialogues, including our inner conversations, from awkward to safer matters. We can say 'but...' or 'anyway...' to ourselves, just as we can utter those words to fellow conversationalists.
>
> (1999: 67)

Billig gives an evocative example of how repression can be both collective and rational, or at least socially beneficial:

> During the apartheid era, (in South Africa) the population of whites would use an outward discourse of race in order to maintain a racist political system....With the collapse of apartheid those old ways of talking have become unacceptable. White speakers cannot be seen to be racist....Internal controls also have to be set in place, so that the thought, as much as the outwardly spoken act, becomes shameful.
> The task for white South Africans...is not merely to keep their mouths shut, but to ensure that they and their children do not think the previously utterable....
> The lesson of Freud is that a certain amount of repression is necessary for the moral order.
>
> (1999: 260)

Neither set of interpretations (psychoanalytic or discursive) makes a judgement about the truth or otherwise of the young women having suffered ordeals to do with racism, and both would acknowledge that racism is of key importance in their lives. However, the examples arguably demonstrate that psychoanalytic ideas are important to research analysts – whether because social relations are psychodynamically organised or because psychoanalytic ideas are so much part of the discourses available to us. It is not, however, possible to choose between the explanations simply by applying them to empirical accounts where research participants invoke such ideas.

If it is not possible to decide between psychoanalytic and discursive analyses in participants' claims that some things are too terrible to be recalled and said (at least at the moment), then can psychoanalysis be said to make any unique contributions to research accounts? In order to consider this issue further, a few examples from a London study of masculinities in 11–14-year-old boys will be examined (Frosh *et al.* 2001). One of the key findings of this study is that boys were emotionally invested in presenting themselves as 'properly' masculine. The pervasive account of what popular boys were like was that they were good at sport, particularly football, 'hard' and visibly disengaged from schoolwork. Most boys felt that they could not measure up to this and, as a result, they expended a great deal of energy on positioning themselves in relation to the hegemonically masculine ideal. Since the hegemonic ideal is also racialised with black boys being viewed as embodying its signifiers, there were both attempts on the part of some white boys to 'act black' and contestation about the signifiers of style:

INTERVIEWER : D'you think some white boys then envy black boys (1) 'cos they think they're stronger?

PAUL : Yeah like, they wanna like, some people wanna be black 'cos (1) they might like be more popular. Like, black people like, don't like really cool. Black people have like black slang don't they an' they call people (.) bro an' that (hands). Like white people don't call each other (.) names like that an' black people call some people some. And sometimes people wanna be black an' that /.../ [11-year-old white boy].

Many studies over the last three decades have highlighted racialised syncretism where young white men (as articulated in the account above) admired and used talk, music and clothes styles developed by young black men (e.g. Cohen 1997; Hewitt 1986; Jones 1988). Given that style signifies prestige and masculine status, and that this is one of the few ways in which young black men can assert greater power, it is not surprising that many boys indicated that racialised style is often a site of contestation, as in the following three examples:

GEORGE : I think I think that because say because I'm white (.) I mean I'm not English or anything but because I'm white they expect me to listen to (.) I don't know (.) Oasis, Blur (*inaudible*) but really but when I was in America so long (.) I've got used to listening to (.) rap, hip-hop, S. R. and B.

BRIAN: : Yes and then because he listens to hip hop black people think he's trying to take away what he likes, he likes hip hop

GEORGE: : They think I'm trying to take away their music) and black people think it's

MAURICE: : I like *starts mimicking African singer* just their's and not his and everyone likes stuff like that but I don't really listen to that I listen to Celine Dion.

INTERVIEWER: : So do d'you get criticised then by black people

GEORGE: Yes yes I do very much) for trying to be black yeah?

GEORGE: : Yes but but that's only because (.) that's only because I lived in America so long.

INTERVIEWER: : How do you get criticised...? [TERRY: Disses you.]

GEORGE: : Uh you're you're trying to be you're trying to be black you're taking the mick you're taking the piss and all this.

MAURICE: : And you're just a white man.

GEORGE: : You you're just white you're just white trash.

INTERVIEWER: : Does that happen to you (.) then?

MAURICE: : Yeah even though I am (.) part of their culture [white group, year nine (13–14-year-olds].

INTERVIEWER: : Right. Do you think that there are differences between black, white and Asian boys?

DAVID: : Not in colour, but what they like, like different songs and stuff like that. /.../ Yeah, different teams, different footwear – say like I like Reebok.

INTERVIEWER: : Mmm.

DAVID: : And black people like Nike and stuff like. I know some white people like Nike as well, and some black people like Reebok, like Darren an Nelson's bruver, 'e likes Reebok....

DAVID: : So like I don't mind what they like or what they don't like.

INTERVIEWER: : (2) Yeah. So what happens if white boys wear the same kind of things that black boys wear?

DAVID: : Erm (.) you get the occasion, where the black person who's goin, 'Oh, you're trying to act like us, you're tryin to act like us' and sayin 'You shouldn't be wearin that cos you're white' but that's bein racist. But all my friends round my area, dey don't what I wear. I've had a pair of Nike trainers before. And dey didn't mind – dey said, 'Oh, dey're nice.'...And I say, 'Fanks', and all 'at.

INTERVIEWER: : (.) Were you trying to black, then, by doing that?

DAVID: : Nah – I was just wearin' dem because it was the latest trend around [12-year-old white boy].

GREG: : Some white boys that hang around with black boys (.) [Interviewer Right] and like they act like black boys....In like (.) this boy in my class (.) he's white but he tries to act like a black lad (.)

INTERVIEWER: : Yeah. W-what do you think of him?

GREG: : Mm (2) I think he's stupid a bit...(.) because he tries to bop too much (.) [Interviewer: Yeah] an he thinks he's too bad.

INTERVIEWER: : What (.) what would (.) you like white boys to be like (.) then?

GREG: : Act like white boys act (.) act the way they act not like

INTERVIEWER: : How, how do white boys act?

GREG: : Not a lot of changes but (.) they should stop trying to (.) speak like black boys cos (.) um, (.) some black and white boys speak differently and (.) they shouldn't try to walk and stuff [black 11-year-old].

It is quite clear from the three accounts quoted above that the white boys and the black boy all construct a story of the attractiveness of 'black style' and of contestation over the racialisation of style and of racialised positioning in relation to style. There is also agreement that it is black boys who attempt to police style with the white boys either denying that the styles they want to be part of are 'black' or that they themselves are trying to be 'black' through what they wear or listen to. The black boy quoted, however, argues that white boys should stop trying to 'act black'. An analysis of these three extracts fits with Connell's (1995, 2000) notion that masculinity is a 'practical accomplishment'. In this case it is racialised and struggled over in schools because it incorporates contradictory power relations. Racialisation (and its intersection with gender in this case) is both a resource in the construction of masculinities and is produced in boys' everyday practices of contestation.

Can anything be added to an analysis that focuses on what is said by applying psychoanalytic notions? Arguably, various psychoanalytic concepts are relevant here – e.g. desire for the Other, disavowal and defence against threat. Desire for the racialised Other has been considered in various pieces of research (e.g. Lewis 2000; Stoler 1995). In this section, we focus only on disavowal. Disavowal is a psychic strategy 'by means of which a powerful fascination or desire is both *indulged* and at the same time *denied* (Hall 1997: 267). Desire itself, according to the psychoanalyst Lacan, comes to the fore when 'someone bars our way to what we desire' (Minsky 1996). All the quotes above indicate that what has been constructed as 'black style' is deeply desired. However, both the quotes from white boys involve accounts that indicate that this style is being indulged while the boys either deny that it is a black style or that they are trying to be black, or argue that it is their culture anyway. Arguably here a focus on language and a psychoanalytic reading produce fairly similar accounts. In both analytic frames, conflict is pre-eminent. However, together they allow a bringing together of socio-cultural and psychic conflicts.

Perhaps then a richer reading and one that genuinely treats individual and social processes as inextricably linked can result – one which recognises that anxieties and contradictions lead boys to use defensive strategies simultaneously to defend themselves against attack and to construct themselves as 'properly' masculine. The issue then becomes one of ensuring that a consistent epistemology is applied. Wetherell suggests that:

> In different ways both discourse theory and psychoanalysis offer constructionist theories of meaning, although in the case of psychoanalytic object relations theories this is usually a partial constructionism. Both note how our access to reality (whatever that might be) is indirect and mediated....Psychoanalysis, unlike relativist discourse theories, suggests limits on this constructionism and often combines it with a realist or critical realist epistemology. Thus it is argued that it may be difficult but it is possible to work out a 'straight' view of reality and indeed part of the method of psychoanalytic psychotherapy is identifying when clients are dealing with reality and when their impressions have been unconsciously distorted.
>
> (2003: 105)

To the extent that psychoanalysis and language-based approaches both use social constructionist epistemologies, the task of reconciling them seems possible, provided that attention is paid to how the analyst is using a social constructionist framework. Perhaps a more difficult criticism concerns the question of who has the right to apply psychoanalytic concepts since psychoanalytic training is a lengthy process that relatively few people undertake. However, arguably, if the concepts are sufficiently well described, they must be open for non-psychoanalysts to apply in research, helped by those who demonstrate, on the basis of knowledge, how this can successfully be done (e.g. Hollway and Jefferson 2000).

The contribution of large-scale data sets to qualitative research on 'race' and racism

In recent years qualitative research has gained status in the human sciences. From a position where it was considered by many only to be suitable for pilot studies, it has become the approach of choice for a substantial number of researchers. As it has generated a large body of publications, there has been a tendency to treat qualitative and quantitative research as antithetical to each other in terms of epistemology, as well as the questions that can be addressed and methodology. There are, of course, researchers who have long advocated the combining of qualitative and quantitative methods (e.g. Brannen 1992). Yet, on the whole, research on 'race' and racism has been differentiated. This does not mean that qualitative researchers entirely ignore the output of quantitative researchers. For example the Policy Studies Institute surveys (e.g. Modood *et al.* 1997) are well quoted in qualitative research, as are some analyses from the 1991 Census – the first to ask a question about ethnicity (e.g. Coleman and Salt 1996; Karn 1997). However, on the whole, the two bodies of research have maintained a binary opposition.

It is possible to see why. For large-scale quantitative analyses are more likely to be presented as atheoretical empiricism than are qualitative analyses that, in many disciplines, have to be theoretically well worked through in order to be acceptable. This leads some qualitative researchers to be dismissive about the possibilities of quantitative work providing meaningful data. At the same time, quantitative researchers recognise that, in an area such as the study of 'race' and racism where policy issues are to the fore, that policy-makers and practitioners want statistical evidence and tend to neglect the contributions made to understandings by qualitative work. So too have research funders tended to privilege quantitative applications over qualitative ones.

The separation of the two sorts of research is, however, problematic. Not only can quantitative research not answer questions about social processes, but also the questions asked, and the terminology used, by quantitative researchers are sometimes not theoretically appropriate (Owen 2001). For example, terms such as 'ethnic community' are used in some analyses, apparently with no recognition that it is meaningless since everybody is ethnicised. Data are presented for groups such as 'Other–Other' (Phoenix 2003), which result when questionnaire answers do not fit with pre-coded concepts. However, they do not denote ethnic groups:

> Statistics are not neutral. They both reflect and contribute to important dimensions of difference and power in society....This is very clear when we talk about statistics of race or of ethnicity. The very language we use is highly charged: terms which some people see as natural may be seen as highly offensive by others.
>
> (Owen 2001: 134).

On the other hand, qualitative researchers cannot answer questions about trends or prevalence that policy-makers may want. More importantly, however, some do not make clear how they have conducted their study and analyses.

In the foreword to an edited collection on lesbian and gay psychology, D'Augelli (2002) argues that a powerful interplay of qualitative and quantitative methods makes it less possible to marginalise lesbian and gay psychology. However, there are also benefits of using both approaches in terms of the understanding that is possible. In particular, demographic data can illuminate the relevance of particular social trends as well as contextualising the processes, meanings and identities elucidated in qualitative analyses. This section of the chapter considers two studies where the combination of large-scale data sets and qualitative data have been used in these ways.

In a study of women in the Irish diaspora, Bronwen Walter (2001) explores the meanings of home and displacement for Irish women in the USA (where they are visible) and in Britain (where they are marginalised).

Her research is theoretically well worked out in that she draws on the notion that we are all interlinked in 'diaspora space' (Brah 1996) in order to disrupt racialised and ethnicised binaries of black/white and outsider/insider. In making connections between spatial and social location Walter uses demographic data showing the trends for Irish-born women to be living in Britain over the course of 130 years and trends in their regional location in Britain over the same period. Equally importantly, she is able to show the large fluctuations in the gender ratio over this period and that there are geographical variations in this. From this, she illuminates the longstanding status of Irish women as labour migrants and how their material location has shifted as regional demand for labour has changed from, for example, textiles in Scotland and Lancashire in the nineteenth century to other occupations in London and Southeast England.

These demographic data illuminate the context of Irish women's lives in Britain and provide a background for understanding what Irish women have to say about their lives. In addition it contributes to the understanding (evident in other studies for black and Asian people among others) that 'being fully integrated into the economy is not the same as being treated as socially equal' (Walter 2001: 162). Walter's study includes documenting the biographies of ten women. This helps to disrupt the idea, which could be produced by a focus on demographic data, that Irish women are homogeneous. Taken together, then, the large-scale quantitative data and the qualitative data provide nuanced, complex accounts of the women's experiences, while locating them in a historical and geographical context.

The second study discussed here as linking demographic and qualitative data is one on children of 'mixed parentage' done by Barbara Tizard and myself (Tizard and Phoenix 2002 [1993]). The study that informed this book focused on the identities of young people aged 14–18 years' old – a quarter of whom had one black and one white parent. In a context where there were few demographic data available on people of 'mixed-parentage', Charlie Owen conducted secondary analyses of Labour Force Survey and the 1991 Census data (Owen 2001; Phoenix and Owen 1996). These secondary analyses indicated that many people are contesting the social proscription on crossing constructed racialised boundaries. There are a rapidly increasing number of people in 'racially' 'mixed relationships' and marked increases in the number of people of 'mixed-parentage'. Thus, despite negative constructions of 'mixed-parentage' and very negative reactions of some people to identifying and publishing work specifically on those in this socially constructed category, the name of which is much contested, the demographic data indicated that it is socially important to understand this group. In addition, it provided the context within which it is possible to comprehend ideological and discursive shifts in regard to 'mixed-parentage'. The major finding in the qualitative (and quantitative) analyses done on the young people's interview accounts was that most identified themselves as 'mixed', even if they claimed other racialised identities in particular social settings. Given the demographic trends it was not surprising that 'mixed-parentage' was a strongly emergent identity.

One major benefit of including large-scale demographic data and qualitative analyses in the same study is that the epistemological approach can be consistent for both sets of data. The result of this is that the criticisms of atheoretical empiricism uninformed by social meaning in quantitative data and of rich, meaningful, but socially decontextualised qualitative analyses are avoided. Instead, there is the possibility of increasing understandings both of trends, current socio-economic circumstances and social processes.

Conclusions

This chapter has contended that a variety of methods have contributed to the profusion of research studies on 'race' and racism. The chapter focused particularly on a relatively new qualitative approach that is frequently characterised as the 'turn to language'. It argued that language-based approaches have helped with the understanding of how everyday discourses construct themselves as liberal and benign discourses of respect and tolerance for cultural difference while legitimating racist and exploitative social relations. They have also demonstrated the complexity and contradiction common to racialised accounts. However, despite the contribution of language-based approaches, some researchers argue that they are necessarily limited since 'there are things that can't be said'. The chapter explored some accounts where young people make an appeal to psychoanalytic concepts and others where psychoanalytic concepts seem relevant. It suggests that it is difficult to choose between analyses that focus only on language and those that apply psychoanalytic notions to the analysis of language and methodology. Yet, since psychoanalytic ideas have 'sedimented' into common sense and psychoanalysis is a rich source of analytic explanation, it seems appropriate to draw on psychoanalytic concepts in the analysis of language.

The final section of the paper explored the opposition between quantitative and qualitative data in general and in the study of 'race' and racism. It used examples of two studies to advocate the combination of large-scale demographic analyses and qualitative analyses within the same epistemological framework for the production of rich, meaningful and contextualised accounts.

3 Researching race and racism

French social sciences and international debates

Michel Wieviorka

I want to begin this article with an anecdote that relates to my own experience in writing and researching racism in France. In 1999, Pierre Bourdieu and Loïc Wacquant published an article in *Theory, Culture and Society* (Bourdieu 1999) in which, in an endnote (p. 53, 11), they referred to my book about *La France raciste* (Wieviorka 1992), the title of which they found 'scientifically scandalous'. They presented me as a 'French sociologist more attentive to the expectations of the field of journalism than to the complexities of social reality' (Bourdieu 1999: 53). The article by Bourdieu and Wacquant was not in itself very profound, as several of those whom the same journal then invited to reply in subsequent issues did not hesitate to stress;[1] the footnote that concerned me was defamatory and revolting. The accusation made against me personally was refuted in a subsequent issue by a review of my book written by Malcolm Brown and Robert Miles, who explained how my work was 'the most significant research' on the study of racism in France and how it 'persuasively expose(s) empirically the dynamics of racism in contemporary France' (Brown and Miles 2000). The main reservation that Brown and Miles 171, expressed about my work was that they found it 'excessively pessimistic in parts'. This criticism was made in 1999 at a time when observers could believe that the Front National (a party that makes political capital out of popular racism) was on the way out. There had just been a split in this party, which had led to a serious crisis. But three years later, after the Front National candidate, Jean-Marie Le Pen, with 17 per cent of the vote, achieved a better electoral score than the socialist candidate whom he eliminated in the second round of the Presidential elections in May 2002, perhaps my critics would be willing to reconsider this reservation, which was the most serious one they made.

This attack on me, and, more specifically, the locus where it took place, hurt me profoundly. Not only did it tarnish my reputation in French – Pierre Bourdieu and his protégé had already attacked me in *Actes de la recherche en sciences sociales* (Bourdieu 1998), a journal written in French, and therefore addressing a public easily able to form their own opinion about the book as it had just been reissued in paperback – but also in English in a journal with an international readership, which addressed a public most of whom do not read the sociology produced in French and were not really able to form their own opinion. In passing, quite apart from my personal case, this does pose interesting problems not far removed from the question, if not of racism, at least of imperialist or postcolonial contempt and the ethnocentrism associated with a position of cultural domination: What sort of community is it that only knows one language, for whom the only thing that exists in practice is the material to which it has direct access and is therefore in English?

The invitation from Martin Bulmer and John Solomos to contribute to this book gives me the opportunity to speak about my actual experience of researching racism, as well as the political and ethical dilemmas that I may have encountered. They would like me to deal with the origins and process of the research; in short, they are encouraging me to present my work in the first person singular. I am very grateful to them, all the more so because, in opposition to a sort of positivism, I consider that there is nothing more important today in the social sciences than to think about the relation of the researcher to his object. Or, if you like: that there is nothing more futile than to postulate a sort of scientific neutrality, an exteriority of the researcher that would enable him to be 'objective' because not involved, or at a distance. It is true that the researcher is not necessarily the person best situated to analyse his own experience, his own subjectivity, to introduce reflexivity into his approach that, in principle, he wishes to be rigorous and scientifically faultless. But who else can assemble the elements required for an effort of this type, at least to begin with? Who is better placed to speak about the research seen from the inside? Who can begin to touch on the aspects that academic books and articles do not usually deal with? When we go to a restaurant we do not normally visit the kitchens. However, I am going to engage here in something that is not dissimilar, avoiding – I hope – any tendency to narcissism or exhibitionism. I am going to present the main themes in an experience of research that I continue to believe is highly instructive and far from banal.

The origins of the programme

New racism

Towards the end of the 1980s I had become convinced that what was special about racism in Western societies was its resurgence and an extraordinary change in direction.

In the literature that was beginning to appear, I was particularly struck by the theme of differentialist racism. In the UK, a few years earlier, Martin Barker had published an unpretentious little book but one which, for me, remains a pioneering study on new racism (Barker 1981). In France, a few years later, similar ideas about cultural or differentialist racism were developed. Pierre-André Taguieff (1988) published *La Force du préjugé. Essai sur le racisme et ses doubles* – a huge, well-documented, scholarly book, clever that it was restricted to a relatively small audience. Almost simultaneously, Etienne Balibar (with Immanuel Wallerstein, 1989) published *Race, classe, nation. Les identités ambiguës*, a more politically committed book. In the USA, psychologists and political scientists who dealt with symbolic racism had positions that were fairly similar. Obviously, racism was being rethought.

At the same time, France was becoming aware of the changes in immigration, which was no longer being defined in terms of labour and increasingly becoming an immigration of settlement. Islam was becoming the second religion in the country (the important book for me and for many others was Gilles Kepel's *Les Banlieues de l'Islam*). Above all, racism was becoming a political issue, with Jean-Marie Le Pen's Front National, no longer an obscure group but a party capable of obtaining high scores in the elections – the shock was the by-election in Dreux in 1983, in which, for the first time, this party emerged as capable of upsetting the classical political game. I therefore became aware of the extent of the rethinking of racism, in the same years as I was becoming aware of the new social and political impact of the phenomenon.

A first research experience

It is true that as a researcher, but also as an individual, I had already been faced with a contemporary experience of racism – that of anti-Semitism in Poland – about which I had published a book in 1984 (Wieviorka 1984). I was forced to deal with this subject during the research on Solidarnosc, in Poland, which I did in 1980–1 with Alain Touraine and a whole group of French and Polish researchers. Right from its beginnings in 1980, I had been fascinated by this total movement that, at one and the same time, rose in the name of the working class, the Polish nation and democracy against a totalitarian form of power that was itself subservient to Moscow. But I am Jewish, of Polish origin, and at the time heard my parents and their friends slating Poland and the Poles, telling me that they were all anti-Semitic; they also criticised Solidarnosc and its leader, whom they described as a bigoted Catholic who was undoubtedly an anti-Semite. With Touraine and his research group, I had gone to study a social movement, Solidarnosc (Touraine *et al.* 1982). But, at the same time, I had used the opportunity when I was there to note down anything that referred to Jewish issues and to anti-Semitism, and whenever possible to do interviews about this question. Between two trips to Poland, I was gathering documents that, in Paris, would later assist me in writing a book. The latter is therefore based on concrete fieldwork experience, but it is, so to speak, an off-shoot of the main research, as well as being, at the same time, an answer to my parents and their friends. For a long period in my life, which did not end when Solidarnosc was liquidated by force in December 1981, I was torn between my profound sympathy for everything to do with a fascinating social movement and my affection for my family circle, who ordered me at best to forget, and, if not, to hate everything to do with Polish society and the Polish nation.

The main theoretical lesson that I drew from this research, which was to be useful to me later, refers to the relation that I observed between the social movement – Solidarnosc – and anti-Semitism; anti-Semitism, in a Poland where there are practically no Jews (a few thousand had survived, many of whom were elderly people, as compared with three million before the war), gained momentum when Solidarnosc was in crisis, when it no longer succeeded in engaging its opponent in a conflictual relationship. When the economic situation became increasingly unbearable and those in political power less and less inclined to negotiate, the dark side of the movement gained momentum, and became populist, nationalist, undemocratic and anti-intellectual, attracted by forms of behaviour tending to reveal an anti-Semitism that the 'real Poles' were beginning to assert. Racism, or, in this instance, anti-Semitism (I will not discuss here whether or not the two phenomena belong to the same category), was the reverse of the movement; in the first instance it was the dark and disturbing side, but also increasingly the reverse of the movement and the beginning of an anti-movement. Being primarily a sociologist of social movements, it therefore became possible for me to theorise racism as being the reverse of the social movement, at least in Alain Touraine's definition of the term.

Institutional circumstances

In 1988–9, I was well placed to be elected to the post of professor at the Ecole des Hautes Etudes en Sciences Sociales. I had just finished a very extensive research programme on terrorism – 10 years' work – and it was out of the question that I would continue to study this phenomenon on which I had already spent more than a decade researching. As part of my candidature I had to present a teaching and research project. At that point, the obvious theme to study was racism. On the one hand, there were the recent developments in French society (the rise of the Front National, the change in immigration, the rise in mobilisation against racism, at that time primarily in the *SOS Racisme* movement), and, on the other, my intellectual interests. Also a factor that has been constant in my work is the concern to study very real social problems and to produce knowledge capable of shedding light on public concerns.

In the first stage, I spent a lot of time preparing myself intellectually, constructing my analytical categories, week after week, during an annual seminar that led to a theoretical book (Wieviorka 1991). This effort was completed with the organisation of a large intellectual colloquium on racism. I was anxious to be in touch with intellectual trends in other countries; I could not accept the navel-contemplating attitude of French research in this area, as in many others, and I wanted to be able to discuss and exchange ideas with specialists from all over the world and from different academic disciplines (Wieviorka 1993). In 1990, I was intellectually ready, by then well established in the Ecole des Hautes Etudes en Sciences Sociales, where the conditions for research were excellent; I belonged to a Research Centre, the CADIS (Centre d'Analyse et d'Intervention Sociologiques), where I found an intellectual environment which was stimulating, creative and congenial. I would never have been able to construct my ideas about racism if I had not been surrounded by people studying the urban crisis and the areas in the *banlieues* (suburbs) where there was a lot of tension. There were also researchers documenting the immigrants' endeavours to construct social protest movements, against racism and for equality, and others working in a comparative dimension who were studying the social and cultural experiences in other countries that included dimensions of racism. In other words there reigned here, under the direction of Alain Touraine – and still reigns there today – a climate that makes this centre outstanding in its production and discussion of knowledge: I could embark on a genuine concrete programme of research on racism.

A programme, a research team, fieldwork areas

Not only have I always conceived my work as a researcher in terms of a combination of working out theory and doing fieldwork, but I belong also to an intellectual tradition where the method of *sociological intervention* is considered by far the best tool in the production of sociological knowledge. The term is used in the title of the research centre (CADIS) founded in 1980 by Alain Touraine, who is also the inventor of this method. Numerous publications, including some in English, present or use this method about which I would only say a few words here (for a fairly general presentation of the method and its applications cf. Clark and Diani 1996).

The general idea that underlies the method of *sociological intervention* is that, while the actors may not be fully aware of the meaning of their action, they are not totally incapable of interpreting it. If we set up an appropriate arrangement, it should be possible to set the actors whose action we wish to study into a context in which they can produce an analysis along with the researchers. Thus, if it is a question of racism, it must be possible to put people who are racists in a position in which they think about their racism, its sources and its meaning, rather than expressing their prejudice and their hatred. More precisely, my initial idea was to bring together, on several occasions, people who were racist, and to have them live through a process during which they would be led to discuss racism and what it involves, and therefore move over to the side of the analysis. The analysis cannot come spontaneously from the people in question, and the role of the researchers is not only to create the conditions of its possibility, but also to introduce it, by presenting ideas, hypotheses and arguments that in some way induce the people who are participating in the research to think (see Wieviorka 1993:

353–61).

Fieldwork areas

It was in this perspective that I set up a team composed of five young researchers, suggesting that we carry out a number of sociological interventions, which, in different situations, would enable us to put racist people to varying degrees in a position to analyse their behaviour.

To begin with, I chose three urban areas that seemed to me to deserve further study. Taken together, these areas would give us a picture that might not be representative but would at least give a fairly varied view of the French arena of racism.

The rise of working-class racism

Roubaix is an industrial town where, in the space of a few years, the social fabric had rapidly deteriorated while, at the same time, the socio-political system formed by the three main actors in the town (the employers, the trade unions and the local authority) had collapsed. The most dynamic part of the population abandoned the town, while immigrants came there in considerable numbers in search of cheap housing and social welfare. In Roubaix, I formed a group of about ten people, some of whom were poor people stuck in council (HLM) housing in a peripheral working-class area with a bad reputation. Others who were not so poor lived in the town centre and were extremely apprehensive about the downward spiral of the town. To contact these people, my researchers and I used intermediaries such as social workers and militants in a local community committee to put us in touch with several people from whom we chose the ten members in our group for the intervention. We explained what we wanted to do to everyone at length: to organise a series of meetings with the group that would take place over a period of time, to discuss the problems posed by immigration at local level. The researchers promised that at the end of these meetings they would present their analysis of the work of the group, their hypotheses, and discuss them with them. It took several weeks to prepare the intervention, to collect the social, political, economic and historical information necessary in Roubaix, to hold a number of individual meetings and finally choose the ten participants in the group. There was no question of saying blankly to the people chosen: 'We want to study you as a racist', but nor was there any question of lying to them. We therefore explained to them that the idea was to think together about the difficulties in their town linked to the presence of North African-origin populations, difficulties which seem to fuel racism. Between March and May 1991, the group hosted, among others, the local Front National leader, as well as the Socialist Party one, a taxi driver who had set up a sort of private militia, the 'Chevaliers de Roubaix', a militant who was well known locally for his role in the urban struggles of the 1970s and 1980s, the mayor, a trio of young *beurs*, etc. In the group meetings, which lasted on average two hours, the researchers (myself and one or two members of my team) said little, presiding over the session and, if necessary, directing the discussion, organising it, sometimes introducing a remark or a comment on the way the debate was going. After this phase of meetings, the group had 'closed' sessions with no guests and there the researchers intervened with considerable force, explaining to the group, for example, that racism, while present in the remarks of its members, was associated with exclusion, their downward social mobility or their social anxieties, as well as with their feeling of a threat to their cultural existence and their national identity. The most outstanding event, in my eyes, in this intervention in which the discussions between the researchers and members of the group were simple, direct and quite cordial, occurred at the end, during the last meeting: the same people who had gone along with the researchers, accepting to enter into an analysis of racism, and no longer uniquely to air their problems, began to utter incredibly, totally uninhibited racist opinions. The research, which had seemed to introduce reason to the group, even appearing to have moved the group away from racism, concluded, finally, with the exact opposite of what had been expected, with an excessive amount of racism, and not by a greater capacity for analysis or thought. My interpretation is that this group was perfectly capable of constructing the theory of its social and cultural misfortune, so to speak. But, once this theory had been outlined with the researchers, the group knew that nothing would change, that the researchers would go home, to their protected worlds, while those who had participated in the research would go back to live in their declining or insecure environments, with no change. By exhibiting an exacerbated form of racism, they had, so to speak, made the researchers foot the bill for the fact that they had outlined an analysis of problems that would remain unresolved. This meeting went on late into the night; I drove home to Paris, ill, and woke up the next day with a high fever.

I will not spend so much time on the other sites where a sociological intervention was conducted along similar lines. In Mulhouse, the economic situation was less dramatic because, after the destructuring of the classical textile industry in the 1970s and 1980s, a process of recomposition took place; unemployment was not so high and several thousand inhabitants of the town found employment by crossing the border, into Switzerland or into Germany. The Front National is strong in this town, where Alsatian identity is quite specific and where it is thought of as being complementary to, rather than the opposite of, French national identity. In this situation, the intervention (in May and June 1991) enabled us to round off the sociological analysis that had already been outlined in Roubaix. It demonstrated that, quite apart from its social sources, racism may also be closely associated with a crisis in the cultural, regional community and the feeling of being in danger of being excluded from modernity. Having strong roots in a local

Alsatian culture that is under threat and belonging to a declining industrial society are one and the same thing; at the same time, and there is nothing paradoxical about this, people have an intense feeling of identification with the French nation. One specific memory haunts me in connection with this intervention: that of an inhabitant of a working-class area saying to a researcher in my team who was interviewing him in the context of preparing the research and setting up the group for the intervention: 'We'll have to bring back the gas chambers.' And, as the researcher, despite our instructions not to react, was unable to hide his emotions, the man added: 'Don't worry. I don't mean for the Jews, but for the Arabs.'

Marseilles is a city with an oral culture where racist remarks explode easily and where cultural differences can be observed much more than in other towns. The forms of discrimination and segregation are numerous, and more visible than elsewhere, while at the same time the local political system that was long open to the various social but also cultural communities – Corsican, Armenian, Italian, Jewish, etc. – shows very obvious signs of exhaustion. The sociological intervention (April to June 1991) here was to reveal not only anti-North African racism but also an extremely virulent anti-Gypsy racism. The 'poor whites' who formed the group expressed primarily a feeling of exasperation, of political impotence and abandonment; they have the impression of being victims, of having been left behind by social change, and they themselves analyse racism as being linked to their conviction that they are the last survivors of a France that has been lost. At the time when the research was carried out, their racism seemed then to be in line with a populism that contained it and set the limits.

The preparatory fieldwork, during which a considerable number of individual interviews were carried out, and the sociological interventions themselves, enabled us to get a more specific image of a France in which the working classes, but also the middle classes, are becoming racist. We discerned four major options, some of which may be combined: the road to social exclusion, the path of the middle classes who want to ensure their peace of mind and keep poverty and immigration at a distance, the road to downward social mobility and, finally, the cultural tradition that is threatened by the outside world (globalisation, the construction of Europe), and from within (immigration). The research itself in fact confirms the more theoretical approach that I had developed previously in *The Arena of Racism* and makes it more precise; it provides illustrations and also enables us to be more balanced.

The crisis in the institutions

At the beginning of the 1990s, if racism was prevalent among the working classes, it also permeated the institutions, either directly or as a consequence of the problems that these institutions were increasingly incapable of dealing with. Thus I decided to include in this research programme two interventions carried out with actors who belonged to the institutions, one with social workers to see how they confronted the difficulties that fuelled racism, and the other with the police.

The intervention with social workers was carried out in Cergy, a 'new town' in the Parisian region, the complete opposite of this France that was ageing badly in Roubaix, Mulhouse or Marseilles. The mayor, who is a friend of a friend, wanted a group of sociologists to study racism in her own town. It was unusually courageous of this elected representative who was taking the risk of having her local authority being labelled as racist. The object here was to study the input of social workers in the processing of social and cultural problems that give rise to racism, or else on the contrary how they developed anti-racist practices that ultimately ended in reinforcing the disease. The group of social workers that we got together (March to June 1990) also met several interlocutors before proceeding with the auto-analysis of its action with the help of the researchers. They admitted very clearly that they were lost. More specifically, they were incapable of defining a clear line of action *vis-à-vis* the cultural differences encountered on the ground, and in many respects equally incapable when faced with the social difficulties of the 'clients' of social welfare. Some of the social workers wanted to recognise and valorise the specific identities, while others only wanted to discuss inequalities and social injustice; on the whole, they had no clear plan of action and were incapable of collective mobilisation, being answerable to the local elected councillors. Here our research revealed the depth of the crisis in social work in France, its difficulties in functioning in the present circumstances of changes in society. I was able to validate these analyses later by going to meet other social workers in other towns and asking them what they thought of the findings of the research we carried out in Cergy.

But should we not go to the very heart of the most central institutions? Another intervention was prepared, this time with the police. To do this, we had to obtain the permission of the highest authorities (in fact, the Ministry of the Interior), and the support of the Institut des hautes études de la sécurité intérieure, which had recently been created and which kindly agreed to help in the research, including financially. I was thus able to meet several dozen ordinary police officers in several towns in France and to choose ten of them who were volunteers for a sociological intervention explicitly dealing with the theme 'police and racism'. Their group met, in the Parisian suburbs, for approximately twenty sessions over a period of four months (October 1990–January 1991). Their interlocutors included a right-wing mayor, well known for his spectacular decisions, which received a lot of media coverage and were considered to be close to racism, an extreme-left lawyer, the director of the national police, and the principal leader of *SOS Racisme*, Harlem Désir. After this series of meetings, this group was also allowed to analyse what had been said and, more particularly, to deal with racism in the police and its specificities, explaining its sources, but also how it worked. Quite obviously, there was a crisis in the police *vis-à-vis* the social difficulties and cultural tensions that the country was experiencing; racism was prevalent throughout the police. Moreover, as a result of their everyday practice at grassroots level, the police contributed to the very production of the phenomenon.

Extensions

These studies were rounded off by another sociological intervention, carried out with a group of skinheads, and by various other studies done in a more classical mode, individual interviews and documents in the Beaujolais area where there is a strong current of rural racism; in Montfermeil, a small town in the Parisian region where the mayor became notorious for his xenophobic, racist and illegal decisions; in an area in the XIIIth district in Paris where a Chinese-origin community gives rise to rumours and racist prejudice; in Sarcelles, a town where, from the beginning of the 1990s, I was able, with my research team, to identify the birth of a new form of anti-Semitism voiced by French Caribbeans and North African-origin immigrants. They accused the local Jewish population of forming a powerful community capable of exercising an influence on local government, whereas they did not have this type of community resource. Ten years later, when a wave of anti-Semitic violence swept France at the time of the second Intifada, these pieces of research were to help me to think about the nature and the actors of this hatred for Jewish people.[2] They were extended by an international comparison in which researchers from my team, on the basis of the main findings of the programme carried out in France, went to the UK, Italy, Belgium and Germany to examine the racism at work in these societies (this international comparison is published in a book which I edited: Wieviorka 1994). Finally, a little later, at the request of the CFDT, one of the main French trade unions, I set up research on racism in employment. Philippe Bataille, a faithful participant in all the previous phases of my programme, took charge of this and enabled the researchers and the trade unionists to think together, on the ground, about racism at work and the means of combatting it (Bataille 1997).

The researcher and his object of research

The book that derives from this programme of research, *La France raciste* (Wieviorka *et al.* 1992) is based on a vast amount of material (approximately 500 hours of individual interviews and over 200 hours of group meetings, all recorded), the production of which constantly posed considerable problems to the researchers.

Meeting with racists can be difficult, and not only when it is a question of skinheads. In some cases, the people met were cautious and suspicious, and asked: Who is this sociologist? Why is he asking these questions? What will he do with them? Who is he working for? In other cases, it was the reverse. Racism was explicit and openly asserted; in these instances, the researcher is challenged to state his position; the speaker would not understand that the researcher was not also racist. The researchers doing the fieldwork, either alone or in pairs, are constantly forced to question their relationship to the object studied and to the people they meet, whether it be in individual interviews or in group meetings. Any complicity is excluded but rejection or repulsion, which could well emerge, constitute an obstacle to a relationship whereby the researchers gain their information. The difficulty is even greater when, in the context of the sociological intervention, the people involved have to be enabled to co-produce knowledge and analysis.

It is to a discussion of some of these dilemmas that I now want to turn.

Interpersonal relationships

In an individual interview, the researcher who wishes to understand and not simply record the facts of the situation has to create a minimum feeling of empathy with the person questioned quite simply to make them want to participate in the discussion. The researcher knows that he is not in a purely neutral position. He has to respect the person being interviewed, take him or her seriously, push them to go as far as possible in thinking about the themes discussed; now, if this person is racist, this type of position is difficult. The researcher in this case may be tempted to conceal his opinions. He may, for example, elicit racist remarks, present himself as having the same ideas and the same prejudices, and put his interviewee at ease by adopting a racist stance himself. I had asked my team to vigorously reject this orientation, just as I had similarly requested them never to put themselves in a situation where they were judging the people interviewed and intimating to them that they disapproved of their discourse. My instructions, which were discussed within the research team, were: we must be researchers the whole time – we are not there either to accept or reject the remarks made, but to understand them and to enable those who make them to think about them. In practice, we have usually been able to maintain this attitude and, often, open up the sphere of analysis: when confidence had been established, if someone made a racist remark, it was possible to say to them something along the lines of: 'That's a racist remark and I think that you made it because what you want to say is that....'

During a sociological intervention, the relationship is constructed and developed in the course of the group meetings, between which, moreover, there are long and numerous possibilities for informal discussions: for approximately forty hours of sociological intervention properly speaking, there are always many more hours of discussion that are not recorded, while nothing is happening, or during the breaks and the meals, without mentioning the preparatory meetings. Therefore of necessity, strong, warm interpersonal relationships are created – because nobody is obliged to participate in this type of research and the participants are not paid, they attend and come back only if they find some sort of intellectual gratification and a pleasant atmosphere. Here, experience quickly taught me that, when confidence had been established, the members of the group knew perfectly well that what we wanted was not to judge their racism, but to understand its sources and its meaning. On the whole, the researchers could be themselves, and as the research progressed it became more and more possible usually to speak of racism once removed as being what we together, researchers and actors, were involved in analysing. A researcher cannot accept the racism that is expressed in the remarks of the participants in a sociological intervention. But if he reacts by saying that these remarks are intolerable, the work will not progress and even runs the risk of grinding to a halt then and there. On the other hand, a totally different situation is created if the researcher succeeds in taking the racist remark expressed as being exactly what should be discussed in the group, if he succeeds, for example, in saying: 'You speak like that, you say dreadful things about Arabs just when we are talking about unemployment in the town, and obviously this is not the fault of the Arabs. I wonder if you are not making anti-Arab remarks because you are unable to mobilise against the people who are really responsible for unemployment....'

But it is not always possible to divert the discussion from the racist remark to an attempt at clarification and analysis. And it would be an illusion to imagine that participants in research directed at distancing, analysing and refuting racism will, in the long run, in real life abandon the racist positions that they have succeeded in analysing. On several extremely painful occasions I have experienced the exact opposite. The first time was in Poland in 1981 at the end of our research on Solidarnosc. In the course of a final meal to which we had invited all the participants in our programme (three sociological intervention groups, approximately thirty people) in Warsaw, one of the members of the group from Gdansk began to make anti-Semitic remarks, criticizing 'Michnik, that little Jew'. Now, a few months previously, when Adam Michnik had come to Gdansk to explain to this group what the KOR – this movement of intellectuals – had done to prepare the terrain for Solidarnosc, this same militant had very deliberately stood up and asked his comrades for a round of applause to thank Michnik in the name of the Polish workers. On a second occasion, I experienced a very unpleasant situation of the same type when, at the end of the sociological intervention with the police, a final meal had been organised for them at the end of the research. During this meal, the police in our group could find nothing better to do than, one after the other, tell racist stories of all sorts, each one worse than the one before, to the utter horror of the research team. Now, a few hours previously, they had been acting as analysts of police racism, demonstrating considerable maturity in thinking and considerable distance in relation to racism in the police itself.

The effects of the research

As mentioned before, the method of the sociological intervention was invented by Alain Touraine, in the mid-1970s, to study social movements. His idea was that the actors' capacity for action was a function of their level of their understanding of themselves. But can an idea of this type be applied to actors who, at the opposite pole of a social movement, are characterised on the contrary by their prejudices, and their incapacity to mobilise in the name of the ideas of justice, equality and projects of emancipation? By working directly and over time with racist actors, have I encouraged them to move away from racism?

My answer will be cautious. When racism appears to be the outcome of social difficulties, of a feeling that one's own cultural integrity is under threat or of the crisis in institutions no longer capable (I recall that we are speaking about France) of fulfilling their republican promises of liberty, equality and fraternity, it constitutes an inappropriate and irrational response to real problems. The research should enlighten those who are willing to participate and move them away from this response. But in practice experience suggests that in fact the impact of the research on participants is very low and the experience of Roubaix recounted above is a good illustration of this observation.

But can the research not have an impact of another type by influencing in particular politicians and those in charge in the public sphere by helping them to improve their action and thus cause racism to decline? Here I would also be cautious. My book, *La France raciste*, got a good reception in the media. When it came out, an important television programme was based on it and used the same title. The book was widely read. I was invited to participate in a great many discussions and its content, I think, was well understood. I have often discussed the findings, more or less confidentially, with people in politics. But, it seems to me, it has had no impact whatsoever on the course of events. At the time when it revealed the social, cultural and institutional realities that, in the course of profound changes in French society, were producing the dramas, self-centredness and fears that lead to racism, it definitely had much less impact on French political life than the books that were limited to criticising the Front National and to hunting down racist ideologies in every nook and cranny. At the most, I am happy to have been invited by the trade union, the CFDT, some years after the book was published, to launch action-research into racism in employment, which meant that my analyses and my approach had been of interest to this powerful trade union organisation.

Finally – something that is not much discussed in the social sciences – did this experience change the researchers themselves? Obviously yes, and at least in one specific way. The adjective 'racist' often has the strength of the obvious and a person or a group are very often described as racist without any hesitation. Now, frequently, in the fieldwork, I observed the existence of a grey area whose borders were fuzzy and whose content was variable, in describing which the use of the adjective 'racist' turned out on further examination to be inappropriate, unfair and excessive. As I write these lines I have in mind the example of a middle-aged couple in Marseilles who lived in a pleasant villa, with a magnificent garden only separated from a council estate inhabited by Gypsies by a wall. This couple lived in fear. When in 1989 the whole world learned of the fall of the Berlin Wall, the young Gypsies had celebrated the event in their own way, by smashing the wall separating the villa from their estate by ramming it with a stolen lorry. This couple were insulted, quite gratuitously, in the street, by very young children. They could not leave their home without running the risk of it being immediately burgled, etc. Their lives have become a total misery. What they said about the Gypsies was not tender, true enough, but was always backed up by concrete and, I think, very real illustrations. This dilemma and other experiences during the research forced me to ask how much of the response we were hearing from people like this was due to racism and how much was due to totally unbearable situations.

In some circumstances, limiting the discussion to social and cultural problems is turning a blind eye to the racist dimension of the issues. But if we restrict our consideration to racism, we stigmatise and discredit all those concerned without exception and over-rapidly. The research taught me to make more of an effort not to reduce everything to simplistic, black and white images; not to separate the world into two camps of good and evil, racists and anti-racists. It also taught me to move away from equally elementary political positions, which believe that it is possible to act on racism by satisfying oneself with confronting it head on, ideologically, and legally, as if the mix of fine feelings and resort to a legal arsenal that might or might not be adequate was enough. In short, it encouraged me to be exceedingly modest and not to believe in quick-fix solutions. If, thereafter, I started on research into urban violence and cultural difference, it is quite definitely on the basis of this experience into researching racism, which in a way constituted an invitation to examine in greater depth issues that are associated with racism and are an integral part thereof.

Notes

1   *Theory, Culture and Society*, 2000, 17, 1.
2   These studies are not included in the book *La France raciste*. They were given to the organisation that financed them, the FAS, and are available in the form of a report.

4   The study of racist events

Hernán Vera and Joe R. Feagin

Introduction

In our research we accent the importance of racist *events*, not just individual prejudices, stereotypes, and discriminatory acts that are the center of most studies of racial relations. In this article, we call on other researchers to focus on these complex and composite sets of human activity and relationships, and to get beyond the methodological individualism dominant in Western social science.

In our 1995 book, *White Racism*, we directed our attention toward what actually happens in situations usually narrated as involving 'race.' There, and subsequently, we have taken 'race' to be a peculiar, problematic, socially constructed type of human relationship. We have purposely neglected conventional categories and taxonomies on which most studies of 'race relations' rely. We have mostly bracketed issues of class, gender, income, occupational status, age, speech, and religion – those factors often considered correlates of or proxies for race. We have taken these factors to represent the general context of the particular racialized events that we wish to research.

Far too much research on 'race relations' neglects or downplays the realities of racist events. Even the term *racism* has disappeared from many mainstream analyses, scholarly and journalistic. One of the world's prominent African American journalists has told us that her newspaper, one of the most influential, has a policy of not using the 'r-word' wherever possible in reporting on racial matters.

In researching white racism, our methodological choices have followed an intent to theorize and explicate 'the racist event' in its many dimensions. We accept Max Weber's assumption that 'knowledge of cultural events is inconceivable except on the basis of the significance which the constellations of reality have for us in certain individual, concrete situations' (1949: 80). We have not studied these racist events merely to construct causal sequences.

Here we chronicle the method followed in studying white racism in the USA, and certain methodological issues we have faced. (We argue elsewhere that much analysis of US racism applies to racism across the globe. See Batur-

Vanderlippe and Feagin 1999.) In the beginning of our work, we had little guidance in developing a method for studying concrete racist constellations. Social scientists have given scant attention to studying events, although there is a growing literature on this subject. About the same time we developed our method, Griffin (1993) proposed an 'event structure analysis' to 'build replicable and generalizable causal interpretations of events.' He examined lynching cases in Raper's 1933 research. Like us, Griffin attempted to understand a socio-historical case 'as both a historically singular event and as an instance of a class of historically repeated events' (1993: 1,096). Like us, he has been concerned with how the order of the reported event-actions could be used for explanatory purposes. We too have asked, how can we use the knowledge gained from a comparison of historical events of the same kind in attempting to understand singular new events of the same kind? How can we generalize conclusions reached in analysis of one event to other events?

Griffin (1993) used a computer program that required answers to dichotomous questions to construct a series of causally connected events. His event analysis is reductionistic, with the advantages and disadvantages of that analysis. Griffin warns us that his interpretation is 'best understood as a selectively empathic causal and interpretive unpacking and reconstitution of the original,' (1993: 1,116) that is, of Raper's original lynching narratives. In contrast, we have moved in an opposite direction. We attempt a more 'packed,' nuanced, complex, and holistic understanding of multi-dimensional racialized events as they play out in context, space, and time. We not only ask about the causality and meaning of the racist events, but also what the actors want to bring into being and what larger structures and processes make their choices and actions possible. For Max Weber, 'the knowledge of causal *laws* is not the *end* of the investigation, but only the means' (1949: 79). We have studied racist events to discover how they imbed, constitute, create, and change social structures and processes.

The idea that racism is a systemic and multi-dimensional *project* is the starting point of our research. We are inspired by ideas on time and space set forth by Jean-Paul Sartre: 'The most rudimentary behavior must be determined both in relation to the real and present factors which condition it and in relation to a certain object, still to come, which it is trying to bring into being' (1963: 91). It is evident in the racist events in *White Racism* and in our subsequent work that white perpetrators of racist events want to bring something into being, even if this goal is maintenance of the racial status quo and privileges. The perpetrators' goals are studied in terms of present factors that condition events and in relation to orientations in space and time. Perpetrators act now, but not just now, for they and their reference groups carry congealed actions of the past into the present – often with an eye to the future. Adopting a holistic viewpoint is important, not only for understanding racism as practiced globally by white Europeans and Americans, but also for the design of anti-racist action. In our view, this anti-racist action should be directed against what is now *and* what is yet to come.

Studying racist events

The concept of the racist event

We have been stimulated in conceptualizing 'racist events' by certain happenings limned in a Canadian Broadcasting System documentary, *Conspiracy of Silence* (1991), as well as from the scholarly and journalistic coverage of the numerous other racist events that were covered in *White Racism*. Here we accent the Canadian rape-murder case of Helen Betty Osborne, a Native American.

We conceptualize an *event* as 'a distinguishable happening, one with some pattern or theme that sets it off from others, and one that involves changes taking place within a delimited amount of time' (Conkin and Stromberg 1989: 173). The adjective 'racist' refers to the fact that, without a consideration of the peculiar historical relationships that are conceptualized as 'racist', it is impossible to understand why, in November 1971, four young white men murdered Betty Osborne, a 19-year-old Native American student. (These happenings took place in the town of The Pas, in Manitoba, Canada.) The same is true for understanding why the Manitoba government did not prosecute the confessed killers until *sixteen years* later. In addition, without understanding white racism, one cannot understand why, three decades later, in 2000, the Justice Minister of Manitoba – who eventually admitted the government's mishandling of the criminal investigation – felt the need to apologize specifically to the Osborne family (Taillon 2000). In studying this case, as in researching other incidents in *White Racism*, a first step is to reach a clear definition of the main research concept – the racist event – and, through observation, analysis, and comparison with similar events, to derive a polished conceptualization of these critical incidents in their multi-faceted implications.

In our work, we have generally highlighted a number of key dimensions of racist events (Feagin and Vera 1995; Feagin *et al.* 1996; Feagin 2000). We do not have the space here to develop these points fully, but we can trace out several recurring dimensions. Among the critical aspects of the racist events on which we have focused are these: (1) the white perpetrators; (2) the targets and victims of color; (3) the immediate context, particularly the social structure, spatial setting, and temporal frame; (4) the panoply of instruments used in the ritualized practices; (5) the playing out of actions in a ritualized and iterative sequence; (6) the psychological and motivational impulses, including socially sanctioned and personal ideologies; and (7) the longer-term aftermath and societal consequences.

In regard to the first dimension, we examine who the white perpetrators are and typically find distinctions among them. Some are principals, the *offi-*

ciants, of racist action, those actively doing the central racist acts. In addition, there are often *acolytes*, who play a supportive role in racist acts, as well as *passive participants* who observe during the initial events and later play the role of bystanders. We will see the importance of these groups when we return to the details of the Osborne case.

As for the second dimension, we assess who the particular targets are and what impact the racist actions have on them. Generally, more than one person is harmed by racist actions, even if one person is the initial target. As a rule, the latter's family and community are not isolated from the occurrence and are harmed as well. Thus, in research on black students at white universities, we have concluded: 'In the process of developing strategies to cope with racial barriers, black and other targets of discrimination are injured physically, psychologically, and socially and forced to waste much energy and time' (Feagin *et al.* 1996: 7). The extreme wastefulness of racism is clear in its impact on the human targets, as well as on the larger society. We accent how those targeted – in the immediate situation or later – are usually more than 'victims,' for they often actively resist white-racist actions. It is often targeted individuals and their communities that force a societal response to white-racist actions.

In regard to the third dimension, we examine the sets and series of racist actions that play out in particular settings and time frames. In the aforementioned analysis of black college student reports of racist actions, where data are available we sort out the importance of social and spatial contexts, and temporal realities:

> This racism is situated in particular places and at particular times as it is practiced by numerous white students, faculty, staff members, police officers, and administrators. Today as in the past, racial discrimination involves erecting physical, legal, and social barriers to make certain places, situations, and positions inaccessible to, or difficult for, members of racial outgroups.
>
> (Feagin *et al.* 1996: 7)

Action sequences in such settings cumulate to form the 'racist event,' that is, the racist scenario taken as a whole. We try to examine the structural contexts of racist actions and probe their nuanced character in regard to both space and time.

The fourth dimension concerns instruments used in the implementation of the racist acts by officiants and acolytes. In a religious ceremony, the 'instruments' would be such things as chalices, incense burners, sacred books, and vestments. In the often ritualized ceremonies of violent racism, the instruments include guns, burning crosses, chains, ropes, and white hoods. In the case of contemporary racial discrimination – violent and nonviolent – the instruments used may include biased bureaucratic reports, hidden inquests, empty review procedures, the touting of equality policies never enforced, denial of earned recognition, exclusionary socializing, and covert maintenance of housing segregation. In addition, denigration of people of color in the media, such as in biased news reporting, involves the use of the media as an instrument of symbolic violence.

The fifth dimension calls attention to the playing out of actions in ritualized and iterative sequences. Sequences imbed actual practices to which actors allocate energy that produces discriminatory consequences, discrimination that ranges from murder to an array of less severe acts. In the workplace, for example, discriminatory actions include lowering salaries and denying promotions. In public settings, they encompass the creation of racialized indignities, such as the refusal of prompt service by white servers at a restaurant and intensive surveillance of black shoppers in stores (Feagin and Sikes 1994). These actions are more than isolated episodes, for they frequently crash in on the lives of Americans of color, indeed by the thousands over the course of a lifetime. Racialized acts are routine, repetitive, and almost always cumulative in effect, with an impact over generations of both those targeted and the perpetrators.

In regard to dimension six, we accent a broader range of issues than conventional socio-psychological analyses of 'race relations.' Looking at racist events, we observe that a hoary racist ideology usually supports discriminatory practices and, as importantly, that a common apology often accents supposedly mitigating circumstances for explaining racist events. As we find in the Osborne case, racist actions are motivated by an array of intensely held attitudes and emotions, including not only racial stereotypes and hatred, but also strong emotions of fear, ignorance, and a sense of personal vulnerability. The desire to cover up difficult issues or to carry out relevant others' orders can also propel whites to engage or acquiesce in racist actions. Significantly, many white Americans know about and watch racist rituals without intervening, and they do not take countering actions for a variety of personal and group-related reasons.

The seventh dimension noted above is, in effect, an extension of previous dimensions – in that in our method we often try to follow the racist actions for a longer term than is conventionally undertaken in 'race relations' research. Often what some might see as aftermath is in fact part of the racist event seen from a longer-distance perspective, as is true for the Osborne case to which we return in the next section. It is also important in studying racist events to pay attention to their significance for the immediate social context and for larger national and international contexts that spiral out like ripples from a pebble thrown into a pond.

The savage murder of Helen Betty Osborne

Studying the case of Helen Betty Osborne, we illustrate some important methodological choices in developing a study of racist events. Let us outline briefly the main of that set of actions and some interpretive questions they provoke. In November 1971, Helen Betty Osborne was walking home on a street of The Pas, Manitoba, a logging town of 6,000. Four white men, aged 18 to 25, cruising in one of their parents' cars, forced her into the car and took her to a park where they sexually assaulted her. When she resisted their violent advances, one man held her while one or more of the others killed her with fifty-six stabs of a screwdriver. Her naked body was found in the bushes of the park. The forensic pathologist described the murder as 'the work of a frenzied killer' (Oake 1989).

Shortly thereafter, many whites in The Pas passed along gossip about the men who had done the rape-murder. Indeed, they bragged about their deeds at a bar. 'All of The Pas knew exactly who the murderers were, a fact later confirmed by the 1998 Manitoba Aboriginal Justice Inquiry,' reported a Canadian editorial (Cockburn 1995). The town's sheriff admitted he had remained quiet for years after one perpetrator 'told him he and the three others had picked up Osborne and that she was killed for refusing to have sex' (Canadian Press 1989b). An employer of one perpetrator and a civilian in the Royal Canadian Mounted Police admitted to having heard about the murderers. Still, the government did not prosecute until 1987, and even then only tried two of the men. A third man was granted immunity for testimony, and the fourth was never charged. One served just six and a half years in prison, and a second abductor was acquitted. Protests and actions by the aboriginal community eventually led to the prosecutions (Canadian Press 1997; Canadian Press 1989a).

While we do not have the space to discuss this account in detail, we see in this brief survey the critical dimensions of a racist event. Note that this event has an array of white participants, including officiants, acolytes, and passive observers. It has one immediate target, yet the larger aboriginal community was greatly affected. The spatial setting, a rugged logging town, is probably important, as is the long period of time that this event simmered in local consciousness. We see also the resistance of the aboriginal community. Also clear is the impact this event had on the regional area and Canadian society. This account raises clear questions of the racial morality at the base of Canadian (and, perhaps by extension, US) society.

Some observations on emotions and understanding

The accounts of these racist events, especially the visual images of the documentary movie, shook us deeply. One initial reaction was that of traditional social scientists. Our training indicated to us that we should set aside our emotions and outrage because that would cloud an understanding of this critical human incident. However, we soon realized that the suppression of our emotions would not in fact remove the blinders from our 'rational thinking,' as the conventional dictum asserting the need for 'value freedom' in sociological research generally assumes (Feagin and Vera 2001). Instead, such suppression of full human reactions would likely make our analysis blind to key aspects of the murderous actions we wanted to study. A holistic sociological approach requires that all human faculties be used for research and understanding.

White-generated racism in Canada and the USA, and likely across most of the world, generally provokes strong emotions and moral outrage among its targets, and, often but not always, those who research it. The conventional social science method would tend to obliterate key aspects of these social phenomena in the research process. In our approach, we reject what Damasio calls the Cartesian error of separating mind, emotions, and body:

> The suggestion that reasoning, and moral judgment, and the suffering that comes from physical pain or emotional upheaval might exist separately from the body. Specifically: the separation of the most refined operations of mind from the structure and operation of a biological organism.
>
> (1994: 250)

In other words, an early methodological decision was that we needed to account for the research consequences of conventional value neutrality, as usually understood, for this might lead us to neglect key dimensions of the event or to observe it with studied indifference to these important dimensions.

Given our acknowledged emotions, we have increasingly tried to implement the methodological option of reflexive sociology, in which our research practice is subjected to the same critical gaze as the social phenomena we study. This is not a new approach in sociology, for Alvin Gouldner (1970), Dorothy Smith (1987), Sandra Harding (2002), and Pierre Bourdieu (1992), among others, have called for this type of social science. Bourdieu (Bourdieu and Wacquant 1992: 6–7), for example, developed a sociological method that combines structuralist and constructivist approaches, and gives special attention to lived experiences of human agents in social dramas, while constantly keeping in mind the social and intellectual assumptions underlying the analyst's approach and methods. Our recursively reflexive approach has enriched our research, and that of our students, with new insights and sensitivities, and has raised our own awareness of an array of epistemological, methodological, and metatheoretical issues (on this impact on sociology generally, see Gouldner 1970: 489).

Racialized emotions

One of the least developed areas in conceptualizing white-generated racism is that of the recurring emotions inherent in these racist actions. In researching the Osborne case, thus, a number of observations and questions about the motivations and emotions seen in the narrated events soon came to the fore. We can note a few of these here.

First, the behavior of the four white men would have been meaningless without a socially sanctioned ideology that views white men as entitled to sexual access to aboriginal women more or less at will. In the town of The Pas, white men 'routinely tried to pick up native women for sex' (Canadian Press 1989b). Beyond whatever desire each might have personally felt, each man exhibited a *collective* sense of racial entitlement and racial superiority. This was seen clearly in the savagery and inhumanity of the rape-murder. This dominant attitude is not just a racial prejudice in the immediate North American scene, nor is it a peculiarity of these four men, for it reflects a general orientation to indigenous peoples that is as old as the first European conquests of these peoples in the Americas (see Sale 1990; Feagin 2000). Beginning at least with the raping and killing of indigenous women by Christopher Columbus and fellow explorers and colonizers in the late fifteenth century, white men have assumed that women of color are not full human beings, but rather are 'exotic animals' available for their pleasure and violence. The rituals of killing indigenous women are clear in the journals of Columbus and other European colonizers (Sale 1990).

The behavior of the young Canadian murderers can be taken to represent an old racist ritual based on a stock of social emotions and 'knowledge,' a set of ideas that seem to entitle white men to abduct an aboriginal woman and expect compliance. Part of this racist *ritual* assumed the right of white men to kill sadistically an aboriginal woman after her resistance. She was not a being with full human rights. Such racist events involve not only a breakdown of empathy across the racial line, but also a full-fledged dehumanization of the racialized other. These indeed define much of the racialization process.

In this case, as in many others like it, this breakdown of empathy and the accompanying dehumanization of the other were not limited just to the principal officiants and the acolytes in the racist ritual itself. Many other whites were implicated. We ask, what are the emotions and understandings of these white bystanders? The young murderers' confession to the local sheriff, their subsequent social acceptance by the white community, and the members of this white community's *silence* are all important in understanding this event. Over time, the white bystanders in effect became acolytes. Apparently, there is a sense among many (most?) of the whites concerned that racist acts, even murder, can generally be performed with *impunity* because the targets are not deserving of full respect and rights. In looking at other such racist events, we suggest examining how important this sense of impunity is for their recurring performance, and assessing which social and political processes guarantee this impunity.

In addition, we view the moral 'values' – here the immoral values – of those involved as being an important feature of this racist event. Seeing these values as immoral and anti-human was important in the long term. Thus, one journalist belatedly covering the story called it, 'One of the ugliest chapters in modern Canadian history' (Zerbisias 1990), and an official governmental report referred to the incident as an 'international disgrace' (Public Inquiry into the Administration of Justice and Aboriginal People 1991). Without these moral understandings and judgments, albeit very belated, there would have been no prosecution, no newsworthy story, and no governmental apology.

Pathology and 'normalcy'

The conventional approach to racist practices by psychologists and psychiatrists – especially in regard to savage practices like those of the Osborne incident and, more generally, aboriginal genocide – places them among the hard-to-understand 'structures of evil.' The psychological perspective may indeed see such social phenomena as pathological and the enactment of unconscious 'object relations' (Bollas 1995: 185). We view this traditional idea of racist events as involving 'pathological' mental structures as a blind alley. The data in the case of Helen Betty Osborne suggest that the white male perpetrators were (before and after the murder) socially integrated individuals and Canadian citizens in good standing – that is, they were 'normal' from a psychological perspective. We see no evidence in the accounts of the racist event that the actions of the perpetrators are so extreme as to be considered psychologically pathological. They certainly were not viewed that way by many other whites in the town at the time.

Events like the Osborne rape-murder are socially imbedded, and the demonstrated prejudices, stereotypes, and racial emotions are *socially generated, called forth, and reinforced*. Sociologist Maurice Halbwachs once observed that his learning and knowledge are not preserved just in some corner of his individual brain, but 'are recalled to me externally, and the groups of which I am a part at any time give me the means to reconstruct them, upon condition, to be sure, that I turn toward them and adopt, at least for the moment, their way of thinking' (1992: 38, 52). Ordinarily, the attitudes and knowledge of an individual are 'part of a totality of thoughts common to a group.' Thus, the ideas and proclivities held by the white men in this case about aboriginal people are not unique to them but are held by many whites not directly connected to this particular event. They made the event possible.

Understanding the *social* embeddedness and *social activation* of racist ideas, attitudes, proclivities, and actions – thus, of racist events – is a central contribution of our sociological approach to contemporary racism. These events are often central to the societies of which they are a part, not some pathological aberration that can easily be rationalized away. For that reason, such events tell us a great deal about the societies of which they are a part. They are, in a word, *foundational.*

Our rejection of racism as just a pathological mental structure does not mean we reject the contributions of psychology and psychiatry to understanding the contours of racism. Instead, we are accenting here the point that researchers must acknowledge the limits of conventional psychological understandings. For the same reason, we turn away from judging the individual morality or immorality of the perpetrators. We are sociologists and do not need to delve into the theological problem of whether those who perpetrate racist events are demonic and 'evil' individuals. Such approaches are not useful for the holistic sociological interpretation that we view as necessary in studying the panoply of past and contemporary racist events.

Crucially, our methodological approach leads us to the view that the events we have observed are – in their communities and at their many recurring points in societal time, and for their actors and observers – unequivocally normal and taken for granted. The conspiracy of silence of the white citizens of The Pas, which assured impunity for the murderers of Helen Betty Osborne, involved far too many people, and for far too long a period of time, for this event to represent an extreme, unique, or individually pathological pattern of conduct.

We do not have the space here to discuss in detail the normalcy of even a few of the many racist events that are similar to the Osborne rape-murder, but there have been thousands in the history of Canada and, more especially, across the USA. One can reflect on the hundreds of thousands of whites who participated actively in, or traveled miles in cars, trains, and buses to witness, the many savage lynchings of African Americans since the late 1860s in many areas of the USA. These lynchings were 'slow, methodical, often highly inventive forms of torture and mutilation' (Litwack 2000: 14). An estimated 6,000 African Americans were lynched by whites between the beginning of Reconstruction (1867) and the present day, in many states of the South and the North (Feagin and Feagin 2003).

At many lynchings, white participants – including children and women – celebrated or picnicked under the hanging bodies of those lynched. They sometimes sent postcards to friends with pictures of decomposing, hanging bodies. Some whites displayed, on walls of their living rooms, pictures of a lynching, sometimes with strands of hair or other parts of the victim kept as memorabilia. An examination of the photographs of lynchings yields smiling white men, women, and children who are posing by the hanging, often charred, remains of black men and women. White police officials often participated or remained aloof while such racial crimes were committed. For these white participants, like those in the Osborne case, such racist events are clearly 'normal,' at least for the regional and national societies at the time. More recent lynchings in the United States – those since the 1960s – have involved ever smaller groups of whites, but such violent actions are still typically imbedded in and perpetrated by groups of whites.

A chronic lack of empathy

Let us reiterate the point that the routine suppression of emotions and empathy is essential to carrying out the operations of racism, whether this involves violent attacks or the more subtle discrimination that is more common in the lives of people of color today. Those whites who perpetrate the racist events clearly exhibit a lack of understanding and empathy across the color line. At some point or another, this seems to involve most whites.

Often, it is not just those who commit the racist acts in the first instance who exhibit a lack of empathy. Consider an example from our book, *White Racism*. There we examined in detail the videotaped Rodney King beating in Los Angeles in the 1990s. In our analysis of these police actions, given our methodological approach, we were not surprised at certain features of the trial of the white officers for beating King. Getting white jurors to suppress their sense of empathy for the targeted black man, to suppress their human emotions about the violence directed at him, was a central part of the successful strategy used by the defense lawyers who got the white officers off. By working hard to get the jurors to sympathize with white officers, and not the targeted black man, the lawyers succeeded in the first trial in getting the officers acquitted for the brutal beating.

This case makes clear our point that researchers should not neglect an understanding of the management and suppression of emotions in the process and later aftermath of racialized events, if they are to truly understand the contours and underlying realities of contemporary racism. Empathy is required of those who wish to understand well any of the important matters relating to the world's great racial divisions.

Conclusion: reflexive research on racism

What then can we conclude about our methodological approach? In our research, we have decided that the emotions and moral outrage that we feel about such racist phenomena have to become, albeit critically and reflexively, an integral part of our research method for studying these phenomena. *All* social researchers imbed their values, emotions, and understandings in their research. It is just that those holding to the traditional 'value neutral' position are generally unwilling to concede this point. In our view, it is better to make these matters public and subject to critical scrutiny as the research process proceeds. Making one's values and emotions open and public does not mean one should not conduct careful, honest, and objective research. It just means much more candor about this process. It can also yield much greater insight into the phenomena being studied.

Thus, we have discovered that to one extent or another we too have been socialized in much of the stock of racist knowledge and values that we observe in the dramatic and everyday racist events. No researchers can really look at their own society as though they were observing a foreign society with different values and norms from their own. While we have never lived in a logging town in Canada, we are part of the same North American society that has denigrated, exploited, and subordinated people of color for four centuries. In researching racist events in North America, we as researchers are, at least in part, analyzing the contexts in which we have grown up. This is true of all researchers working on issues in their own societies. Under these conditions, as Gouldner noted, the scientific enterprise cannot be concerned with 'discovering' truth 'about a social world regarded as external to the knower, but with seeing truth as growing out of the knower's encounter with the world and his effort to order his experience with it' (1970: 493). Thus, continuing reflexivity is central to the social research and interpretation process.

In addition, racist events, wherever they occur, have individual and social consequences – such as torture, death, a conspiracy of silence, or failure to act by police – that are profoundly inhumane and anti-human. What is the standard for this judgment? As we see it, the standard is a broad human rights perspective on which there is a substantial and growing international consensus. From this international rights perspective, racist events are clearly immoral, and to describe them in neutral terms is to flinch from a probing analysis and deep interpretation.

White perpetrators of violent and other forms of racism, at least since the end of the Second World War, must be cognizant of the agreed-upon immorality of racist practices. Denying this reality is no longer plausible due to of extensive international efforts and decrees on human rights and racism. For example, in the late 1940s, the United Nations ratified an extraordinary document called the Universal Declaration of Human Rights. This is now internationally celebrated and indicates a growing consensus across most of the world's societies on what are basic human rights. Every person is viewed as having a broad range of rights by virtue of being human, rights that transcend the authority of any particular government. 'All human beings are born free and equal in dignity and rights,' and 'all are equal before the law and are entitled without any discrimination to equal protection of the law.' One article of the Universal Declaration also asserts that 'Everyone has the right to an effective remedy...for acts violating the fundamental rights' (United Nations 1995).

This international perspective on human rights was accelerated and reinforced by the Nuremberg trials of German Nazis after the Second World War, trials that established the view that some acts are 'crimes against all humanity,' and are to be condemned from the standpoint of principles higher than those of particular nation-states (Sjoberg *et al.* 1995). German Nazis were put to death on the grounds of this new global understanding. In summary, then, there is a strong international human rights standpoint for judging racist events as crimes against humanity. This is an important insight that can be reflexively imbedded in the research carried out on such common events.

5   Researching 'mixed race' experience under slavery

Concepts, methods and data

Stephen Small

Introduction and goals

This chapter describes and discusses the conceptual framework, research methods and empirical data used to examine the experiences of people of mixed African and European origins (usually termed 'mixed race') under nineteenth-century slavery. The goals of the project were to evaluate the extent to which Blacks of mixed origins enjoyed preference over Blacks during slavery, and why. Was the work that they did easier than that done by Blacks? Were they more likely to become legally free? Did most of them have rich white fathers who privileged them? Answers to these questions require a number of methodological and conceptual tools, and a range of data sources. In a book soon to be published by New York University Press, I explore these arguments for the island of Jamaica and the state of Georgia in the USA, focusing on both the enslaved and the legally free populations. These two territories were selected because of their radically different demographic profiles – in Jamaica enslaved Blacks always outnumbered Whites, while in Georgia Whites always outnumbered enslaved Blacks. These demographic profiles are usually used to explain differences in the treatment and privileges enjoyed by Blacks of mixed origins (Jordan 1962, 1968). In this chapter, I discuss the methods and data for the enslaved population for Georgia alone, in order to highlight some of the key methodological issues.

Genesis of the research and the questions

I have worked on, and taught about, the circumstances of Blacks of mixed origins as compared with Blacks, under slavery, and in the contemporary period in the USA and England, since the 1980s. Most work by scholars in this area has been about the expressed identities of people of mixed origins, especially in the USA (Spickard 1989; Root 1992). However, I have been far less concerned with attitudes and identities than with institutional experiences, material resources and ideological articulations by dominant groups (Small 1989, 1994a). When I got to the University of California at Berkeley in 1984, as a graduate student, I completed my Ph.D. dissertation on that topic. I then turned to a different topic and period – race, class and gender in the 1980s (Small 1994b). However, I continued to give papers on slavery, and I then returned directly to the issue of 'race mixture' under slavery in 1995, when I decided to collect more data to publish a book. This was prompted in large part by my return to the USA, to a teaching position in African American Studies at the University of California at Berkeley. I then spent several years, including several lengthy visits to Jamaica and Georgia, collecting data. The book was finally finished in 2004 and will be published in 2005. What this means is that I had much more time to work on this project than might normally be the case – though that was far from intentional as much of it was due to distractions, some professional, some not, as well as a couple of moves to new jobs across the Atlantic. But it does mean that I have had the advantage of thinking through the issues over a long period, coming across scholars working on these areas and benefiting from their insights.

This project is closely involved in my personal life as well, my father being Black and my mother White. Growing up in Liverpool in the 1970s, generally being called 'nigger' by Whites, and 'half-caste' by some Blacks, and seeing my mother abused by other Whites because she was married to a Black man, I was always conscious of being mixed. I continually pondered many issues to do with my circumstances and identity, to do with the criteria and language for defining race, and when I ended up, quite unexpectedly, at university, I took the opportunity to study many of these issues. The fact that I am still studying them must surely date back to this time. While I have always striven to be professional in my approach to these questions, I have little doubt that many personal concerns continue to inform my research.

What were the goals of my project? My review of the literature on the circumstance and attitudes of Blacks of mixed origins under slavery provided a general wisdom – one reinforced in the social imaginary of films and literature. It suggested that, under slavery, Blacks of mixed origins were 'better off' than Blacks believed to be of pure African origins. It was argued that enslaved Blacks of mixed origins got better jobs – working in the house and in trades – as compared to Blacks, who were usually condemned to the fields; that they got better resources such as food and clothing; that they were more likely to be legally freed; and once legally free were more likely to be successful. The typical explanation is that these Blacks of mixed origins had rich White fathers, or were the mistresses of White men who legally freed them, and that Whites preferred them over Blacks, for certain jobs; or that Whites usually legally freed them where Whites were outnumbered by enslaved Blacks (Berlin 1974; Williamson 1984). An extreme example of such privilege is Amanda America Dickson, who became the richest woman of color in the USA when her White father, a wealthy master-enslaver, left his substantial fortune to her (Leslie 1995).

I was unhappy with a number of things in this argument. There seemed to be a narrow base of evidence, and an extensive base of extrapolations for many of the arguments. For example, many analyses focused on exceptional communities such as New Orleans, Charleston and Savannah – thus using an unrepresentative sample of the elite legally free people of color, rather than a representative sample of all Blacks of mixed origins, including the enslaved (Berlin 1974). Much of the evidence came from white travelers visiting exceptionally large plantations, rather than from a range of plantations and farms of different sizes (Olmsted 1863). In fact, most agricultural units in the USA were small, and the proportions of enslaved persons of different colors on them were highly variable, with some plantations having no Blacks of mixed origins at all, and others having a majority of Blacks of mixed origins on them. I could not see how most Blacks of mixed origins could be house servants in such circumstances.[1] Besides, there is substantial evidence from people of color, for example, in biographies, that suggests a different picture. Also, I knew that most White men were not rich, but poor, and while there was clear evidence that many rich White men legally freed their lovers or children of mixed origins, I had also come across substantial evidence that many, perhaps most, White men abandoned them. In any case, I had not found a clear data set that assessed the exact number of White men, rich and poor, with kids of mixed origins, nor how they treated them. I felt that any decisive answer to the larger question required such a data set. Similarly, I knew that the word 'mulatto' was misleading, not to mention offensive, and that it did not automatically mean a person defined as a 'mulatto' had a White father. I found many 'mulattoes' who had no White fathers – that is, they had two parents of mixed origins, or one Black parent and one parent of mixed origins. Individuals in such circumstances had no White father to privilege them and therefore it was necessary to know exactly how many were in such circumstances.

Finally, in the argument that working in the field was more oppressive than working in the house, there were gaps. For example, I knew that there were various types of field labor – gang labor and task labor – and I was unsatisfied by the idea that house labor was automatically easy, or invariably preferred by the enslaved. I presumed that it entailed long hours of work, constant surveillance, less autonomy for those enslaved, and was more likely to put women of color in a position where they would become the victims of sexual abuse. In other words, too many things seemed wrong with this argument and some closer inspection was required

I felt it would be better to look at all Blacks of mixed origins, enslaved and legally free, in a range of circumstances; to see how many had White fathers, rich or poor, or no White father at all, and how many actually had privileged positions in houses or trades. Also, where they had White fathers, how many of these fathers actually legally freed them? I felt that it was better to look at evidence of various kinds, especially evidence provided by the enslaved themselves, rather than just evidence from Whites; that it was better to look at a range of types of field labor, and at house labor in detail. I felt it was better to look at all Blacks, enslaved and legally free, on plantations of different sizes and with different crops. I also felt it was better to examine such questions at the level of a state rather than for the whole USA. This was the ideal model. Unfortunately, the data simply do not exist to answer all of these questions, and what I ended up with was the best approximation to this that I could achieve. I found substantial data for Georgia that enabled me to come to significantly different conclusions from those that prevail in the literature. I describe this process, methodology, concepts and data in this chapter.

What I found was that Blacks of mixed origins were dispersed across a wide variety of plantations of different sizes, including those in which they were a majority of the workers and thus unlikely to be only in house jobs. I discovered that most Blacks of mixed origins did not have White fathers at all and, that if they had White fathers, these fathers were more likely to be poor, self-interested and irresponsible, offering no privilege to their mixed offspring. I also found significant evidence from Black sources to demonstrate significant abuses experienced by Blacks of mixed origins. I found that housework was particularly grueling and was the context of sexual abuses of enslaved women, while some types of field labor had hidden compensations for those who survived its rigors. When I looked at the legally free population, it was clearly disproportionately people of mixed origins. But I found that most Blacks of mixed origins were born legally free, rather than being manumitted, and that there were large numbers of Blacks of mixed origins among the runaways.

The research process

Terminology and concepts

The perceptive reader will already realize that I have used a number of words and terms that are not common in the literature on 'race relations'. These include 'enslaved' (instead of slave), 'Blacks of mixed origins' (instead of mixed race), 'legally free' (instead of free) and 'master-enslaver' (instead of slave-master). I use these terms because, for a long time now, I've been unhappy with much of the language used in work on race, and with the ways in which it is often used uncritically. Nor am I the only person unhappy with such language (Banton 1977; Miles 1982; Miles and Small 1999). It is important in the research process to recognize that you don't have to use the language used by your colleagues or predecessors. The quest to find entirely satisfactory language is a fleeting illusion; however, there are some words and concepts that are preferable to others. I want to raise discussion of two groups of concepts.

The first is what I call the foul language of 'race relations' – words that are used as if simply descriptive and neutral, when in fact they hide a power relationship and/or are offensive. I mean words like 'non-white', 'mixed race', 'miscegenation', or like 'slave-master', 'slave-mistress'. I prefer not to use the word 'non-white' at all because it takes a minority of the world's population and categorizes the majority, negatively and condescendingly, in contrast to this minority. Just thinking about 'Black' and 'non-Black', or 'people of color' and 'people without color', quickly highlights the mischief that these words perpetrate. Rather than 'mixed race' I prefer to use the phrase 'Blacks of mixed origins', which I introduced in 1991 (Small 1991). As I argued then, in the context of slavery, the African ancestry of this group was a greater determinant of their status and life experiences than was white ancestry. Similarly, as I've written elsewhere, 'slave-master' invests a finality and legitimation to a relationship that was always challenged by those enslaved. I prefer to use the words 'master-enslaver,' 'mistress-enslaver' and 'enslaved'. In my opinion, these words necessarily highlight the contestation that was inevitably present under slavery (Small 2002). The words that I reject are historically created concepts, frequently offensive when introduced, historically defunct and unnecessary. These new concepts are more jarring; are more likely to make a reader uneasy and think about them. They are far preferable. And any researcher in this field should be prepared to introduce their own concepts. But a word of caution. If you attempt to do this, you will be opposed by colleagues, and by publishers, who will try to squeeze you into the straitjacket of convention, whether scholarly convention, or the convention of an English dictionary. Some of my most difficult, and time-consuming, fights have been with editors and publishers, trying to prevent them from deleting or changing these words, usually substituting them for the words I have rejected. I think it's a fight worth having and I'm ready to do it at any time.

The second group is the new concepts that arise out of your research project. These cannot be figured out in advance, and some will not be clear until you are well into your research process. But you should be clear at the start that, as you develop your research, you may need to challenge or entirely reject extant concepts, or modify them, or create an entirely new set of concepts. This realization may begin as uneasy feelings about what is in the literature. Or it may spring from an immediate outright rejection of the terms and concepts in the literature. Let me describe two concepts – housework and fieldwork – that I have interrogated directly for my study of Georgia. I was very unhappy from the start with the argument that Blacks of mixed origins were 'better off' than Blacks because they worked in the house not the field. The presumption here was that housework was inherently better than fieldwork, and thus invariably chosen over fieldwork.[2] That housework was less strenuous, there was less likelihood of contracting disease or of being whipped, and those doing housework had privileges such as access to better food, or clothes, or to 'White culture'. In contrast is the view that all fieldwork was inherently bad – the idea of a gang of enslaved persons with an overseer and/or 'slave driver' working from dawn to dusk, especially in a scorching mid-day sun, and at the crack of a whip. This is a notion very much based on a movie representation of slavery – such as is found in *Roots* or *Mandingo*.

When we actually look at the evidence, the story is more complicated. First let me acknowledge that there is considerable evidence suggesting that housework had many advantages, including the many expressed preferences of enslaved Blacks and Blacks of mixed origins themselves for this kind of work. But there is significant evidence suggesting that it could be as bad or worse than fieldwork. House servants, in close proximity with 'master-enslavers' and 'mistress-enslavers', were subject to demands for work 24 hours per day, were under constant surveillance and subject to sexual abuse. If a 'master-enslaver' woke up in the middle of the night with sex in mind, it was more likely he would satisfy his desires with those closest by, rather than tracking off to the site of the field-enslaved persons possibly half a mile away. Evidence for such practices comes from the diaries of White women that describe their own plantation or that of other White women. It also comes from the diaries and/or narratives of women of color (Fox-Genovese 1988; Clinton 1982; Craft and Craft 1999). And fieldwork was far less homogeneous than imagined. A key distinction here is between gang labor and task labor. In Georgia, and across the USA, cotton agriculture was based on gang labor, but rice agriculture was based on task labor. Under the system of gang labor, the work was less physically strenuous than rice, but the enslaved were under constant surveillance, and had longer working days and fewer options for autonomy and for growing their own crops. And while rice was more murderous – the mortality rates were far higher – nevertheless the working days were shorter, there were greater opportunities for autonomy and for growing crops for consumption or sale. It is no surprise that under rice cultivation in coastal Georgia, enslaved persons had greater opportunity to maintain African culture, and controlled a substantial economy – one upon which Whites were greatly dependent for food and supplies (Smith 1985; Wood 1995). Detailed information for the elaboration of these experiences comes from the diaries of master-enslavers, while the so-called 'Slave Narratives' also provide substantial information (Dickson 1870; Rawick 1972; Starling 1985). While much of this has been said in the literature on slavery generally, the findings have not yet been applied to the debates on the relative experiences of Blacks and Blacks of mixed origins.

Literature review

The first step in my project was to carry out an extensive literature review. During this process I read published books primarily for their footnotes and methodological appendices, rather than for their content. I wanted to know where the archives were and what collections of historical documents were housed in them. And, conscious that there were substantial distances between myself and them (I was then living in California), I wanted to develop a strategy and criteria for which ones to visit first. Most of the archives that I used were in Georgia. I was able to visit Georgia in 1996 for an initial reconnaissance, and I used that opportunity to go to the main archives, for a preliminary view. This included the Georgia Department of Archives and History (GDAH), the rare books collection in the Woodruff Library at Emory University, both in Atlanta, the Hargrett Rare Books and Manuscripts Library at the University of Georgia in Athens, and the library at the Georgia Historical Society in Savannah.

The literature review also demonstrated that considerable primary data could be obtained on microfilm. Let me give three examples. First, many books published in the nineteenth century were already housed in the University of California at Berkeley library, or available there on interlibrary loan. Second, one can access substantial data via microfilm collections from major libraries across the USA – these were obtained on interlibrary loan.[3] Third, data on the nineteenth-century Federal Censuses can be gained in the same manner. There are also options for other data to be gathered locally. For example, I discovered that the Church of Jesus Christ of Latter Day Saints (the Mormons) have genealogical collections at their local temples that are open to the public. There is such a temple in Oakland, California, and I was able to access data from the 1850 Federal Census already housed in that library's collection or via loan from another collection. Similarly, there is a regional archive of the US Census in San Bruno, California, which had documents on microfiche. I also got a small grant from the University of California at Berkeley library to buy the 1850 Federal Census data for the 'schedule of slaves'.[4] The overall goal at this stage should be to access as much of these data, especially primary data, while you are at your home campusx, making you better prepared for research visits out of town. It also means that when you visit other research sites you can spend most or all of your time accessing materials and data that are not available anywhere else but at that particular site. However, let me emphasize that while a literature review is indispensable, it is always incomplete. Your project will always be unique, and previous publications do not tell you every archive or collection that they looked at, but usually only those that they used and cited in their published work. They will certainly fail to mention very substantial collections simply because they were not used.

In addition to the literature review, I also contacted scholars who had previously worked on the subject, especially those who had worked in the archives that I wanted to visit. They told me of other scholars and graduate students currently working in the field, and about sources about which I was previously aware. For example, James Walvin in the History Department at York University in England gave me numerous contacts, as did Professor James Roark in the History Department at Emory University in Atlanta, Georgia. Most of these scholars were responsive, but some were not. And I met other researchers, including a couple of female graduate students, who told me that, in general, they have not received the kind of response to their inquiries that I had received. The power of gender and social status continues.

In the archives

During my preliminary trip to the archives, I wanted to see what they looked like, how they were laid out, what were the procedures for accessing documents or for making photocopies, and verb a range of other practical matters. My initial inclination when I arrived in the archives was to dive deeply into the first apparently useful primary documents that I came across. This was a mistake. It is far better to spend several days – even a couple of weeks – reviewing what is in the archives generally, what materials are in the open and closed sections: locating descriptive catalogues of the collections, using name and subject indexes, getting a good overview of the entire collection. This is a difficult thing to do – the urge to get right on with the primary documents is tremendous – but it is a process that will prove to be extremely beneficial for understanding the collections as a whole, and for helping you decide exactly what is in the archives, and in what order you should go through the documents.

Be clear that in the majority of archives with original documents you will not be allowed direct access to the materials. The staff at the archives will subject you to close scrutiny and security. This is often a surprise to young researchers who think archives are just like libraries, with all the ease of access. Not so. You will usually be allowed to take into the archive only pencils and individual sheets of paper, and will have to request documents at very specific times of the day – maybe up to several hours in advance. This means you will have to be very well organized and anticipate the material that you will need. It might be better to ask for more than you need, because it is easier to return material than to wait for more to appear. In the GDAH, I was searched every time I went in and out of the main collection – as were all the people consulting the collections. Historical documents may be several hundred years old (most of the ones I consulted were from the mid-nineteenth century) and are extremely rare and valuable. The archives don't want you defacing or destroying them. At the GDAH, a person is on duty at all times to ensure that you do not turn the pages of a rare book in an inappropriate fashion. This can be quite disconcerting at times – but you'll get used to it.

It will be indispensable to develop good relations with archive staff. Apart from providing the necessary introduction and overview of the archive's collections, they can direct you to lesser-known collections, tell you what is or is not in specific collections, and inform you of, and put you in contact with, others working on your area of research at any particular time. With years of experience, and many projects under their belt, they can give you insights and short-cuts worth a barrel full of diamonds. But there can also be unexpected moments. One very difficult moment happened when I was quite legitimately allowed access to the closed shelves in the GDAH and there was no assistant there. A few minutes later, an assistant showed up, saw me and panicked – thinking I was stealing documents, or at least concerned that I was there without staff supervision. However, the guard on duty (who had a gun) recognized me, as I had already been there every day for several weeks, and the tension was deflated. However, the staff spent the rest of the day anxiously trying to understand how I had been allowed entrance unaccompanied, and it was a very uncomfortable situation and I can't help feeling that they looked at me more closely in the following weeks.

It is important to keep detailed, meticulously organized notes of what is in the various collections in the archives. Be sure to note exact names of collections, exact folio numbers (the large folders that often contains several documents) and the exact folder numbers (smaller files with smaller numbers of documents). After you have left the archive, you will almost certainly forget much of what you have seen and therefore will need a detailed record of what is there, for when you get back to your home base. These notes will be indispensable, not only if you need to go back (which is time-consuming and expensive), but also in case you need to contact a locally based research assistant to locate specific items for you – a far more-cost-effective option. In Georgia, I was fortunate to work with several graduate students from Clark Atlanta University in Atlanta, and they provided valuable assistance during my visits, and even after I had left.

A key suggestion that proved indispensable came to me easily. When I told a colleague I was going to archives, he advised me to get a big photocopy budget and photocopy everything possible – because once you have left, it will be expensive to get back. This seemed obvious, though I did not have the intention in my mind at the time. I proceeded to do exactly what was suggested and I never regretted it.

While in the archives, I found a whole series of books of Georgia county histories that were not available in the library at Berkeley. Most of these were written by residents of the county, who got old and wanted to record the history of their county. These books provided lots of additional information, insights, names, places and dates, and also the opportunity to cross-check other data I had collected. But be careful, very careful. The majority of these writers were amateurs, and many were pretty poor ones at that. Significant data they provided were unreliable and some of them were simply incorrect. Many statements of fact were no more than impressions. So if you use them, be sure you have an independent source of verification.

Let me mention one more insight from the research process. Given the mass of documents in an archive, it is difficult to know exactly what to read and what to bypass. You can use clues from previous books, and use the name and subject indexes in the archives. But if you only do this then many documents will still be missed. For example, one afternoon I looked at a book that seemed an unlikely suspect and it produced an entirely new lead. The book concerned a young White Northerner who had moved to Georgia and, after trying to help an enslaved person to escape (successfully as it happened), was himself arrested and imprisoned. For no apparent reason, I just kept reading it, though the first forty pages or so had almost nothing to

say about my topic. Then all of a sudden the issue appeared with a specificity and concreteness surpassed only by its abhorrence. The author
described how, while in prison, the prison guards would bring in Black
women of mixed origins night after night. He then went on to describe how
this practice – White men using women of mixed origins for sex – was
pervasive in Georgia, and ended up with a story of one White man who had
raped his enslaved woman, and then, when her child, his daughter, was
barely a teenager, had raped her (Paine 1851). Now I knew that rape was
pervasive, but I did not know how common incestuous rape was, especially
that committed by White men against their daughters of mixed origins, as I
had not seen it in any published books on Georgia. But then I saw more and
more examples of it. As I discussed it with some female graduate students in
my department, they told me of novels and poetry in which incest of this
kind was addressed, suggesting that they were better sources for a practice
unlikely to appear in sociological or historical documents. They were right –
I could find little other data in my sources, but I found a publication on the
extent of incest in the White South, along with some data from 'Slave
Narratives', which explored the issue further (Bardaglio 1991). It was
patently clear that only Black women of mixed origins could be the victims
of such a practice – a repugnant and deplorable practice – what I call the
atrocity singularly reserved for Black women of mixed origins.

Primary data sets

Space constraints do not allow me to describe the data for all of the questions posed in this research, so here I address only some of the more
important and difficult ones, particularly those that convey the range of data
sets available. As mentioned above, there is no centrally located, comprehensive data set for these kinds of historical questions. What exists is a range of
data sources, of varying levels of comprehensiveness, detail and reliability.
The trick, the essential requirement really, is to find out which ones are the
best, to access them in a cost-effective and practical way, and to ensure that
you have a means to cross-check their accuracy. It is useful here to discuss
some of the primary data collected for this study in the traditional categories
of qualitative and quantitative data.

The qualitative data collected were diverse, disparate and numerous – as
is entirely normal in historical projects of this kind. The goal was to obtain a
range and diversity of documents and texts covering all aspects of life in
Antebellum Georgia. I was especially concerned to obtain data from people
of color because their evaluation of the status of work, and the significance of
color, was often different from that of Whites. The priority was to find out
what existed, and where the documents could be found – that is, in which
archives they were located. What types of documents did I use? First, I used
manuscript sources from a range of plantations, farms and urban employers,
including letters, diaries, wills, memoirs, autobiographies, work routines,

bills of sale and financial accounts. Second, I used contemporaneous publications – by individuals and organizations – like city and county histories, agricultural treatises, economic and political texts, accounts of travelers, abolitionist papers and an array of religious writings. Third, I used newspapers of various kinds at city, country or state level. These were especially useful for accounts of enslaved persons who escaped – they provide immense individual detail of physical characteristics like color. Fourth, I used federal, state, county and municipal government documents including population surveys, laws, court records, minutes of meetings and debates, financial reports and probate records. In the USA, there is a range of sources of data providing oral and written testimony by people of color, enslaved and legally free, known collectively as 'Slave Narratives' (Rawick 1972). These include letters, memoirs and biographies, interviews and court testimony. There were significant amounts of these data available for Georgia.

The most important and the most interesting quantitative data set that I used, and the one that I think adds most to my analysis of these questions, comprised the original returns to the 1850 Federal Census, that being the first one in which data on the 'race' of the enslaved was recorded. In the 1850 Federal Census, the population of what it called 'negro slaves' was divided into two categories – 'Black' and 'mulatto'. The enslaved persons were listed by owner, and data were also provided for sex and age. These data were reported on a separate schedule – Schedule II – and the original returns can be obtained on microfilm from various sources.[5] I collected these data so that I could assess the numbers and proportions of Blacks of mixed origins on plantations of different sizes in cotton and rice agriculture. I did this so as to estimate the extent to which Blacks of mixed origins were located in the most privileged jobs on the plantations.

Space does not permit me to go into detail here but let me convey the main idea. The Federal Census for Georgia in 1850 recorded a total enslaved population of 381,682, of whom 22,669 were listed as 'mulatto' and 359,013 as Black. With the help of several research assistants, I carried out the first 100 per cent count of race and gender across agricultural units of different sizes for the entire state. I organized these data into the following categories: units that had no Blacks of mixed origins on them; units that had only Blacks of mixed origins on them; units that had a large proportion of Blacks of mixed origins on them; and units that had a small proportion of Blacks of mixed origins on them. In 1850, there were about 38,450 owners of enslaved persons and my count reveals that about 8,800 (23 per cent) of them owned at least one person of mixed origins, while 29,650 (77 per cent) owned none. In addition, I found a significant number of agricultural units with large percentages of Blacks of mixed origins on them, and a small number of units that were exclusively Blacks of mixed origins. Drawing from these data, I argue that the majority of household servants were probably Black, and that large numbers of Blacks of mixed origins most definitely worked in agricultural labor for the whole year or part of it. Now it is certainly true that the Census has problems. For example, some planta- tions in the coastal rice counties indicated that they had no 'mulattoes' among their enslaved population, but inspection of the documentary records for individual plantations demonstrates that there were in fact 'mulattoes' present. In these instances the master-enslavers simply lied, perhaps because they did not feel it was important to provide this information. However, this was in a small number of cases and the Census still remains the best quanti- tative data set for this question.

The main lessons

There are several general lessons that apply to the use of historical data for sociological questions. First, an extensive literature review is indispensable in order to assess the state of knowledge on the topic, and methodologically for helping locate the key collections of historical documents, and where they are archived (that is, where geographically). This will also tell you the names of the specific collections within the archives. It is then your respon- sibility to go beyond the collections cited – these are not the universe of all collections relevant to your own project – and to do so by systematically using indexes of various kinds, as well as following some intuitions and unlikely trails. During this preliminary review, and before you get to the archives, you should try to locate substantial data available via microfilm from major libraries, and important plantation collections. You should also contact scholars who have previously worked (or are currently working) on the field and develop good relations with them and with archive staff. This will save you substantial time and money.

A second lesson is to be critical of the extant concepts, to reject those that are offensive or inappropriate, to develop your own concepts and be ready to stand your ground in defense of them when you are attacked because they diverge from convention, cannot be located in an English dictionary or are cumbersome. The fight will be worth it and in the long run they will make more of a contribution to the field than you realize. Try to figure out ques- tions and concepts in advance, though remain somewhat flexible – you might find other questions that are more interesting or more analytically insightful.

Third, when you get to the archives, spend time getting a comprehensive overview of how the various collections are arranged and keep meticulously organized and detailed notes of what is in them. Take photocopies galore, anything you think you might use, and bring them back to home base. Be prepared to spend substantial time following leads of various kinds, and expect that trails that bring you to a dead end are simply par for the course.

Finally, for the empirical data sets, be sure to review quantitative and qualitative data sets as appropriate, and to cross-check them for important and key issues. You will have to delve into a wide range of sources of various levels of reliability and usefulness over a long period of time, so extensive record keeping is indispensable.

Conclusion

This chapter has sought to describe the conceptual framework, methodology and empirical data sets used to research the experiences of people of mixed African and European origins under nineteenth-century slavery in the USA. I briefly described the conventional wisdom on these issues prevalent in the literature, and I identified a number of problems with the assumptions and data used to support this conventional wisdom. I then described the various methods that I used to collect data for these same questions in Georgia. I described the research process, highlighted key issues to do with the language and terminology employed in this research, and provided concrete examples of the data collected as well as practical issues to take into account in collecting such data. I believe that many of the insights derived from my particular research endeavors are applicable to others doing historical research, especially historical sociology.

One of the major problems that we face as academics is to do with the conceptualization and formulation of our research project. This is often a question of theory and of epistemology. A second set of problems has to do with the trials and tribulations of the research process. This is more often a question of practicalities. In both endeavors we are confronted by the finiteness of time. The issue is how to avoid uncritically genuflecting to the conceptualizations of previous generations of scholars (whose concepts and assumptions continue, in many respects, to burden us) and how to escape being swallowed up in the vastness and variety of the resources. There is also the tricky question of how to write up our project – but that is not a question that I have had time to address in these pages. In respect to these questions, a clear methodology – conceptual clarity, the specificity of sources and a definite strategy for accessing them – becomes a device for escaping from the prison of the finiteness of time. But this is not just about making life easy for yourself, because these criteria also serve as a device for constructing a story that has authority – it has authority because it has rigor, depth, is systematic and comprehensive.

For my specific project, I was unhappy with many of the assumptions in the literature, with some of the key concepts and with the empirical data used to answer the questions. After considerable review of the literature, and collection of data, I was able to offer counter-arguments based on better data. I argue that Blacks of mixed origins certainly enjoyed many privileges and considerable advantage when compared to Blacks presumed to be of unmixed origins. But I found that these have been considerably exaggerated and that, when we take a fuller account of all Blacks of mixed origins and all Blacks, the picture is more complicated. Far fewer Blacks of mixed origins had rich White fathers than is imagined and far fewer were to be found in housework. In addition, housework reveals substantial problems not previously acknowledged, while fieldwork, especially task labor, had a number of compensating factors. Even one of the most privileged of all Blacks of mixed origins under slavery – Amanda America Dickson – was the product of sexual coercion, her White father aged over 40 at the time of her birth, her mother aged 13 (Leslie 1995: 37). Privilege it certainly was, but it was not without its costs. Nor did the majority of Blacks of mixed origins get this. Neither Booker T. Washington nor Frederick Douglass got any benefit from their White fathers. And even in communities presumed to be privileged, there were strict limitations. As Johnson and Roark point out, in South Carolina during slavery 'all but six out of a hundred free Afro-Americans were desperately poor', and 'for most, life was a never-ending struggle to make ends meet' (Johnson and Roark 1984: 60). My argument is that any assessment of the circumstances of Blacks of mixed origins generally throughout the states – even those in the stereotypically privileged communities of New Orleans, Louisiana and Charleston, South Carolina – requires an analysis of the kind described in this chapter. Without such an analysis, any conclusions reached are likely to remain empirically biased, conceptually impaired and theoretically flawed.

Notes

1   That is because the usual assumption is that Blacks outnumbered Blacks of mixed origins on the plantation and were put into the fields to work, while Blacks of mixed origins were kept in the house and trades. But on plantations where Blacks of mixed origins outnumbered Blacks this was hardly likely, and was extremely unlikely on plantations where there were no Blacks of mixed origins enslaved at all.

2   The presumption is also that it is factually correct – that there were more Blacks of mixed origins in the house than the field. I argue that the demographic imbalance in favor of Blacks makes this unlikely – and that it is more likely that the majority of house servants were Black, not Black of mixed origins.

3   For example, Scholarly Resources in Wilmington, DE, publishes extensive collections of primary data on microfilm for slavery and for other periods in African American history.

4   In the Federal Censuses through 1860, there were separate schedules for the 'free population' and for the 'slave population'.

5   It is quite easy to borrow these returns on microfiche, via interlibrary loan, from the Federal Bureau of Census.

6 Three rules I go by in my ethnographic research on race and racism

Mitchell Duneier

Hakim Hasan is a book vendor and street intellectual at the busy intersection of Eighth Street, Greenwich Avenue, and the Avenue of the Americas – a.k.a. Sixth Avenue. He is a sturdy and stocky 5'7 African American, 42 years' old. In the winter, he wears Timberland boots, jeans, a hooded sweatshirt, a down vest, and a Banana Republic baseball cap.

Hakim is one of many street book vendors throughout Greenwich Village and New York City generally. Most of these specialize in one or more of the following: expensive art and photography books; dictionaries; *New York Times* bestsellers; 'black books'; new quality mass-market and trade paperbacks of all varieties; used and out-of-print books; comic books; pornography; and discarded magazines.

On Sixth Avenue alone, among the vendors of new books, a passerby may encounter Muhammad and his family, who sell 'black books' and an incense known as 'the Sweet Smell of Success' at the corner of Sixth Avenue and Eighth Street. Down the block, an elderly white man sells bestsellers and high-quality hardcovers on the weekends. At Sixth and Greenwich (across the street), one encounters Howard, a comics vendor, also white, and Alice, a Filipina woman (Hakim's sometime business partner), who sells used paperbacks and current bestsellers.

It goes without saying, perhaps, that one good way to find out more about people is to get to know them at first hand, but this is more easily said than done. When I began, I knew that, if I was to find out what was taking place on the sidewalk, I would have to bridge many gaps between myself and the people I hoped to understand. This involved thinking carefully about who they are and who I am.

I was uneasy.

One of the most notorious gaps in US society is the difference between people related to race and the discourse revolving around this volatile issue. Though there were also differences between our social classes (I was raised in a middle-class suburb, whereas most of them grew up in lower- and working-class urban neighborhoods), religions (I am Jewish and most of them are Muslim or Christian), levels of education (I hold a Ph.D. in sociology and attended two years of law school, whereas some of them did not graduate from high school), and occupations (I am a college professor of sociology and they are street vendors), none of these differences seemed to be as significant as that of race. Actually, the interaction between race and class differences very probably made me uneasy, though I was unaware of that at the time.

When I stood at Hakim's table, I felt that, as a white male, I stood out. In my mind, I had no place at his table, because he was selling so-called black books. I thought that his product formed the boundary of a sort of exclusionary black zone where African Americans were welcome but whites were not.

It is interesting that I felt this way. African Americans buy products every day from stores owned by whites, often having to travel to other neighborhoods to acquire the goods they need. They must shop among whites, and often speak of enduring slights and insults from the proprietors of these businesses. I myself rarely have to go to neighborhoods not dominated by whites in search of goods or services. None of the book vendors ever insulted, offended, or threatened me. None of them told me I was not welcome at his table. None of them ever made anti-white or anti-Semitic remarks. Yet I felt unwelcome in ways I had not felt during previous studies that had brought me into contact with African Americans. This was because many of the conversations I heard were about so-called black books and because the people participating in them seemed to be defining themselves as a people. (Actually, there were also white customers at Hakim's table, though I didn't know it at the time.) I felt out of place. Also, I wanted the trust that would be necessary to write about the life of the street, and race differences seem a great obstacle to such trust.

One day, before I knew Hakim and after I had concluded that these tables were not an appropriate place for me to hang out, I walked by his book table on my way to an appointment. I was surprised to see for sale a copy of *Slim's Table*, my own first book:

'Where did you get this from?' I asked, wondering if it had been stolen.

'I have my sources,' Hakim responded. 'Do you have some interest in this book?'

'Well, I wrote it,' I responded.

'Really? Do you live around here?'

'Yes. I live around the corner, on Mercer Street.'

'Why don't you give me your address and telephone number for my Rolodex?'

His Rolodex? I wondered. This unhoused man has a Rolodex? Why I assumed that Hakim was unhoused is difficult to know for certain. In part, it was due to the context in which he was working: many of the African American men selling things on the block lived right there on the sidewalk. There was no way for me to distinguish easily between those vendors who were unhoused and those who were not, and I had never taken the time to think much about it. I gave him my telephone number and walked off to my appointment.

A few weeks later, I ran into an African American man, Carl Thomas, who had been in my first-year class at the New York University School of Law. (Carl went on be the lawyer who would bring the beating of Abner Luima to the attention of the press and was the first attorney to represent him before Johnny Cochran took over the case.) Purely by coincidence, he told me that he was on his way to see a book vendor from whom he had been getting some of his reading material during the past year. It was Hakim.

I told my classmate about my interest in getting to know Hakim and explained my reservations. He told me that he didn't think it would be as hard as I thought. Hakim had apparently gone through spells of sleeping at my classmate's home with his wife and children.

A few days later, my classmate brought him to meet me in the law school lounge. When I told Hakim that I wanted to get to know him and the people at his vending table, he was circumspect, saying only that he would think about it. After another few days later, he dropped off a brief but eloquent note at my apartment, explaining that he didn't think it was a good idea. 'My suspicion is couched in the collective memory of a people who have been academically slandered for generations,' he wrote. 'African Americans are at a point where we have to be suspicious of people who want to tell stories about us.'

During the next couple of months, Hakim and I saw each other about once a week or so on our own. On a few occasions, we met and talked at the Cozy Soup 'n' Burger on Broadway. It seemed that we had decided to get to know each other better.

Early one morning a few months later, I approached his table as he was setting up and asked, 'What are you doing working on Sixth Avenue in the first place?'

'I think there are a number of black folks in these corporate environments that have to make this decision,' he replied. 'Some are not as extreme as I am. Some take it out on themselves in other ways.'

It had not occurred to me that Hakim had come to work on the street from a corporate environment. Learning this about him has been significant as I have worked to understand his life on the street. In the universities where I teach, I meet many African American students who believe that it will be very difficult for them to maintain their integrity while working in corporate life. Many of them have come to this conclusion by hearing of the experiences of relatives and friends who have already had problems; others have themselves sensed racial intolerance on campus. Yet, in choosing to work on the street, Hakim had clearly made what would be a radical, if not entirely incomprehensible, decision by the standards of my African American students. Once we had discussed some of these issues in depth over the subsequent weeks, Hakim volunteered that he felt comfortable letting me observe his table with the purpose of writing about it, and I began to do so.

In fact, Hakim probably did not feel comfortable. In an afterword to *Sidewalk*, he later wrote:

> Mitchell Duneier recalls that he was thoroughly surprised when, during our first conversation at my book vending table, I told him that I had a Rolodex. His surprise was a matter of social context. But what if I had not mentioned the word Rolodex to Mitch? Because the word Rolodex is associated with people who work in offices, and because I was perceived as a 'street person,' my use of it stood out. It caused a shift in Mitch's perception of me. I am now inclined to suggest that this book would never have been written if it had not been for this conversation, which challenged his assumptions about me and my social status.
>
> In the first chapter Mitch recalls his difficulty in convincing me to become a subject – at the time the sole subject – of the book. Indeed, I found myself hearing the decree of my mother, whenever she had to leave my siblings and me at home alone: *Do not open the door for anyone while I'm gone.*
>
> If I defied the maternal decree and opened *this* door, on what basis would I weigh Mitch's intentions? How could I prevent him from appropriating me as mere data, from not giving me a voice in how the material in his book would be selected and depicted? How does a subject take part in an ethnographic study in which he has very little faith and survive as something more than a subject and less than an author?
>
> Because I believe my disastrous experience in the corporate world was the effect of racism (a claim many whites these days liken to that of the proverbial boy who cried 'Wolf!'), I asked myself, 'Can I expect Mitch, as a white sociologist, to understand why that experience led me to work as a book vendor on Sixth Avenue in the first place?' The idea of race as a lived experience could not be avoided; at the same time, if I made the mistake of denying Mitch *his* humanity on the basis of race, without giving him a fair chance, there would have been no way for me to know whether he could write about my life accurately.
>
> I did not know how Mitch would construct an account of my life on these blocks. Would he conduct his research as a descendent of a socio-logical tradition which historically has found it all but impossible to write and theorize about blacks, especially poor blacks, as complex human beings? I worried this way, oddly enough, even after reading Mitch's first book, *Slim's Table*, despite its insights into the lives of working-class black men, because my life, not the lives depicted in that book, was at stake.
>
> I am still trying to understand how Mitch and the people whose lives he documented developed relationships on several New York City Streets where race and class conflicts derail most efforts to transcend such barriers. Does this mean that people sometimes find ways – the

will, actually – to work through their phobias and prejudices on these streets? Is it a matter of being willing to listen to one another with respect? Does it hinge on the sheer willpower of a subject, in this case myself, who was determined not to be reduced to theoretical formulations or mere 'data'? Given the vast inequalities, racial misunderstandings, and violence found on the street at every turn, I believe there was some measure of good luck involved here – the kind of luck scholars and 'subjects' of different races, classes, and genders will need when they encounter one another in the field.

I could not imagine a more eloquent statement on these topics than Hakim's. When we use the word 'luck', we are often referring to mere good fortune, but we are also referring to factors that have not yet been identified. While acknowledging that there is a tremendous amount of luck involved in any fieldwork project actually coming to fruition, it is essential to characterize the concrete things we actually *can* do in order to increase the chances that good fortune will be on our side. In reflecting on my field experiences researching race and racism as a white male, I have developed a few rules for myself as I go about doing my work.

> First, don't begin with the assumption that special rapport or trust is always a precondition for doing successful fieldwork. And don't be so presumptuous as to believe that you have trust or even special rapport with the people you are trying to write about, even when it seems you do.

On 8 June 1996, I appeared on Sixth Avenue at about 6.00 a.m. Ron, whom I recognized from the time I had spent on the block (but whom I had never met), was already there. I had heard enough about his violent episodes to think that I had better wait until Marvin arrived before I approached.

Marvin appeared half an hour later. He greeted me and introduced me to Ron, who, it turned out, had been expecting me. As the two men began unpacking magazines from crates that a 'mover' named Rock had transported from Marvin's storage locker, Marvin told me to watch how the magazines are displayed, with the foreign fashion titles placed at the top of the table where they will catch the eyes of passersby.

As I joined in the work, I removed a tape recorder from my bag. Ron looked down at the machine and scowled. He hardly spoke that day. I put the tape recorder back in my bag, never having turned it on.

I was wearing the same clothes I had been wearing in the classroom a few days earlier: a blue button-down shirt, beige pants, and black shoes. Even if I had dressed differently, I would have stood out. My speech and diction alone would have made me seem different. Had I tried to downplay these differences, though, Ron would have seen through such a move immediately.

So right away on the block I was being a person not unlike the person I am with my friends in casual settings, my family at home, and my colleagues at work. Of course, in each of these settings, I adapt somewhat, accentuating some traits and downplaying others. In small ways I am not aware of, I doubtless did the same as I began my work.

Using myself as a participant observer, I was there to notice by taking part, trying to observe and retain information that others in the setting often thought unimportant or took for granted. I had research questions vaguely in mind, and I was already making mental comparisons between what I was seeing and what the sociology literature had to say. I was there simply to observe and record, and I was asking the people working the sidewalk to let me be there.

One of the most difficult situations I faced as I tried to make an entry into these blocks was avoiding the conflicts that already existed. Hakim, with whom I had become closely associated, got along well with everyone on Sixth Avenue except Muhammad. But if I was to get to know all the men on the block, it was essential that I not be viewed as especially associated with Hakim.

The act of 'getting in,' then, sometimes led me to be less than sincere about my connection to Hakim. Fieldwork can be a morally ambiguous enterprise. I say this even though I have never lied to any of the persons I write about. The question for me is how to show respect for the people I write about, given the impossibility of complete sincerity at every moment (in research as in life).

The gulf between the other vendors and myself was much greater than it was with Hakim. How could I expect these men to trust me? The vendors were wondering the same thing. One conversation captured on my tape recorder illustrates this. I had been interviewing one of them, who had been holding my tape recorder, when I got called away. While listening to the tapes a few months later, I came across the conversation that ensued after I left. (The participants, who forgot the tape was running, have asked me to conceal their identities in this instance.)

'What you think he's doing to benefit you?' X asked.

'A regular black person who's got something on the ball should do this, I would think,' said Y.

'He's not doing anything to benefit us, Y.'

'I'm not saying it's to benefit us,' said Y. 'It's for focus.'

'No. It's more for them, the white people.'

'You think so?' said Y.

'Yeah. My conversations with him just now, I already figured it out. It's mostly for them. They want to know why there's so much homeless people into selling books....I told him because Giuliani came in and he said nobody could panhandle no more. Then the recycling law came in. People voted on it.'

'Case in point,' said Y. 'You see, I knew he had to talk to you. I can't tell him a lot of things 'cause I'm not a talker.'

'I told him in California there's people doing the same thing that we're doing. They do it on a much more higher level. They are white people. You understand?'

'Yeah.'

'They have yard sales.'

'Yeah.'

'They put the shit right out there in their yard. He knows. Some of them make a million dollars a year. But what they put in their yard, these are people that put sculptures. They put expensive vases. These are peoples that drives in their cars. All week long, all they do is shop.'

'Cooking for stuff,' said Y. 'Like we go hunting, they go shopping.'

'Right. Very expensive stuff. They bring it and they put it in their yard and sell it. And they do it every weekend. Every Saturday. Every Sunday. So they making thousands. He's not questioning them: How come they can do it? He's questioning us! He want to know how did the homeless people get to do it. That's his whole main concern. Not really trying to help us. He's trying to figure out how did the homeless people get a lock on something that he consider lucrative.'

'Good point,' said Y.

'You gotta remember, he's a Jew, you know. They used to taking over. They used to taking over no matter where they go. When they went to Israel. When they went to Germany. Why do you think in World War II they got punished so much? Because they owned whole of Germany. So when the regular white people took over, came to power, they said, "We tired of these Jews running everything."'

'But throughout time the Jewish people have always been business people. But they love to take over.' Y laughed.

'Of course,' X said, laughing hysterically. 'That's what he's doing his research on now. He's trying to figure out how did these guys got it. How come we didn't get it?'

Y laughed.

X continued laughing hysterically, unable to finish his next sentence.

'I don't think so,' said Y.

'But he's not interested in trying to help us out.'

'I'm not saying that, X. I'm saying he's trying to focus on the point.'

'I told him that, too,' said X. 'Everyone he talk to, they're gonna talk to him on the level like he's gonna help them against the police or something like that. They're gonna look to him to advocate their rights.'

'No. I don't think that, either. I think it's more or less to state the truth about what's going on. So people can understand that people like you and I are not criminals. We're not horrible people. Just like what you said, what happens if we couldn't do this? What would you do if you couldn't sell books right now?'

Hearing those stereotypes invoked against me made me realize that – conventional wisdom to the contrary – participant observers need not be fully trusted in order to have their presence at least accepted. I learned how to do fieldwork from Howard S. Becker, and one of the things he taught me – I call it the Becker principle – is that most social processes have a structure that comes close to insuring that a certain set of situations will arise over time. These situations practically require people to do or say certain things because there are other things going on that cause them to do that, things that are more influential than the social condition of a fieldworker being present (Becker 1998). For example, most of the things in a vendor's day – from setting up his magazines to going on hunts for magazines to urinating – are structured. This is why investigators like myself sometimes can learn about a social world despite not having had the rapport we thought we had, and despite the fact that we occupy social positions quite distinct from the persons we write about.

It was hard for me to know what to make of that discussion between X and Y. Maybe they were 'just' having fun, but I don't think so. Though I was not astonished by what I heard, I had no idea that X harbored those suspicions toward me as I had gone about my work on the blocks throughout the summer. In this sense, fieldwork is very much like life itself. We may *feel* fully trusted and accepted by colleagues and 'friends,' but full acceptance is difficult to measure by objective standards and a rarity in any case. If we cannot expect such acceptance in our everyday lives, it is probably unrealistic to make it the standard for successful fieldwork.

At the same time, participant *observers* like myself who do cross-race fieldwork must, I think, be aware that there are many things members of the different races will not say in one another's presence. For blacks in the USA, it has been necessary to 'wear the mask' – to quote the black poet Paul Laurence Dunbar, who wrote:

> We wear the mask that grins and lies,
>
> It hides our cheeks and shades our eyes, This debt we pay to human guile;
>
> With torn and bleeding hearts we smile, And mouth with myriad subtleties.

Dunbar's words are no less relevant today, for, as a survival mechanism, many blacks still feel that they cannot afford to speak honestly to whites. Surely, it would have been a methodological error for me to believe that apparent rapport is real trust, or that the poor blacks I was writing about would feel comfortable taking off the mask in my presence.

I believe that some of the vendors may have let me work out on Sixth Avenue with them because they eventually saw what I was doing nearly the way I did; others merely wanted to have me around as a source of small change and loans (something I discuss later in *Sidewalk*); and a few others may have decided to put up with me so that there would be a book about them and the blocks. But it would be naïve for me to say that I knew what they were thinking, or that they trusted or accepted me fully, whatever that might mean.

Second, begin research with a humble commitment to being surprised by the things you learn in the field, and a constant awareness that your social position likely makes you blind to the very phenomena that might be useful to explain.

Once while listening to tapes I had made on the street, I came across a dialogue between two unhoused men – Mudrick telling Keith that the Assistant Manager kicked him out of McDonald's for not being a 'customer' when he tried to use the bathroom. A comparison I did not plan to make was suddenly evident: Mudrick is an unhoused vendor. He works on the street. I am a professor. I work in an office building. The unhoused vendor, a 57-year-old black man, has just relied on the goodwill of a teenage black boy with the title 'Assistant Manager' to let him use the bathroom. I, by contrast, had been using the bathrooms of local restaurants whenever I pleased.

We are told by the methods literature to ask questions that will enable us to dialogue with theory, questions that are important in the real world, or make some contribution to the literature. What we are not told is how to overcome blinders that may derive from differences between ourselves and the people we write about. These blinders influence the conception of questions, and the determination that certain topics should be noticed in the first place.

I had often seen men urinating against the sides of buildings or in cups during my years working with the vendors, but this had never registered as important enough to jot on a note pad, or think about twice. It was so much part of my taken-for-granted reality that it did not merit note. I had probably assumed that the men who were peeing against the side of the Washington Square Court condominium were just lazy, and no different, by the way, from all my upper-middle-class male friends who do the same thing when they are in the middle of the golf course and are too lazy to go back to the clubhouse to take a piss. This is the kind of male behavior I have taken for granted throughout my life. And the things we take for granted often do not end up in our field jottings.

On the tape I had just listened to, I was confronted with a single conversation that posed a challenge to my taken-for-granted assumptions. Mudrick had been *excluded from* the McDonald's bathroom. As an unhoused man, he was not peeing against the condominium out of the same kind of laziness I had observed in my upper-middle-class white friends on the golf course. But why, if I had been working out on the street every day and night with these men, had I not *understood* this to be a problem? How was it that, while working with the housed and rehoused vendors, I had not noticed this basic aspect of their lives, let alone conceived of it as a research issue?

As an upper-middle-class white male, I had skin and class privileges that the men I was working with did not have. As I thought back to the previous summer on these blocks, I thought of the hundreds of times I had crossed the street and darted to the back of Pizzeria Uno without once wondering if anyone would deny me entrance. Though we were occupying the same physical space and engaging in common activities out on the street, my experience of urinating (and, I would later learn, of defecating) had been radically different from that of the men I worked with. This is part of the reason I did not perceive it as a research topic. The fact that I *did* finally consider it, that I did ultimately recognize a research issue, came from a constellation of lucky circumstances, one of which being that, while listening to the tape in my office far away, I happened to have been in need of using the bathroom, which made me particularly sensitive to the issue of peeing when I heard that 5-second snippet of tape that might have otherwise run by unnoticed.

Now here is a question. What if I had not belonged to a more privileged social position than my subjects? What if, instead, I was poor and black and similarly excluded? I would surely have understood this to be an aspect of daily life, but would I have understood it to be a topic? I don't know the answer, but one possibility is that being excluded from public bathrooms is so taken for granted on the street that it is rarely discussed. I never heard anyone talk about it during the previous summer, and the discussion I *did* hear on the tape was hardly that, more like a reference to an incident that did not deserve elaboration. I do not believe that someone from the same social position as the vendors would necessarily have seen exclusion from bathrooms as a research topic, any more than my colleagues at the university would see the circumstances of bathroom use on the eighth floor of the social science building as an interesting research issue.

I suspect that a black male professional researcher might have had less difficulty than these men gaining access to local public bathrooms, but I cannot be certain. Researching race usually entails researching class and it is often difficult for researchers to know if they are being treated differently from the people they write about due to skin, class, gender privileges, or by some interaction between them. Despite the social differences between us, it is possible that I would have arrived at an understanding of this situation if the men had talked about it. They did not. I remain uncertain as to how to interpret their silence. Did they simply find this to be an unremarkable aspect of their struggles as unhoused men, since this form of exclusion was so routine? Or did they want to protect me (and themselves) from further humiliation and embarrassment by not discussing my own racial and class privileges as a white upper-class academic? I have routinely noted that people who experience race and class discrimination tend to be quite sensitive toward the feelings of those who do not share their experiences. In fact, in my experience neither blacks nor whites in the USA talk honestly about race in the other's presence.

Though I constantly obsess about the ways that my upper-middle-class whiteness influences what I see, I must emphasize my uncertainty about what I do not see and what I do not know I missed.

Third, try to overcome the disadvantages that derive from your social position by consulting with your research subjects, as well as with scholars and intellectuals who once shared the social position of the people you are writing about.

After completing the draft of the original *Sidewalk* manuscript, I gave it to Hakim and asked him for his comments. He read it and brought to my attention a major limitation. As he saw it, my study focused too closely on him and not enough on the vendors who occupied other spaces on Sixth Avenue. As I listened to what he had to say, I realized that we needed to have a sustained conversation about the material in the manuscript. I proposed that we teach a course together at the University of California-Santa Barbara, where I was that year. Hakim was clearly well read, and I had admired his pedagogical relationships with young men like Jerome. Surely my students in Santa Barbara could benefit from working closely with him. I told my idea to Bill Bielby, the chair of my department, who arranged for Hakim to receive a lecturer's salary for the 10-week course.

Hakim and I taught a seminar for undergraduates called 'The Life of the Street and the Life of the Mind in Black America.' In it, we discussed a number of books that Hakim had sold at his table and spoke in detail from the draft manuscript, showing the students how 'black books' entered into the lives and discussions of people who came to Hakim's table. As a teacher, Hakim was organized, insightful, and patient with students on subjects of race, class, and gender, although the discussions were sometimes quite heated.

My research focus was evolving in the seminar as I continually listened to Hakim and came to get a sense of what might be gained if the book included a more comprehensive view of the street.

Sometimes it was the suggestions of African American scholars that led me back to the field with new ideas and questions I had not thought to ask. In trying to understand why black women don't get entangled to the same extent as white women by street harassment in encounters with poor black men, for example, I was helped by the suggestion of a black Wisconsin sociologist, Franklin D. Wilson. He thinks that, because the black women share a racial history with the men on the street, they do not feel responsible or guilty for the men's plight and so are less willing to excuse the men's behavior toward them. Surely a white scholar could have had that insight, but none of those who read my chapter did. I suspect it comes out of Wilson's particular life experience, from situations and people he has known.

Another thing that has helped me has been my collaboration with the African American photographer, Ovie Carter, whose professional and life experiences enable him to give me good advice. Ovie is 52 years' old, was born in Mississippi, and grew up in Chicago and St Louis, before serving in the Air Force. He joined the *Chicago Tribune* at the age of 23. He has worked in Africa as a photojournalist but has spent most of his career covering poor neighborhoods in Chicago. Shortly before our work began on this book, his brother moved in with him from the streets as he made his way off crack. Consequently, Ovie has a deep appreciation for the anguish and problems associated with addiction. Ovie read and commented on all the chapters in *Sidewalk* as I wrote them, and the long hours we have spent together have helped me to understand aspects of life on Sixth Avenue that I would otherwise have been blind to.

All these circumstances have worked for me at times, but there is no simple way to overcome ingrained racial bias, inexperience, or others' suspicions. Perhaps the best starting point is to be aware that a different social position can have a serious effect on one's work, and one can do better work by taking them very seriously.

7　On unsteady ground

Crafting and engaging in the critical study of whiteness[1]

Ruth Frankenberg

White Privilege

> *Today I got permission to do it in graduate school,*
> That which you have been lynched for,
> That which you have been shot for,
> That which you have been jailed for,
> Sterilized for,
> Raped for,
> Told you were mad for –
> By which I mean
> Challenging racism –
> Can you believe
> The enormity
> Of that?
>
> (Frankenberg, 1985)

First, here is a one-sentence introduction. My research engages whiteness. Next, a comment on that introduction: the statement 'my research engages whiteness' could not have been made, meaningfully, at the time, around 1980, when I began the political inquiry that would lead me toward that work. This is so because, at that moment, the notion of 'whiteness' was not present in the political or intellectual worlds of which I was a part. This chapter cannot, then, proceed as though an area of study or an entity to be examined was 'there,' and I simply moved toward it and began an investigation. For me, as indeed for many scholars, the crafting of the field took place alongside and as a result of the research undertaken. In this chapter, I will discuss that process and its effects by reference to close readings of my own work, using them simultaneously as data and as analytical resource.

Take two: A standard mode of introduction to the work of any scholar is by reference to her/his scholarly products. Noting that I have already violated the conventions of that project by beginning this essay with a poem rather than a scholarly quotation, let me state that my first book, *White Women, Race Matters: The Social Construction of Whiteness*, was published in

1993. It is an ethnographic book based both in an intimate relationship with the subject of study itself and upon in-depth, life-history interviews with thirty white women resident in the USA. My second book, an edited collection, *Displacing Whiteness: Essays in Social and Cultural Criticism*, was published in 1997. It is by intention interdisciplinary, international, and multi-ethnic/multi-racial in terms of authorship. In the years between and after the publication of these two books, I have authored a series of essays on whiteness. These have entailed cultural observation and analysis, both of the field of study itself, and of whiteness in the wider world. Of these, one was auto-ethnographic. This current essay is not, then, my first opportunity to mix together the analyses of self, other, field, and socio-cultural context.

Take three: All research starts out with a purpose; much research responds to a crisis. My original commitment to studying that which I first called simply 'race privilege,' later 'white women's enlistment into privileged locations in a system of racial domination,' and later yet 'the critical study of whiteness' began as a response to the following:

1   a 'legitimation crisis' in the theory and practice of white feminists, first posed in the USA and later in Europe and elsewhere;
2   a critique of power relations in the representational disciplines of cultural anthropology and sociology; in particular the examination of the capacity of particular kinds of subjects to name, 'represent,' and speak about other kinds of subjects;
3   a new dimension to the scholarly critique of colonialism – one that, rather than 'leaving colonialism in the past,' demanded that one examine the traces of its continued significance in the present.

It was from the convergence of all these crises that my discussion developed and that the naming of an entity, concept, and subject/object of study called 'whiteness' emerged.

Take four: Now, speaking in the present tense. In this essay, I draw on my 20-plus years of work in an arena currently known to some as 'the critical study of whiteness,' to others as 'whiteness studies.' My own naming of this work leans toward the first option, given that my work has been from the beginning anchored in critical engagements with the interwoven histories of racism and colonialism. This naming makes of 'whiteness' a process as much as an object, and a site that must from the outset be deemed problematical. By contrast, the term 'whiteness studies,' I have often feared, reifies or makes 'always already existing' an entity called whiteness. Naming whiteness without qualification might also lead one to forget to engage it critically. Additionally, the name 'whiteness studies' has at times been too readily assimilable to a kind of 'me-too-ism' following from the development of fields of racial-ethnic studies from the 1960s onward.

The very naming of fields of study is at once signal and symptom of the histories and effects of one's scholarly work. Whenever a field of study is created, the histories of other fields are invoked. Analytic strategies are adopted, developed, and deployed. Boundaries are put in place; strategies of representation are justified. In short, choices are made about precisely how infinity is to be carved out and rearticulated. I offer, here, a social constructionist reading of my own scholarly work. I would argue that the process mapped here is not simply a depiction of my work but of the construction of knowledge in general.

Discussion of the crafting and practice of my research entails documentation of several interwoven processes. The first of these is the naming and renaming of the field of study in question. The second is the continual remaking of the 'referent,' in this instance the continual revision of white people's sense(s) of self and positioning. The third is the ongoing reconception of the researcher/theorist's own location in connection with the field. This latter point does not, I must emphasize, suggest that I am in any sense 'no longer white,' despite the assertion of some proponents of 'the abolition of whiteness' that this might be a possibility (Ignatiev 1997). Rather, it refers to the inevitability that one is constantly learning more about and thus revising ideas about one's field of study, and that, with equal inevitability, the world that one studies does not stand still.

I propose, sharing much with interdisciplinary cultural studies, that one must not, indeed intellectually *cannot*, presume any kind of stability or transparency in the articulation of a research area of this kind (Grossberg 1997; Slack 1996). As Lawrence Grossberg argues, it is not the case that the practitioner of cultural studies enters into a pre-existing field, documents it, and reports upon it in its pristine form. Rather, the practitioner encounters a problem, more or less inchoate (here referring to 'problem' *and* to 'practitioner'), and strives to make meaning, alone or with others, out of that which she or he encounters. Further, she or he strives to make transformative meaning, to rearticulate that which pre-existed her/his arrival on the scene. Moreover, as will be noted toward the end of this piece, rearticulation may sometimes be for better, sometimes for worse, and sometimes simply sideways in direction, rather than forward or back.

In this essay I develop a 'reflexive/recursive' reading of my scholarship. Commenting on my own method and analytical work as they have developed over two-plus decades reveals that not just method and analytical practice, but also the content of the research and theorization, are *themselves* 'reflexive/recursive' in process, content, and outcome. The analysis of my work as 'reflexive/recursive' is applicable not just to my journey, and indeed not just to critical race studies, but also more broadly to others committed to interdisciplinary, poststructuralist research into socio-cultural problems.

I use the term 'reflexive' in the sense that, I would argue, the positionedness of the researcher/theorist must be examined and accounted for. It should be further clarified that the word 'positioned' is not used here in an essentialist 'I am *this*, therefore I think *that*' fashion. Rather, for me the term signals my recognition of the impossibility of any Archimedean, objective, or 'all-seeing' stance. However, insisting that the place from which one undertakes research is as complex as the socio-cultural setting from which one sets out to document one's subject of study does not by itself account for one's perceiving capacity. For the researcher's perspective is also connected with a politicized, thinking consciousness such that one's mode of interpretation will be connected with communities of meaning in significant ways. Thus, one's research practices will be amenable to formation and transformation in ways that are, perhaps, only fully explicable well after the fact of perception itself. Thus examining and accounting for one's positionedness is a difficult business, and the notion of recursive reading becomes critical to the interpretive journey.

I use the term 'recursive' to suggest that past conclusions are not necessarily closed. Rather, they are potentially open to re-examination and revision, and also available as resources for later research and theory. Thus, theoretical results can become the 'data' of future work. Conversely, data can be recognized subsequently as having already been positioned (more or less consciously from the standpoint of the author) and, hence, unconsciously theorized before the conscious theorization process ever began.

An example of this latter point is that, as any researcher conceives her/his interviewee sample, she or he inevitably makes decisions about the boundaries of class, race, gender, region, etcetera, placed around her or his data set. Likewise as she or he designs her or his information-gathering tools, she or he will perforce decide what to ask and by what means to do so. Simply stated, these basic processes are never transparent, never anything other than located, and as a result, directive as much as they are objective in intention and result. Subsequent revision, rethinking, or supplementation of one's beginning premises then potentially makes visible that which was taken as *a priori* at an earlier stage.

All of this generates directions and caveats about the methods and actualities of the research process. First, it is important to see one's work as always 'situated,' as positioned rather than conceivably general in its point of origin. Second, given the recognition that one's work is 'positioned' work, it is critical to be self-conscious about what that positioning *is*. Third, as one undertaking self-conscious work, an author should seek to move consciously rather than naïvely from the composite pre-existing formal and informal knowledge bases of self and other that will, by definition, be giving it shape. Fourth, as the work proceeds, is in dialogue with spaces outside itself and perhaps has impact on these, the new work has the potential to revise that which the author has done before. Here the notion of recursivity again takes center stage.

Analysis of a poem, 'White Privilege' (epigram, above), makes possible an intial discussion of how knowledge is framed, about the situatedness or positionedness of my work, and about the non-closedness of the work as presented in 1985. One can see in it the working of a reflexive-recursive approach to my (and for that matter, anyone else's) intellectual activity.

The poem was written early in my work, 3 or 4 years beyond my dawning recognition that 'white privilege' amounted to a problem to engage with, and signaling the moment when I formalized that recognition into Ph.D. research. Thus, I speak of 'permission to do *it* in graduate school' (italics not in original). The 'it' is referred to in two different ways: one that remains unnamed in the poem, the undertaking of research; and another stated explicitly near the end of the poem, that of 'challenging racism.' This latter naming proposes, then, that the foundational premise and goal of my work was in fact challenging racism. Further, it suggests that my activity is connectable with a range of other activities, gestured toward in the list that begins near the start of the poem. In play here are processes endemic to all of life activity: organizing one's conception of the phenomenal world, and connecting together formerly disparate aspects of it.

Embedded in the poem is an analytical frame about the premise of challenging racism, its relationship to me, and its relationship to my work. I am marked in it as distinctly different from an other or others, a 'you,' who has been lynched, shot, jailed, sterilized, raped, accused of insanity, for 'do'(ing) precisely that which I have just received permission to undertake.

Key to my sense of positioning is awareness of an array of histories of racial disciplining, with some practices more clearly gendered than others. The narrating voice of the poem speaks most directly to the targets of racism or at least to its challengers, not, for example, to uninvolved spectators. And it ends by commenting on the 'enormity' of the difference between the location of the 'I' who writes and the 'you' who is addressed. What one sees here, in short, is a description of the emergence of research from within a specific, delimitable context.

But in addition to those analytical presences, analytical absences must be named here. Perhaps the most significant of these, from the vantage point of the present, is that I do *not* name a generalized state of being white, 'whiteness.' The words 'white' and 'privilege' in the title of the poem support one another linguistically as descriptors. However, the phrase 'white privilege' does not yet constitute name or noun. Thus the 'it' that I am about to undertake is nameable in response to another entity that *is* already a noun – 'racism.' Evidently, it was at that moment far easier to name white privilege by reference to what it was *not* (not lynched, not shot, not raped, and so on) than by reference to what it *was*. All that my poetic voice articulated about that self is that it had scholarly access to the means of challenging racism. And the term 'enormity' seems to stand in for the causative agent of the difference between the 'I' and 'you' of the poem.

As such, the '*that*' of the study ('can you believe the enormity of that?') is connected causally with the '*it*' of the activity that I was about to undertake. This then is the grammatical frame that amounts to the title words of the poem. 'That/enormity' plus 'permission to do it' signals 'White Privilege.'

Revisiting that poem, 17 years after it was written, and then turning to *White Women, Race Matters*, it is possible to examine the path traveled, documenting the movement from one point to another in analytical and also empirical terms.

I will not, here, reiterate my findings in that book, for to do so would be too consuming of time and space. Nor, although this is a chapter on methods for research, will I revisit a discussion of the challenges that I faced while seeking to interview white women on a topic at times invisible and at other times 'taboo.' These questions are engaged in detail in the book itself (Frankenberg 1993: 23–42). Instead, I will comment on the ways in which my depiction of my work in *White Women, Race Matters* iterates in reflexive and recursive terms the crafting of the project itself. That iteration revises, supplements, and clarifies that which was stated in the earlier articulation of the project. As such, it enables a continuation of that which is under consideration in this chapter, namely analysis of how research is undertaken and how meanings are made.

In fact, the very title, *White Women, Race Matters: The Social Construction of Whiteness*, signals both transformation and stability in the work. For by now, there is a noun, a name, *Whiteness*, to replace the earlier 'White Privilege' used in 1985. There is the promise of some content – examination of the 'social construction of whiteness' – to supplement or even stand in for the list of 'nots' in the poem. Meanwhile the *double entendre* of the phrase *Race Matters* connects directly with the terms 'challenging racism' and 'enormity' called forth in the 1985 text.

In 1985, there was no clear name for the poem's subject, nor for its fellow travelers. However, by 1993, there are three names, 'white women,' 'race,' and 'whiteness,' connected with one another, and potentially with the 'White Privilege' and 'challenging racism' of the 1985 text. The foundational framing is then similar. But in the 1993 text, there is linguistic plenitude where, in 1985, there were more questions than answers available. In 1993, there is a set of named subjects under consideration – white women. This contrasts, one might say, with the 'you' addressed in the poem – a racially ambiguous grouping that, while not *necessarily* not white, still seems not to be white (to be not-white) by definition or necessity. (To put this less legalistically, although white persons have been punished for challenging racism, the immediate vision that comes to mind in the poem is that of men and women of color.) In the 1993 voice, white women, white people, and whit*eness* are very much present and at stake. There is a plea to '*White Women*' offered simultaneously with a statement that there is a set of 'matters' connected with that collectivity of individuals. The subtitle of the book, *The Social Construction of Whiteness*, further articulates that a grouping or collectivity of persons is available to be invoked. Also, having invoked that set of persons one can, must, and will, it is implied, analyze its coming into being in the text to follow. My purpose in this detailed reading of one poetic text and one book title is not to engage in word games, but to underline the fact that one inevitably crafts one's object/subject of study at the same time as one analyzes it.

Thus far, I have primarily discussed the intellectual and political framing of my work. However, as I will now make clear, as a cultural critic, ethnographer, and at times auto-ethnographer, *others'* voices and experiences are critical to my own work, whether as intellectual and political colleagues or research subjects. I am interested, looking back to the 1985 poem, to see a singular rather than plural voicing of my cry – '*I* got permission to do it in graduate school' despite the more obviously plural dimension in the poem of the 'you' that 'challeng[ed] racism.' Reading recursively, one can note that the authorial voice depicted in 'White Privilege' is thus limited, perhaps overly narrow by implication, in its description of my situation. Reading it in context, however, one could conclude, correctly, that in the mid-1980s the voice of white, anti-racist academia was small indeed. Thus despite the presence, around the planet, of other anti-racists, including some who were also feminist and/or also white, and/or also scholarly feminists, the sense of aloneness was meaningful, at least in subjective terms.

On a different level, however, I was not objectively alone as I 'got permission to do it in graduate school.' For as noted above, three political-intellectual crises and areas of critique, one in feminism, another in anthropology and sociology, and a third in the analysis of colonialism's legacy, sparked my own intellectual questioning and concerns. These three critical sites did not present me with anything like a cardboard cutout or 'boiler-plate' for my work. For one thing, my work on the critical study of whiteness developed alongside and in dynamic interaction with the fields just named. But these fields certainly provided me with some of the tools with which to undertake my own research project. As such, all three – the second and burgeoning third waves of feminism, critical ethnographic practice, and colonial discourse studies – were crucial to it.

The other indispensable resources for my work were the voices of women interviewed for *White Women, Race Matters*. In naming these voices as a resource, one must note that there is no transparency here, either. The decision to take an ethnographic route toward seeking answers to my questions has its own complex history, one from the individual to the global and from the personal to the political. Also, given the origin of my work in part in feminist scholarship and in the critique of ethnographic practice itself, the 'why,' 'with whom,' and 'how to' of ethnographic work were sites of contestation. Lastly, as noted above, creating an interviewee sample at a time and place wherein whiteness was, for the most part, 'hyper-normal' and thus apparently invisible, or 'taboo' and as a result under pressure to remain invisible, meant that even invoking speech entailed consciousness of context and of one's own situatedness within that context.

In sum, a complex webbing of methods, communities, theories, and modes of practice were – What? Available to me? Required of me? – as I moved from the first inklings of an idea to one of its moments of actualization, the completion of a dissertation and later a book called *White Women, Race Matters*. The next critical question is, then, what makes this transition happen? Who (plural and, of course, including me) made it possible for that process to take place? Part of the answer will have to be that the sheer scale of this process, albeit limited and singular (one book in relationship to four developing fields of intellectual inquiry, thirty white women interviewed for a particular number of hours), makes it difficult to fully account for its production.

Still, using a recursive reading strategy, one can comment upon the book, noting the traces upon it of those resources just listed. Opening the text at the start of Chapter 1, one sees a clear transition from race privilege depicted as 'not' in 1985, to race privilege depicted as actuality. This is signaled by the first words of the first chapter, 'My argument in this book is that race shapes white women's lives.' As in the earlier depiction of self and race privilege as 'not like' rape, lynching, assassination, and so on, connections are made here between concepts that were ostensibly unconnected with one another. Thus '*In the same way* that both men's and women's lives are shaped by their gender [italics not in original]...white people *and* people of color live racially structured lives.' Pieced together here are one *a priori* from feminist theory (gender shapes the lives of men as well as women) with two from race studies (race hierarchy exists; racism entails privilege as well as oppression). By logical extension, a bridge can now be built between the two ('*any system of differentiation* shapes those on whom it bestows privilege as well as those whom it oppresses') [italics not in original].

All of this makes possible the beginning of that which, in cultural studies, is named *rearticulation* of one's understanding of the phenomenal world. Moving down the paragraph, it is argued that, 'in a *social* context [italics not in original] in which white people have too often viewed themselves as nonracial or racially neutral, it is crucial to look at the "racialness" of white experience.' Here, once more connected with the fundamental premises of feminism, anti-racism, and cultural studies, knowledges are seen as inherently social. Thus rearticulation is not a matter of intellectual transformation alone, but rather has social consequences, just as the earlier articulation was also social in origin.

Finally, this first paragraph makes clear the other way in which the investigation to follow is not only a theoretical one. Rather, it relies upon the presence of living subjects, and situated ones at that, examining 'white women's places in the racial structure of the United States at the end of the twentieth century.' The promise to examine 'white women's lives as sites both for the reproduction of racism and for challenges to it' leaves ambiguous the question of agency, of who has or will initiate challenges to racism. This is, of course, part of that which is investigated in the text.

The second paragraph leads into the analytical consequences of the first one, stating that 'If race shapes white women's lives [something proposed by reference to several of the intellectual fields drawn upon, and demonstrable thanks to interview data], the cumulative name I have given to that shape is whiteness.' In the elaboration that follows, the presence of all of those resources is palpable. Yet it also innovates in relation to them. It is now stated that whiteness has several linked dimensions:

> First, whiteness is a location of structural advantage, of race privilege. Second, it is a 'standpoint,' a place from which white people look at ourselves, at others and at society. Third, 'whiteness' refers to a set of cultural practices that are usually unmarked and unnamed. This book seeks to begin exploring, mapping and examining the terrain of whiteness.

Beginning in the middle of this description, one may note that white subjects are named in the plural ('a place from which white people look at *ourselves*' [italics not in original]). Moreover, from the leverage point of the first paragraph of the text, the term 'whiteness' has been given a formal status. It is now deemed not only a noun but also, perhaps even more importantly, a location. It is then a dynamic, relational site; thus it is the converse of a 'not.'

There are several ways in which whiteness as named in the above, three-part definition links directly with the concepts of race and racism. Here are the most obvious ties to the 1985 description of the work already in progress. Yet it must be noted that 'race privilege' is here deemed something more exact, and at the same time more general, 'structural advantage.' This, one might argue, signals a shift from the empirical to the analytical and from the particular to the foundational.

The second part of the definition of whiteness makes another large-scale connection, that between 'structure' and 'subject.' The mode of naming it here owes much to feminism, given the use of the concept of 'standpoint,' revised and rearticulated from its Marxist origins by socialist feminists in the decade leading into my own research on white women. Indeed as noted a few pages later in the same chapter, my own crisis in relation to feminism centered in part on the collapse of the idea of an unqualified 'feminist standpoint' once racism was brought consciously into the picture. The third aspect of the definition engages directly the foundational understanding of ethnography, that cultural practices are crucial resources by means of which to understand all aspects of human society. Yet by insisting on the veritable converse of ethnography, looking for that which is *un*named and *un*marked for most of the research subjects, the method to be undertaken here challenges the conventions of ethnographic practice.

A final sentence sums up my plans to apply the definition ('This book seeks to begin exploring, mapping and examining the terrain of whiteness'). In a linguistic irony that was to my memory unconscious at the time, here is a plan to engage that which is unmarked, unnamed, but also structurally advantaged or dominant, by means of metaphorical strategies more frequently reserved for the dominated in the context of colonizing activity. Methods of examination formerly both reserved for peoples and communities marked 'other,' and indeed central to 'othering' those communities, are turned around and applied to whiteness – a site that, as is argued in the book, had been brought into being by the very 'othering of others' itself.

This close reading of the start of *White Women, Race Matters* demonstrates, it is hoped, how an argument was generated in one instance. I have not, of course, covered the whole of the text, or even the greater part of it. Instead by focusing very closely on the ideas that led me into the research that culminated in *White Women, Race Matters*, I hope to have made visible the ways in which neither ideas nor empirical reality themselves are ever self-evident. Given this, as argued at the start of this essay, it becomes critically important to be thoroughly conscious of the situatedness of one's knowledge, to be able to disclose the traces of one's work, ideally at the start, but if not that, at least retrospectively.

There is a saying that 'the more things change, the more they remain the same.' However, I am not compelled by the veracity of that idea. For, I would argue, it turns out that both change and sameness are complex processes, and often co-existent ones at that. I will complete this paper with some comments on my more recent work on whiteness, and the ways in which it can be connected with what has gone before.

First, an updated definition of whiteness:

1   Whiteness is a location of structural advantage in societies structured in racial dominance.
2   Whiteness is a 'standpoint,' a location from which to see selves, others, national and global orders.
3   Whiteness is a site of elaboration of a range of cultural practices and identities, often unmarked and unnamed, or named as national or 'normative' rather than specifiably racial.
4   Whiteness is often renamed or displaced within ethnic or class namings.
5   Inclusion within the category 'white' is often a matter of contestation, and in different times and places, some kinds of whiteness are boundary-markers of the category itself.
6   Whiteness as a site of privilege is not absolute but rather cross-cut by a range of other axes of relative advantage or subordination; these do not erase or render irrelevant race privilege, but rather inflect or modify it.
7   Whiteness is a product of history, and is a relational category – like other racial locations, it has no inherent but only socially constructed meanings; as such whiteness's meanings are complexly layered and variable locally and translocally; also, whiteness's meanings may appear simultaneously malleable and intractable.
8   The relationality and socially constructed character of whiteness does not, it must be emphasized, mean that this and other racial locations are unreal in their material and discursive effects (see Frankenrberg 2001: 76).

It hardly needs to be stated that this definition of whiteness has grown since my earlier iterations. While points one, two, and three are close to those that appeared in *White Women, Race Matters*, here are five additional ideas about whiteness. But these later points are not, it should be noted, new ones to me. Their content is not absent from the book in which the three-point definition first appeared. Rather, they elaborate or extrapolate upon what was already there. Over the years, in a succession of talks and published articles, it has proven necessary to add each of these definitional points.

Why, then, did I not name them earlier on? Why did I not pull them out from the book text and mark them? I do not, I must confess, have simple answers to those questions. When they were finally marked or, more accurately, pulled out from the body of the text itself, this was the result of my interactions with readers/listeners responding to the book, including students, colleagues, and others. They are primarily the result of my recognition of what it is that needs to be paid attention to, about whiteness, in any or even in all contexts. They result from further recognitions, very often dialogical in emergence, of what might remain *un*marked, if I do not underscore it.

I would further propose that the making of steady ground – the crafting of a space called whiteness – actually makes it possible to further disturb, question, complicate that very ground. It becomes possible to make that ground unsteady again, but in meaningful rather than random ways. Here, then, one continues to categorize and document the small parcel of infinity to which one has been assigned. I state this primarily as a part of my own contemplation upon the crafting of knowledges, noting that one does not always know or notice all that one actually knows. The moral of the story – keep thinking, and keep listening. One sees, here, the benefits of recursivity in scholarly practice. The more things change, the more...what? They remain the same? The more they become different? The same and yet different, or different and yet the same?

A more complex instance of development, recursivity, and reflexivity, of the *changing* same, may be examined in another example. 'The Mirage of an Unmarked Whiteness' was written for a 1997 Berkeley, California, conference on 'The Making and Unmaking of Whiteness.' This was, its organizers said, 'the first major academic forum to assess the state of research on whiteness' (Rasmussen *et al.* 2001: 4). The event signaled, I suggest, not so much the coming of age of 'the critical study of whiteness' as, perhaps, the coming to '*doxa*' of the word whiteness itself. After a scant decade or so, a word, 'whiteness,' previously barely in existence in the academy, had become a concept. And as elsewhere, this was the result of dialogical recognition of that which could and should be named.

However, by the time that the proceedings of the conference were published, a full 5 years after the event took place, the term was so recognizable, at least for some, that it now needed to be qualified, questioned, made problematical. As expressed by the co-editors of the conference proceedings:

This book comes at a moment when questions about the status and project of whiteness studies need consideration. Is whiteness a useful category of analysis? Does it help explain or illuminate ethnoracial differentiation, division or domination? Is whiteness a useful category for political action? What, if any significance does it have for organizers and political officials? How does whiteness figure into various racial vocabularies? Does looking closely at whiteness help to sharpen or does it obscure the analysis of race? Does studying whiteness further marginalize the experiences of groups long left out of the historical record? In other words, is 'critical whiteness studies' the Trojan horse through which the study and perspective of whites will be recentered in studies of race and ethnicity?

(Rasmussen *et al.* 2001: 1)

It is striking, first, that the processes of representation, categorization, and compartmentalization had clearly been underway with respect to this word, widely enough for them to be debated be and even disputed. Whiteness, these authors acknowledged, was the site of contention and debate among the organizing group. At the time of that volume's writing, whiteness was (or was it?) seen to be related to the analysis of race and ethnicity, as well as (or was it?) to political activism, and to the practice of historiography (again, or was it?). In other words, clearly whiteness existed, conceptually. It had a knowable place in the academic and political lexicon. There seemed no longer to be any question that there was a "there," there.' Yet a concern flows through the editors' list of questions. Thus, they ask repeatedly, is the concept of whiteness of benefit, or is it a hindrance? Worse, is it a 'Trojan horse,' an intentional disruption to the very arenas of work of which it is claimed to be a part?

My own essay, written and later revised for publication in the proceedings of that conference, engaged a particular, to my mind key, question about the 'there' of whiteness (Frankenberg 2001). For it had struck me, from some 'where,' that the notion that whiteness is an unmarked racial category needed to be revisited and interrogated anew. The origin of this 'where' raises interesting questions. On one hand, from the very start of my initiation into an awareness that issues of racism would entail re-examining my own racial identity, I had learned, forcefully, that my mentors of color were all-too-conscious of my whiteness. I also came to understand, about myself, and about many but not all of my white peers, that our sense of our race was blurry at best, repressed, suppressed, or invisible much of the time. On the other hand, it took me longer, and emanated from a different 'where,' to translate that awareness into a simple analytical distinction, one that recognized that the 'white gaze' was different from that of people of color when it came to 'seeing whiteness.' A trigger to my own thinking in this regard was an article written by bell hooks, 'Representing Whiteness in the Black Imagination.' Here, hooks draws on autobiographical writing and analysis to make clear to her readers exactly *how* uninvisible white people were to her and her kin and community (hooks 1992). Yet I remained, some*how*, at least partially enmeshed in the idea of whiteness as an unmarked racial category and location. Which, looking back, and indeed contemplating the present, both is, and is not, the truth (Frankenberg 1995).

Re-examining my earlier work, I find that I had argued that whiteness is *sometimes* an unmarked category, rather than *always* being so. Thus in *White Women, Race Matters*, I had said, 'white people have *too often* viewed themselves as nonracial or racially neutral,' and ' "whiteness" refers to a set of cultural practices that are *usually* unmarked and unnamed' (Frankenberg 1993: 1, italics not in original). Yet I had theorized its unmarkedness by white people, far more thoroughly than its sometime markedness. This is, perhaps, part of what made it possible for me to argue in my own discussion of my work, both at the 1997 conference and in the 2001 text,

> [O]ne of the truisms about whiteness with which scholarly critics of whiteness frequently operate at the present time is that whiteness is an unmarked category. Indeed it is one with which I myself worked for a number of years.
>
> (Frankenberg 2001: 73)

This 'flattening' of my own argument made it possible for a further level of over-simplification to take place when the editors of *The Making and Unmaking of Whiteness* followed my lead. They proposed that, in their volume, 'Frankenberg departs from her own earlier influential argument that whiteness is an unmarked category and instead claims that whiteness is by no means invisible to everyone' (Rasmussen *et al.* 2001: 15).

I offer here just a partial summary of my 2001 essay, 'The Mirage of an Unmarked Whiteness.' It asks how and why whiteness has emerged as a concept at different moments in history, and what has enabled it to, as it were, seem to disappear, despite its continuing salience on the socio-political landscape. The 'mirage' of an unmarked whiteness thus signals a double negative: whiteness *seems* to be unmarked, but is in fact rarely so. Rather, I remind myself and readers of the paper, it is more consciously seen by some subjects, white and of color, than by others. Further, the paper suggests, one can track and account for the apparent amnesia of white people with respect to the existence and salience of whiteness as descriptor of identity and subjecthood. I propose, in this regard, that attention to the concept of hegemony helps one to comprehend the 'now-you-see-it, now-you-don't' character of whiteness. Finally, I comment that I had perhaps been overly optimistic in the past, in imagining that urging 'race-evasive' white people to 'see their whiteness' might lead toward ways of seeing that are also 'power-evasive.' On the contrary (as also observed in *White Women, Race Matters*), modes of naming and seeing whiteness can move backward and even sideways, with respect to the history of ways of seeing race, rather than inevitably forward. Thus, I note in the 2001 essay, some of the most recent ethnographic work on whiteness has signaled white race-cognizance coupled with power-evasion.[2]

What might one learn from this story? On the most mundane of levels, I might note here that I misquoted myself in the 2001 essay, arguing that the notion of whiteness as unmarked was one with which 'I myself had worked for a number of years.' I might note too that the editors of *The Making and Unmaking of Whiteness* took me at my own word, and agreed with a statement that was, looking back, really a partial truth. Yet there is more to the situation than that. The idea that 'the unmarkedness of whiteness is one that I had worked with for several years,' is indeed true. But further, and even more importantly, I suggest, the unmarkedness of whiteness is an idea that *worked with me.* For just as my white peers and colleagues were, for the most part, raised in acceptance of the not-racialness of whiteness (their own not-racialness) I too had been raised with that way of seeing (or rather *not*-seeing) my racialized self. This is, then, how my own memory as voiced in the 1997/2001 essay both spoke and did not speak the truth about my knowledge of the racialness of whiteness, and its social construction.

Recursivity reaches a high point, here. One of my arguments in 'The Mirage of an Unmarked Whiteness' is, precisely, that even the most vigilant of white anti-racists and white theorists of whiteness can 'forget', without warning, aspects of their own analyses of race and of whiteness.[3] I can then learn, from rereading my own 2001 essay, precisely how it is that I 'forgot' my own prior analytical conclusions. Likewise, by rereading my own 1993 text, I can rediscover that even then I 'knew' that for white people, their racial identity was 'too often,' 'frequently,' but not 'always' unnamed and unmarked. And, recursively, I discover once more in reviewing my work in order to write this essay that, for me, whiteness has 'too often,' 'frequently,' but *not* 'always' been an unmarked racial category.

I began this essay by reference to the three terms, 'recursivity,' 'reflexivity,' and 'social constructionism.' Here, I suggest that the three come together. For in this journey of naming, marking, and unmarking whiteness, it becomes, I hope, obvious that my analytical strategy has been to document my own positioning, together with that of my colleagues and more broadly that of my peers, in the making of an argument about whiteness. Moreover, I hope it is clear that all of our positioning, *in* texts, *prior* to writing texts, and *after* texts have been written, owe as much, perhaps more, to their social contexts than to anything that might be deemed entirely individual. This, then, suggests a principle to which I have always held strongly: the best that one can do in scholarly work is to recognize its situatedness and strive to work consciously from within the parameters of one's location.

Notes

1   I would like to thank Lata Mani for her comments on this paper.
2   Frankenberg, 'The Mirage of an Unmarked Whiteness,' Rasmussen *et al.*, *The Making and Unmaking of Whiteness*, 88–92: 48,96. For my earlier expression of the three 'discursive repertoires' by means of which whiteness has been named, see *White Women, Race Matters*, 13–16; 137–90.
3   Frankenberg, 'The Mirage of an Unmarked Whiteness,' 77–81.

8 Naming the unnameable
Sense and sensibilities in researching racism

Philomena Essed

Introduction

Many years ago the then teacher of my ballet class used to have this typical line in response to groans and moans over muscle-straining exercises: 'This is not a tea party!' We would chuckle and keep at it. I have thought about this expression more than once in relation to, sometimes fanatically negative, responses in the Netherlands to my books on everyday racism. In challenging the myth of Dutch non-racism, *Alledaags racisme* (1984, – extended English edition, *Everyday Racism,* 1990) became subject to heated debate, reinforced when I published a second, more theoretically driven book *Understanding Everyday Racism* (1991). The controversy, part of which has been documented, never ceased (Prins 2000). In contributing to this volume, I am also taking the opportunity to reflect on the Dutch discomfort with the notion of racism, and what that has meant and means for researching racism to others, and to myself.

Admittedly, at first unpleasant comments upset me because, still a student and naïvely confident that innovation and quality matter, I could not put these attacks in perspective. Gradually, I understood that pioneering work comes with the price of taking the heat, in particular when it concerns a critical paradigm. In this chapter I draw partly, but not exclusively, from these experiences. Originally trained in the traditional way to keep the personal out of the scientific text, I was fortunate to discover through feminist theory the limits of the (masculine) masquerading of the positional self (Harding 1987; Wolf 1996). In the course of the chapter, I interweave my road into racism research with a national story embedded in an international context of race critical research (Essed and Goldberg 2002b; Goldberg and Solomos 2002). Hopefully, a certain degree of explicitness about life experiences, political, social and other motivations that have influenced me and others can be a helpful tool for critical students and researchers who want to explore new ways in researching race and racism.

Astonished by the dismissive response and as a way of understanding more about the (gender and racial-ethnic) politics of academic research, I wrote an essay called *Academic Racism: Common Sense in the Social Sciences*

(Essed 1987). It addressed the paradigmatic (and political) controversy over the authority to speak, an issue that has gained momentum in cultural studies and beyond (Roof and Wiegman 1995; Collins 1998). I had claimed in *Everyday Racism* that targets of racism can offer knowledgeable insights when it comes to defining when, where and how racism is manifest in everyday life. Established (white) intellectuals, for whom the word racism sounded too extreme for the Dutch situation, responded with adamant denial. At that time, the local response felt 'very Dutch'. But in due course I would learn that the denial of racism was not a typical Dutch phenomenon and not unique in academic circles either. Whether racism is nameable or unnameable in discussing societal problems is subject to continuous political struggles, the parameters of which are shaped by political forces. Periods of assertiveness among (racial-ethnic and white) dissidents – the civil rights movement and black power in the USA (1960s–70s) or anti-racism in the UK (late 1970s–80s) – have been met with subsequent political repression in the periods that followed. My interest in the role of intellectuals was relevant, because elites play a significant role in allowing or preventing the word racism from being used in politics, media, education, business or international politics (Lauren 1988; van Dijk 1993b; Lauren 1998; Wodak and van Dijk 2000). In *Academic Racism,* I analyzed examples where scholars used common-sense opinions rather than referenced arguments to support their view that racism might be out 'there' but not over 'here'. The denial of racism was in its effect a form of racism. I also covered texts from highly respected scholars. I was annoyed with what I felt mounted to smugness and lack of self-reflection about race, ethnicity and gender in Dutch academia – the term whiteness did not yet circulate at that time. *Academic Racism* was sharp: I faced up to the phenomenon, called it for what it was, and then…I felt a bit intimidated myself. The Dutch academic community is small, the same names saying the same things, no anonymity concerning the texts I was critical about. For me, to call racial-ethnic statements in the text of A or B paternalistic, denigrating, contributing to racial-ethnic inequality, would surely be read as my having said something like: A and B are racists – all hell would break loose. I was wary about my critique coming across as personal. I did not publish *Academic Racism* other than as a working paper that some of my colleagues have used in methodology courses.

Today, protest against racism in the Netherlands has been silenced and the topic of racism has all but disappeared from Dutch research agendas. This situation has urged me to reassess the topicality of *Academic Racism* and to incorporate a few excerpts from that piece in this essay, in order to illustrate the politics invoked by doing racism research and the methodologies involved. The mechanisms operating to deny racism then are sadly relevant today still and not only for students in the Netherlands. I am also thinking of students of racism in other countries, for instance Southern Europe, the Scandinavian countries and Iceland, where references to 'racism' are relatively new in public discourse (Rútsdóttir 2002). It is not unlikely that the word racism meets similar negative emotions, skepticism, denial or other counter-forces as it has in the Netherlands. Take for instance the ironic title of a recent publication about racisms throughout Europe at the end of the twentieth century: *Even in Sweden* (Pred 2000) – generally perceived as the European model of social justice and equality.

The crusade against the word racism in the Netherlands (and to a lesser or larger degree against those representing the paradigm of systemic racism) got shaped at an early stage, in the 1980s, the period when the issue of racism first emerged on academic and political agendas. Without suggesting any fixed evolutionary development, it might be helpful to realize that, even when there is ample literature now about the nature and manifestations of racisms in South Africa, the USA, Canada, Australia, Brazil, Europe and other locations, in each and every country exposure is and has been the result of persistence and stamina against national forces insisting that 'our case' is special, not as bad as the others. In *Academic Racism,* I commented:

> You often hear that the Dutch situation is 'special' because the Dutch word 'ras' cannot be understood as the exact equivalent of the English word 'race', and that therefore the term racism cannot be applied to the Dutch situation. It is interesting to note that, until late in the 1970s the English had their own arguments against applying the term racism to race and ethnic relations in their country. The following quotation about English self-perceptions could just as well have been written for the Netherlands:
>
>> English people are used to thinking of racism as a Bad thing, but they are convinced that it is always happening somewhere else. It may go on in part of Africa or in the United States, but it is not an English phenomenon....It is...generally agreed that even if there is any manifestation in England of racism, the situation in this country is so different from that in any other country you care to name that we have nothing to learn from the history of other countries, or from the most immediately contemporary happenings in them.
>>
>> (Dummett 1973: 14)

The 1990s have witnessed uses and abuses of the label of political correctness, a move to the right all over Europe, the gradual acceptance of open anti-immigrant discourses and a new Dutch 'boldness' where more and more people make it a point to say anything they feel like including verbal Islam bashing (LBR 2002). In its newsletter of January 2002, the European Monitoring Center on Racism and Xenophobia reported that the Council of Europe has expressed concern about the Dutch labor market: This is 'one of the areas where discrimination still appears to be most widespread. The effectiveness of existing criminal law aimed at combating racism and discrimination is limited, notably due to difficulties in the enforcement of the relevant provisions. Of concern also is the general climate concerning asylum seekers and immigrants' (EUMC news, 2002, 9: 3, www.ecri.coe.int).

In the aftermath of September 11th, violence against (in particular Muslim) immigrants has increased, and so has anti-Semitism. Assimilative pressures have intensified; the words of 'asylum seeker' and 'refugee' have lost their meaning, coming to signify 'fraud'; while 'problems' are too easily associated with unwilling, ungrateful or culturally backward *allochtonen* (unique Dutch concept referring to ethnic minorities, to those considered not (really) to belong to the Netherlands). This is not to deny the challenges all countries face in times of global migrations and multi-ethnic configurations. Furthermore, in the new millennium, *diversity* is becoming a policy catchword, indicating that the Netherlands is coming to terms with the fact that at least the larger cities are multi-ethnic, multi-racial (Essed and de Graaff 2002). The generous welcoming of the word diversity has also to do with the fact that it has a more optimistic ring to it than racism. After two decades of complaints that 'you cannot say anything any more without being accused of racism' there are no critical concepts left to name, and it is necessary to understand the coherence between various exclusionary phenomena such as: preference for one's own circles, contempt for women with a headscarf, whiteness (and maleness) of board-rooms and university chairs, indifference about and hostilities against illegal immigrants, irritation about ethnic difference, or taken-for-granted beliefs in the superiority of the Dutch way. The term racism – one among other relevant explanatory notions in this context – has been pushed out of Dutch everyday discourse, in political circles as well as in academia.

It is likely that human feelings and emotions have influenced mainstream intellectuals to react strongly against what they might have read as importing US and UK notions of racism into the Netherlands. By creating space in this essay for emotions behind scholarly productions I hope to open up the debate about researching racism in a different way. I have felt inspired by recent initiatives to focus on race, gender and ethnic identity in topic choice and fieldwork experience (Twine and Warren 2000; McClaurin 2001).

Racism *'verbum non gratum'*

Racisms have always included biological and cultural dimensions, ideologically embedded in what David Goldberg calls naturalism and historicism – philosophical underpinnings in the shaping of racial states (Goldberg 2001). Theories of race served to account for stages of evolutionary progress in human control of the constraints of nature. Different from the USA, expressions of racism in the Netherlands are less about race purity and whiteness than about cultural-ethnic differences and European-ness as representing a superior level of civilization (van Dijk 1984; van Dijk 1987; Mok 1999). This view is not commonly accepted among Dutch scholars who hold on to the national self-image, among other things, of progressive tolerance (for instance, religious pluralism, individual freedom of sexual expression, non-racism) and moderation (meaning free from extreme political trends, while subdued in the expression of negative or positive – including critical – emotions). Few if any mainstream social scientists posed the question whether it makes sense at all to elevate the Netherlands morally, a country with a long colonial history, when it comes to the problem of racism. For a while I suspected that this was due to a disposition to shun self-criticism. I still do not know whether that is true, but a journalistic article about a recent global survey caught my attention. It identified the Dutch as the nation with the highest degree of self-satisfaction in the world (ANP press release, 3 July 2001, www.accenture.com). Was it lack of knowledge, fear or riding the waves of a superior national identity, which contributed to the situation where the word *racisme* (Dutch for racism) has become *verbum non gratum*? As I will show later, I am also referring here to publications of social scientists who seemed genuinely concerned about ethnic inequality and who have written critically about prejudice and discrimination. By the time I published my second book *Understanding Everyday Racism* (1991), the stage had been set for an even more forceful assault in which the same arguments of the 1980s would surface.

Organizing my notes in preparation for this chapter, I consulted a few colleagues in the Netherlands who have published about (cultural) racism. How has their work been received over the years?

> I am doing research in inner-city areas where I come across a lot of racism. But these days when it is politically correct to be against political correctness you cannot use the word racism anymore.

Another one comments:

> Generally I have had few negative reactions to my work on racism. It depends on the wording you use. It has been my experience in the Netherlands that the word racism triggers all kinds of comments and objections, whereas research on stereotypes and prejudice is seen as much more acceptable.

Subsequently, I went through a pile of copies of *Migrantenstudies*, the main (and only) Dutch journal for studies of the multi-ethnic society. I had in my possession four volumes per year over the period 1994–2002. Topics included all and everything about ethnic minorities and the Dutch society. But only two articles focused explicitly on racism, one from a scholar who has invested over the years in empirical research on common-sense racism in the Netherlands (Verkuyten 1995). The other article was about Belgium (Witte 1999). Having said this, I immediately confess that I have never tried to publish in this journal either. I felt increasingly more comfortable writing in English where there was more intellectual and ideological space for issues of race and racism.

About paradigms and methodologies

There is no impartiality with respect to social injustices. Indifference or speaking out can be a matter of choice and scholars have the tools to expose racial discrimination. This is what the Dutch scholar Frank Bovenkerk might have thought when he initiated, through a series of projects, the postwar discussion on racial discrimination in the Netherlands. This was an engaged social anthropologist whose early research consisted of social experiments, a formula imported from the UK. Put simply: There are two candidates applying for a job, or renting an apartment, white candidate X and ethnic candidate Y, with similar income or professional profile, and the only variable is skin color or ethnicity. If the ethnic candidate is rejected and, subsequently, the white candidate gets to be accepted, that is seen as discrimination – not as racism, a term Bovenkerk (and with him others – see later below) preferably reserved to refer to an abstract ideology of white superiority. His book, *Because They Are Different* (Bovenkerk 1978), opened many eyes to the problem of racial discrimination in the Netherlands. Today, social experiments continue to be used on a European level as a method to identify institutional discrimination (Wrench 1996).

I too read Bovenkerk's book, which provided me with tools to rethink and see in a different light some of my, otherwise pleasant, experiences in high school and at university. I pondered about and reassessed (white) Dutch reactions towards family and friends. Until that time, my most relevant (conscious) identification was womanhood, the feminist movement my context, the women's bookstore my favorite location. But I was one among very few students and feminists of color. More and more, I discovered that 'we' women, and among them wonderful friends, were similar but at the same time not, a theme Adrienne Rich had written so eloquently about in *Disloyal to Civilization. Feminism, Racism and Gynephobia* (Rich 1970).

The reworking of a course paper into an article for the critical Dutch feminist journal *Socialisties Feministiese Teksten* became my first public struggle with the everyday contradictions between cross-cultural sisterhood and racism (Essed 1982). The next step, a focus on racism in the everyday lives of women of color, came naturally. And I was not alone. I would discover later that women of color all over the world, from Germany to India, from the USA to South Africa and from the Philippines to Brazil, have been the vanguard in linking gender and ethnicity, in exploring the gender dimensions of racism, and the racial dimension of patriarchies and gender systems.

The concept of everyday racism was a paradigmatic shift away from the positivism of Bovenkerk's social experiments. It felt unethical in my view to ask black or ethnic test subjects to go through real experiences of rejection in order for the researcher to establish that there was discrimination then and there. Even when black candidates agree to 'act' as job applicant, the party who discriminates does not fake it at all. The rejection adds to the repertoire of everyday humiliations, and revives earlier experiences of racism in the life of the candidate. Arguably, it gives comfort to have a team of researchers share the burden with you rather than to face discrimination on your own, as would usually happen. A (morally) less offensive version involves cases where, *after complaints from ethnic youngsters*, an anti-discrimination bureau applies the social experiment method to a specific disco in order to register and take (legal or political) action. This introduces the question of whose voice counts. Would it not make sense to listen first to what ethnic minorities had to say, to explore through probing and questioning what life felt like in a white-dominated society, to see dominant society through the eyes of those who were considered not to belong, not to be part of the norm? I knew from my own experiences as a woman of color and from many conversations with others how experiences of discrimination could eat at your heart, chip away at your self-confidence, cause anger that had to be repressed, could cloud your mind in circular thinking of how you should have responded differently, how you should have challenged the perpetrator, but did not....It simply violated my sense of integrity to have people agree to go through new discrimination on top of what they already go through in ordinary life.

I did not reject positivistic approaches as such – systematic observations and quantitative data are necessary to distinguish between incidents and patterns of discrimination. But social experiments did not provide sufficient context. Descriptive observations lacked theoretical depth and explanatory power. I wanted to understand *why* ethnic groups were discriminated against, and what discrimination could tell us about Dutch society. I was intrigued by what it meant when people would say about subtle discrimination that they *intuitively knew* what was going on. I wanted to understand the analytical complexity of how targets of covert rejections and humiliations in everyday life recognize racial or ethnic undertones of certain events.

Armed with a tape recorder I went to interview black women in the USA and in the Netherlands. In in-depth conversations we spoke about a range of experiences, about feelings and expectations about everyday interactions they took for granted. I found important differences having to do with the US (historical) obsession with race purity and segregation. But there were also many similarities between the two countries. Women in both countries were repeatedly accused of stealing, cheating and laziness. Black women were seen as sexual objects, as loose and approachable. Underestimation, invisibility or – over-visibility, when excelling – were common. So were downgrading and continuous assimilative pressures in (integrated) schools. In the Netherlands, women felt burdened by continuous exposure to negative discourse about minorities – often in their face. In case of protest, there would be accusations of oversensitivity – can't you take a joke? – a reaction common too, I learned later, in stories of Afro-German women (Oguntoye *et al.* 1986). Whatever the negative experiences, there was this wall of white determination: it could be anything, but not racism. Ironically, and in light of the above, the response to *Everyday Racism* by those who disagreed was that I called 'any' negative experience a form of racism. It was probably a sign of the times, feminist methodology still in the process of claiming space and authority (Nencel and Pels 1991), to reject my methodology as wrong and unscientific. But I did take this critique to heart and in *Understanding Everyday Racism* would pay extensive attention to the method-ology and frameworks of interpretation (Essed 1988; Louw-Potgieter 1989; Mellor *et al.* 2001). And guess what: the critique of some *feminist* methodol-ogists, now a more established field, would be that I had placed too much emphasis on methodology (Prins 2000). But let's not get ahead of the story.

The power of words

Books and publications are just words. The impact of these words, the degree of authority attributed to their meaning, depends on how the words are taken, whether they are helpful to others, whether they enrage others, whether your words are taken as arguments to legitimate policies, and so on. In the early 1980s, in preparation of *Everyday Racism,* I used to browse weekly through second-hand bookshops in Amsterdam and, occasionally, in London. I literally bought any book about racism I could put my hands on, invariably in English, as next to nothing had been done in this area in the Netherlands. I read moral and intellectual support in the writings of a gender and racial-ethnically diverse assembly of critical intellectuals of their times in the USA (among others Ralph Ellison, Troy Duster, Stokely Carmichael and Charles Hamilton, Angela Davis, Adrienne Rich, Thomas Pettigrew, Herbert Blumer, David Wellman) and in the UK (Ann Dummett, Annie Phizacklea, Stuart Hall, Chris Mullard, the seminal book *The Empire Strikes Back: Race and Racism in 70s Britain* (1982)).

With their critique of racism, researchers can influence public opinions, government policies, work, education and other social institutions (Collins 1998: 83). The fact that the audience can be much broader than fellow academics and students is a source of power, but it also makes the researcher vulnerable to all kinds of reactions in and outside the academic community. Personally, I had never given much thought to the possible implications of researching racism. With *Everyday Racism,* I had just completed my MA in social anthropology and was in the process of applying for a Ph.D. scholar-ship. I saw myself as a scholar-in-training who happened to be interested in the issue of racism. I was overwhelmed by the fact that *Everyday Racism* hit national headlines. Even less prepared was I for the attacks that would soon follow. I mention one particular intervention against the paradigms concerned with everyday racism, racism in school textbooks, in the media, and so on. The intervention I am referring to is worth noting, not because it expresses disagreement with my understanding of racism, but because of the particular format of the critique: It was used as the national test for the subject of Dutch in the final exams of 1987, comparable to the British A levels. Yearly, thousands of 18–19-year-olds take this exam.

The text of the exam was called *The Misunderstanding*, (an edited version of) an essay by Frank Bovenkerk, first published in a Dutch weekly. One of my nieces took the 1987 final exams, which is how word got to me that 'I' was in 'her exam'. I had been pleasantly surprised to hear that the national exam committee had decided to choose a text on the issue of discrimination and racism, but I was equally concerned about *what* would be said about these problems. I presumed that the exam committee used this particular text on discrimination, because it expressed what they perceived as a non-controversial, that is, a commonly accepted or at least pedagogically responsible point of view. The students were not asked to comment on the line of argumentation. They had to make a summary of the text in 500 words maximum. In order words, in order to pass the exam successfully they had to accept the authority of the text – and therewith the exam committee's view of the racial-ethnic status quo, presented by way of the author. This seemed to me a powerful instrument to influence young people in their thinking about discrimination and racism.

Curious about what 'being in the exam' could be about, I asked a friend of mine, Diana, a teacher herself, whether she could get me a copy of the text. Diana was a maths teacher. We were in the same group of women of color who met monthly to talk about culture and belonging, about racism and other matters of concern. Diana and her husband had been the target of racial harassment from a neighbor. When they could not take it any more they went to court – and won. Diana kindly gave me a copy of the text and the scoring sheet.

The Misunderstanding is an ambivalent, at times contradictory, piece. Bovenkerk expresses concern about the prevalence of racial discrimination, because it keeps ethnic minorities from moving up the social ladder, in particular in the labor market. He states that racism in its raw forms – 'negroes are genetically more ignorant' (page 2, line 20) – is rare in the Netherlands. Racism occurs more frequently in disguise (line 22). But, he makes sure to assert, it is absurd to call the Netherlands a racist country (page 2, lines 10–12) and he insists racism is certainly not a remnant of Dutch colonial history (page 4, lines 117–26).

> The word racism used to represent a theory, a coherent set of statements about the inferiority of other races. But today this word is also used to refer to negative opinions about another culture, even to the point where an unfriendly comment, a rough gesture, or a denigrating look can result in the reproach of racism.....The word [racism] loses meaning when it is used to refer to any real or imagined unpleasantness against ethnic groups or their individual members. Philomena Essed applies

that notion like that in her popular book *Everyday Racism*. Imagine: The complaint of a heavily pregnant black lady that 'white' tram passengers do not offer her a seat is taken for racism.

(page 2, lines 12–16; 27–31, translation PhE)

Was this also the voice of (white) masculinity? This was the second time in reviewing my work that Bovenkerk dismissed as relevant, let alone even remotely possible, that there could be racial undertones in comments about the sexuality of black women. In an earlier review about *Everyday Racism,* he referred to an example where a black nurse has a male patient, an elderly man, commenting to her (approvingly) that boy oh boy, 'you people have such firm behinds'. Here is what Bovenkerk had to say – after he explained between brackets that by 'firm behinds', the patient means 'fat buttocks':

The ill manners where 'white' tram passengers do not offer their seat to a pregnant black woman, or the comment about a fat behind: are these examples of acts resulting from 'an ideology of racial dominance and oppression?' Look, don't give me that!

(Nederland racistisch? *Intermediair,* 9 November 1984, page 49,
translation PhE)

In all fairness to the author, Bovenkerk did not dismiss entirely that pestering against minorities happens regularly and that even racism occurs. Informed like no other about the devastating impact of institutional discrimination, he has also lobbied successfully for the introduction of posi-tive action in the Netherlands (preference for ethnic candidates in situations of equal competence), an instrument that I did not embrace uncritically (Essed 1996; 2002). But where Bovenkerk argued at length about what racism was *not* about, he did not say *what* the subtle racism he acknowledged as occurring frequently was exactly about and *how* that was different from the bulk of examples I was writing about. The predicament had to be solved outside the arena of scientific arguments. Bovenkerk went on to discuss a project about white inner-city dwellers' complaints that they used to be so helpful and supportive to Turks and other newcomers, but what did they get in return: noise and dirt, and refusal to adapt to the Dutch way. Worse: when you object you are accused of racism (page 3, lines 45–94). In support of these voices, Bovenkerk suggested a *political* argument against using the word racism to refer to these complaints:

The political danger of a definition of racism that is too flexible is that they [native Dutch who feel that their complaints about ethnic minori-ties fall on deaf ears], and I mean many more residents than only those from the decayed city areas, will be driven into the arms...of the extreme-right.

(page 3, lines 90–3, translation PhE)

The Misunderstanding ends with a plea to reverse the situation:

> In my view it is...necessary...to reverse the possible relation between discrimination and racism. If direct and indirect discrimination continue to persist that will cause a race problem, not the other way round
>
> (page 5, lines 172–3, translation PhE)

Academic racism

At the time the national exam committee decided to use Bovenkerk's essay, I had little clue about the authority of words, that *who* spoke and *when* and *in which medium* and *who else was on the speaker's side* was as important as *what* was being said. It was not quite pleasant to find myself the object of attack and ridicule, but I was resolved not to show any of that. I believed that any evidence of vulnerability would be like acknowledging defeat. Moreover, negative response (mostly from intellectuals, in contrast to social workers, feminist activists, teachers, health workers, the police, NGOs and others who invited me to engage with them) challenged me. I wanted to know: What is the role and responsibility of scholars in relation to the reproduction of racism? How do other key players in the field define race and racism? These questions I addressed in *Academic Racism*, originally produced as a working paper for the then Center for Race and Ethnic Studies at the University of Amsterdam – the closure of which in 1991 marked the end of an emerging Dutch school of research in the race critical tradition (Essed 2002).

When I came across Charles Tilly's *Durable Inequality* ((Tilly 1998) it reminded me of *Academic Racism,* where I wrote about networking and emulation in reproducing the denial of racism. 'Old-boys-networking' is not necessarily a question of conspiracy. Networking is not typically an instrument of established groups – it is only that established groups have more efficient infrastructures to effectuate preference for like-minded folks. The preference for sameness, for familiarity, for people we feel we can trust because they look like us, or are members of the same club, is probably part of a more complex phenomenon we have called *cloning cultures* (Essed and Goldberg 2002). The cultural and social cloning of ideas, of paradigms and social constellations, an issue that deserves more attention than I have been able to give in this chapter, has probably reinforced the denial of racism. I end with a few examples from the 1980s. My concern is not the specific individuals involved, all well-intentioned scholars, but the authorizing of their opinions through the social status of the speakers and/or the relative importance of their assignment. One has to keep in mind that the emulation of ideas through (powerful) networks continues to be a fundamental instrument of durable inequality (Tilly 1998). The related silencing and self-silencing of critical racism research(ers) has meant that 'anti-anti-racism' arguments have remained largely unchallenged – and as topical today as in the years of 1984 and 1985:

> In *Judgement and Discrimination* (Köbben 1985), an article first published in a main quality newspaper, Bovenkerk's former teacher, André Köbben, respectively chair and director of two high-status institutions, the ACOM (Advisory Commission on Minority Research) and the COMT (Center for Research on Social Conflicts) describes himself as a 'benevolent intellectual' (p. 57) with respect to the issue of prejudice. He states that it has become clear from his experiences that it is better to have reservations against 'accusing' anyone of being 'prejudiced' because it aggravates people to hear somebody say that to them (pp. 56–7)....Racism, let alone the power relations it stands for, are not even mentioned. The reluctance to use the term racism could already be inferred from an earlier COMT (see above) inquiry among union members (de Jongh *et al.* 1984). The report quotes a range of statements made by the union members, expressing hostility against foreigners and rejecting union support for ethnic minority equality claims. However, the researchers insist upon classifying their findings as forms of 'stereotypical beliefs, prejudice and myths' (p. 222)....They argue that they have a problem with the notion of racism: One of their interviewees, they say, voted for the racist Center Party, but it appears that he nevertheless goes fishing regularly with his migrant neighbor. The researchers were puzzled whether such a man should be called a racist (p. 222).

> In a major study, the same year, commissioned by the ACOM (see above), which advises the government on ethnic issues, the researchers evaluate a range of international studies of prejudice, discrimination and racism (Elich and Maso 1984). The report aims to give an 'objective' international overview of academic studies of prejudice, discrimination and racism in view of formulating subsequent research policies for the Dutch context. From the very beginning, the word racism is consistently placed between quotation marks. In light of this, their main conclusions are predictable from the start, namely that racism should not be considered a social problem in the Netherlands. Elich and Maso see racism as a mere 'polemical' word (p. 11).

(adapted from *Academic Racism*)

Concluding remarks

In the early 1990s, I got invited to a conference on Managing Diversity in the USA. I was told that this was the first time this particular academic association was focusing on issues of race and gender. It had taken lots of effort and lobbying to come this far. On my panel, an African American graduate student presented a paper about racism in US business schools. She spoke from a black lesbian point of view. Afterwards a few people rushed towards her in positive acknowledgement. Others seemed to distance themselves. A small group of African American attendants commented: 'She should not have done this, coming out as a black lesbian and talking openly about racism. Somebody should have warned her not to do this. She may have ruined her career.' When I asked why this was the case, the answer was: 'In our system you first graduate, then you work towards tenure, and only when you have tenure you are free to say what you want.' How awful, I thought. Fortunately, our Dutch system is different.

While writing this essay, the event came back to me, and I realized that my academic career might have been less politically stressful if I had been a follower rather than a pioneer, if I had been willing to compromise intellectual integrity in exchange for the protection conformity offers. I had to find out the hard way the risks and retaliations when you do not emulate ideas, do not adapt to dominant paradigms – the Bovenkerk response was mild compared to abusive language, gossip and insinuations in weeklies and daily newspapers (Prins 2000). Painful as that has been, it has also made me more acutely aware that the general principle, the bottom line in and outside academic work, should be human respect, not humiliating one another – a theme Avishai Margalit writes so brilliantly about in *The Decent Society* (Margalit 1996). In retrospect, I can imagine that for some readers (the emotion behind) my 'sharp pen' has been difficult to swallow, if not infuriating. The interweaving of political interests, paradigmatic controversies, gender-ethnic-racial and other identities, social positioning and emotions of authors and audiences is a complex phenomenon. I must admit, researching racism without conceptual sharpness would be like running through mud. Messy. At the same time, transparency and space for the human being behind the researcher can help us to appreciate, at the right moments and for fitting purposes, sense *and* sensibilities, rationality *and* fears, conceptual rigor *and* political strategizing.

The theory of everyday racism, a concept grounded in the analysis of experiences of Dutch and US women of color, has been shaped by women's studies. Its emphasis on the lived experience and the significance of everyday life, my commitment to produce change and my skepticism about the desirability and the possibility of value-free research are all key methodological principles of feminist research (Blackmore 1999). With Dutch academia privileging whiteness and masculine values of detachment and neutrality – 95 per cent of full professors are (white) men (Balen and Fisher 1998) – the ideological climate did not always work to my advantage. It has been strategically wise to publish in English, thereby communicating with an international network of more experienced researchers in racism research. I recommend that also to students and emerging scholars in other non-

English-speaking countries, trusting that most international racism researchers are open to engaging with students from across borders and oceans. When you are under attack, the intellectual or moral support from well-established scholars who have gone through similar experiences gives immediate relief. But it also puts things into perspective. Another advantage of writing in English was that it helped me to qualify the Dutch critique. Both books about everyday racism have been published in Dutch and in English, but negative critique was almost exclusively limited to the Netherlands – different from outside reviews from the USA, UK, Canada or South Africa (Prins 2000).

The more knowledge you have about a problem, the more flexibly you can relate to the issue. With more competence came more confidence and relative distance – which is certainly not the same as so-called objectivity or neutrality. In my current thinking, the problem of racism has more modest proportions in relation to other systems of injustice. In the second half of the 1990s, I broadened my view to include more explicitly multi-dimensions of identity (Essed 1996). Gradually, a positive (advisory) engagement has developed with NGOs, unions, policy-makers, consultants, managers, leaders and others. In that process, practical situations have become a testing ground for theory, and in theory development I can imagine more easily the practical implications. Inspired by these experiences, I am defining new research questions focusing on leaders who are not clones in a tradition of predecessors disposed to reproducing exclusions and more inequalities. I am looking at critical women in leadership, most of whom had to carve out their own paths.

Advisory work requires continuous assessments of *what* you think the other party is open to hearing or listening to, as well as strategic insight in *how* you communicate that. Here, I can only agree with Köbben, Bovenkerk and others that, depending on whom you work with, words like discrimination or racism can cause too much consternation to be useful. My advisory work and popular publications focus almost exclusively on human potential and possibilities for change. But scholarship is a different matter. The body of critical knowledge I engage with is invaluable because it keeps me on my toes, alert to conflict of interest and abuse of power in dealing with practical or political matters. Therefore I cannot go along with those who, for political or strategic reasons, avoid critical words like racism in their research.

Freedom to think critically is the oil of knowledge production, the most basic condition for scholarship. But once you acquire through study and research, in-depth, documented, comprehensive knowledge of racism, there is no way back. One cannot undo critical knowledge. There is no way not to recognize racial and other injustices once you have learned how to see them. One can only hope that critical knowledge be used fearlessly, but with wisdom – with respect for one another as human beings.

Acknowledgements

For her very insightful comments, I thank my colleague Lorraine Nencel who graciously read a first draft on awfully short notice. David Goldberg helped me to improve the text with editing advice. Many thanks!

9 Writing race

Ethnography and the imagination of *The Asian Gang*

Claire Alexander

Introduction

One morning in early November 1996, I found myself – for the first, and undoubtedly last, time – on a film set. It was 7.30 a.m., raining and bitterly cold, and I was standing in a housing estate in East London, wearing only a thin salwaar kameez and a deepening scowl as the day crept on, seemingly unending and unproductive. I had gone, under some protest, with Yasmin, the Bengali woman who ran the project I was working in, in response to a call for Asian extras for a new British film, *B. Monkey*. The film was a 'love story/thriller' about a teenage girl who joins 'a gang', but is redeemed by her love for a teacher with whom she runs away to Yorkshire, only to be pursued by the aforementioned gang....I'm not sure how it ended, but I imagine with happiness for the heroine and well-deserved, probably bloody, punishment for her socially pathological teenage friends. By 4 p.m., having done nothing all day but shiver and drink tea, I didn't really care.

My eventual career-making role was to walk up a staircase with shopping bags while the heroine and one of her 'gang' friends ran down. They were, possibly, the most excruciatingly banal moments of my life. Through the repetition of these meaningless moments, as the minute-that-never-ends wore on, however, the invidiousness of my position became increasingly explicit and oppressive. Yasmin and I were the only Asian women on set (there was also one older Asian man) and it was clear that our role was to provide 'ethnic colour' – literally and figuratively – for the gang scenes. In search of an authentic inner-city backdrop, the film was located in a condemned block on one of the poorest housing estates in London. When this proved not quite 'authentic' enough, the film crew imported three White skateboarders from a public school in Hampshire, and a burned-out estate car for added urban grit. The presence of Yasmin and myself was, it seems, as additional 'reality' props – walk-on markers of inner-city deprivation and decay. It was a disturbingly surreal experience, being transformed from an 'urban ethnographer/anthropologist' with a morning to spare and her own 'traditional costume' (to quote the casting agency) into the object of a racialised gaze that constructed me as the embodiment of ghetto unfabulous 'Otherness'. Still more disturbing was the clearly demarcated (raced, gendered and generational) boundaries of this construction of so-called 'cutting-edge' reality – the metal barriers that held apart the local residents, particularly the young Bengali men who gathered around watching, with a mixture of bemusement and increasingly vocal derision, as their homes and lives became BBC gangland fantasy.

A few days later, I turned up at the offices of the *Times Higher Education Supplement (THES)*, clutching a feature article based around my research. Reflecting partly on my experience on the film set, the article questioned the insistently negative media portrayal of Asian communities in Britain: the obsession with arranged marriages, runaway girls and cultural break-down, and the unremitting demonisation of young Asian men, symbolised in the rise of a series of new 'folk devils' – the Underclass, the Fundamentalist, the 'gang'. The article had been agreed in principle with the Features editor, who had previously published an article on my earlier research, *The Art of Being Black*, but it was late, so I decided to deliver it in person. The Features editor, a White woman in her early forties, came down to meet me – her face fell visibly when she saw me, and she seemed flustered. I don't think I embodied her image of 'Dr Claire Alexander'. Later, when I had heard nothing from her, I called her and she told me that the article had been rejected. It was, she said, 'too positive and unrealistic' (which was ironic for an article about negative media portrayals). In addition, she said she felt my approach was 'too subjective' and that I had become 'too close' to my subject matter – I needed to step back and be more objective, to see what was 'really' going on.

These events are, admittedly, rather trivial, perhaps even banal. It is, however, their very banality – their everydayness – that makes them of significance in reflecting on the process of ethnographic writing; particularly of 'writing race'. While in Britain academic ethnographic writing has fallen into a decline, it is also true that what Renato Rosaldo calls 'the ethnographic sensibility' (1989: 39) has also undergone a series of transformations into other media – it has gone 'undercover', to re-emerge in the guise of documentaries, reality TV, drama and film, photography and literature, not to mention the stalwarts of 'investigative journalism', and the slew of government-commissioned reports on 'the state of race relations/multi-ethnic Britain'. The underpinnings of classic ethnography – its traditionally unmediated claims to truth and experience, to objectivity and innocence, to knowledge rather than politics – can be seen to form the uncontested foundation for the myriad imaginings of raced and ethnic 'reality' in Britain today.

The media fantasies of *B. Monkey* are, then, more than simply B-movie hokum; they form part of an inscription of racialised knowledges that define and legitimate dominant landscapes of race. More than this, however, this process of representation has implications for the production of ethnographic texts, in whatever form they appear – in particular around the claims to 'authenticity' and the silencing of alternative voices that this entails. While this is hardly an original observation (Clifford and Marcus 1986; Clifford 1988; Rosaldo 1989), I would argue that the critiques of ethnographic authority since the 1980s have had little or no impact on the production of ethnographies of race and ethnicity in Britain. Indeed, unreconstructed ethnographic ideologies have served to reinscribe the naturalisation of racial and ethnic difference in popular, academic and policy terms.

Against this background, the production of ethnography cannot but assume a conspiratorial stance; despite authorial intentions, the danger is always that the ethnographer becomes part of the naturalisation process – and this is more the case when the ethnographer is 'a native'. If as an extra, my body was enough to make me a legitimating symbol of ethnic alienness, as an 'ethnographer of colour', I could not help but wonder if the process of 'writing race' was actually much different. As an ethnographer, my body serves to write me inescapably, if ambiguously, into my work – for the Features editor, I was too 'native' to be professional, too close to be objective, and altogether just too 'Asian'. More generally, it marks me alternatively as gatekeeper, apologist or traitor. The ambivalence of my position – as ethnographer and as 'folk devil', at once writing and being written – is not a comfortable one, nor can, or should, it be easily inhabited as an emblem of either 'authenticity' or 'innocence'. The issues of positionality are crucial to the ethnographic enterprise, but this is not to reduce them to narcissism – to what one reviewer of *The Asian Gang* called 'irritating self-indulgence' (Ruggiero, 9 November 2001). Rather, for me, what Kamala Visweswaran (1994) has termed 'homework'[1] is about a politics of location that refuses the comfortable and artificial 'Truths' of the traditional ethnography, and disrupts the authorising gaze.

This chapter aims to trace the contours and pitfalls of adopting an ethnographic approach to race and ethnicity in Britain. Drawing on my ethnographies of Black and Asian youth, *The Art of Being Black* (1996) and *The Asian Gang* (2000), the chapter will reflect on the role of ethnographic authority, specifically in relation to the position of 'native' ethnographers. More particularly, it seeks to explore the issues of location, authority and disruption that are part of the construction of racial 'knowledge'. By exploring the constraints upon the production of my own ethnographic texts, and strategies for 'dislocation', the chapter argues for the explicit recognition of the 'partiality'[2] of the ethnographic voice and its ambiguous implication within broader political processes.

'Writing race': ethnography, authority and truth

It is perhaps true to say that in Britain, unlike the USA, ethnographies of race and ethnicity have come to occupy a peculiarly controversial space, torn between claims of the primacy of 'field experience' by the anthropologically rooted descendants of the 'race relations' school (Banks 1996),[3] and accusations of neo-colonial control by later generations of (particularly Black) scholars, activists and cultural theorists (Centre for Contemporary Cultural Studies 1982; Gilroy 1987; Sharma *et al.* 1996). The division centres crucially on opposed views on the role of culture as an object of analysis, with the 'ethnicity' theorists privileging a traditional holistic and institutional version of cultural boundaries (Benson 1996), and the sociology/cultural studies writers advocating a neo-Marxist perspective of cultural construction and resistance (Hall 1992) – what might be captioned as the opposition of 'old' and 'new' ethnicities, or the imagination of identities as 'being' or 'becoming' (Alexander 2002).

In the wake of the critique of 'ethnicity studies' in the 1980s, which savaged the culturalist bias of 'pathology sociology' (Keith 1992),[4] the field of racial and ethnic research has become a bifurcated arena, with a clear division emerging between the sociological focus on race and racism, and an anthropological emphasis on 'cultural difference' (Benson 1996). While the 'new ethnicities' revolution (Hall 1992) has, to some extent, challenged this division and reinvigorated a multi-disciplinary engagement with 'culture' and difference – certainly at the level of theory and cultural production – in the ethnographic 'field', the 'old ethnicities' approach still holds sway. Particularly in relation to Asian communities, the triumph of what Modood terms 'the mode of being' over 'the mode of oppression' (1992: 55) has perpetuated a traditional anthropological version of culture (Rosaldo 1989) built upon a largely unreconstructed Malinowskian vision of ethnographic fieldwork.[5] This vision is built upon the reach for what Sue Benson terms a 'double authenticity' (1996: 48), which privileges at once a reified version of 'authentic' cultural difference and the authenticity of the field experiences of the anthropologist in accessing and translating this 'difference'.

If the notion of ethnography as science has not survived the 1970's crisis in anthropology (Rosaldo 1989; Clifford and Marcus 1986), it is nevertheless the case that residual ideals of truth and objectivity remain stubborn features of much ethnographic research and writing on ethnicity in Britain.[6] The link between ethnography and experience remains a powerful emblem of authenticity, with 'the field' as a central organising principle. George Marcus has thus argued that 'the regulative ideals and framing presumptions of what it is to do fieldwork very much remain in place in anthropology's professional culture' (1998: 3). 'The field' carries with it, Marcus argues, ideas of boundedness and of 'Otherness' – it is a travel destination to be discovered rather than a standpoint, a relationship or a process. Fictions of 'experience', forged in the process of 'fieldwork' amongst the not-so-new natives 'at home', have continued to justify the search for 'self-created worlds' (Ballard 1994), and the position of their 'translators'. Fieldwork then serves as a guarantee of the authority of the ethnographer and of the authenticity of the object of the study. It provides a means through which boundaries are traversed (by the anthropologist, *not* her informants), negotiating a complex process of 'insider/outsider' status, through which claims of

'first-hand' knowledge and detachment are validated. 'The Field' also functions as a guarantee of 'innocence' (Van Maanen 1995); of disinterested
involvement and the pursuit of a native 'Truth' (Rosaldo 1989), uncompro-
mised by the messiness of power inequalities or transgressive subjectivities.

While the legacy of the literary turn in anthropological theorising has
largely debunked the claim to unmediated knowledge and objectivity,
placing ethnographic writing as part of a process of structuration, dominance and exclusion (Clifford and Marcus 1986; Clifford 1988; Rosaldo
1989), in practice, 'writing culture' has been transformed at the level of style
rather than substance (Marcus 1998). Ideas of culture and cultural boundaries remain largely intact and unscrutinised – which has serious
implications for the construction or deconstruction of racial and ethnic
'difference' (Alexander 2002). It is ironic, but significant, that, even in the
wake of the mainstreaming of the deconstructive turn in ethnographic
writing, 'race' has remained largely invisible as a point of transgression or
disruption. If they appear at all, notions of partiality and positionality have
entered into ethnographic practice of 'writing race' as a watered-down and
half-hearted gesture – reflexivity by rote. Rather than precipitating a crisis
of representation of 'the Other', the triumph of auto-reflexivity has rein-
scribed a valorisation of the ethnographer's experience in a dual movement
of self-absolution and self-serving credentialism (Back 2002). Issues of
power, divisions of class, race and gender become obstacles to be negotiated
or overcome in the search for the ultimate ethnographic truth – at best, they
vitiate these claims; more usually, they constitute guarantees of the authenticity and centrality of the ethnographer as Hero/ine within a new
ethnography-as-quest narrative.[7]

It can perhaps be argued, then, that a purely descriptive reflexivity has
formed part of a new disciplinary habitus – a necessary genuflection at the
altars of power and difference, neatly packaged in a short methodological
chapter, or section of a chapter, before going about ethnographic business as
usual. I myself have been guilty of such a strategy: in *The Art of Being Black*,
the methodological reflections were limited to a small sub-section, which
glossed over the often fraught and ambiguous relationships that constituted
the fieldwork. My reasons were simple, if insufficient: it was my doctoral
research and I did not want to give any space to those critics to dismiss the
work as subjective or unprofessional – one of the dilemmas, I suspect, that a
lot of young Black academics face. As it was, I think my silence on my positionality made it easier to dismiss me as a wannabe ethnographer in native
costume.

While there has been critical work on the role of gender in fieldwork
(Stacey 1988), very little ethnographic work fully explores the contours and
tensions of conducting fieldwork within a wider racialised landscape, preferring to isolate itself from broader political implications – or, rather, ignore
its implication within them.[8] It thus writes *across* race (Benson 1996), privileging narrative or literary concerns over a more rigorous critique of

ethnographic practice and ethics (Marcus 1998). Roger Ballard, for example, argues in *Desh Pardesh*: 'Ours is *a literary representation* of values, styles and strategies of South Asian Britain, but it is *not a representation of what their political interests and concerns might be*, and should never be so regarded', 1994: x, my emphasis).

It is significant to reflect on the opposition of a merely 'literary' representation and a wider political field, and on the complete silence on issues of power in ethnographic production and reproduction: so much for the contribution of *writing culture* then.

The mediating/controlling figure between fictive 'inside' and legislative 'outside' is that of the ethnographer. As argued above, the conventional view of the ethnographer is that of a neutral observer, a traveller across cultural borders and, once safely returned, a translator of cultural truths. The notion of 'participant-observation' carries with it a number of assumptions: first, the privileging of experience − of 'participating' as a means of discovering cultural truths; second, the primacy of the ethnographer's gaze in discerning and purveying these truths; third, of a regulated and limited engagement with 'the Other' under study within the clear boundaries of 'the field'. While the move towards conducting ethnography 'at home' has necessitated a rethinking of the notions of border crossing and translation, it is nevertheless the case that research on race and ethnicity in Britain has centred on the discovery of internal 'tribes' that reinscribe the Self/Other dynamic of traditional ethnography. The ethnographer and her subjects are positioned through discourses of difference and hierarchy − of race, ethnicity, culture, gender, class and so on − which may or (more usually) may not be rendered explicit. The implicit normalcy of this dynamic − usually White/Other − is, however, interrogated and subverted if these axes of distinction are compromised in any way; for example, through the growth of 'native' research. The consequences are both ambivalent and insightful in redefining the limits and possibilities of ethnography as a tool for researching 'race'. For myself, as one of very few 'ethnographers of colour' in Britain, these tensions are at once productive and constraining. It is to the role of the 'native' ethnographer in 'writing race' that I now turn.

Black enough? Native ethnography and the politics of 'writing race'

In 1996, my first ethnography, *The Art of Being Black*, was published. Although it was one of the only ethnographic monographs on Black British youth to have been published in recent years, somewhat naïvely, I had not really expected the attention it would garner. In the few weeks following, articles appeared in a number of national newspapers, including a slightly bizarre piece in the national Black newspaper *The Voice*, which asked a number of Black celebrities whether they felt being Black was actually 'an art' (most, unsurprisingly, felt it was 'natural'). Other reviews were uniformly critical – not so much of the contents of the book itself, but of the fact it had been written at all, and even more of the writer. A review by Darcus Howe, former activist turned media darling, commented that 'There are enormous problems with this methodology, primarily with the capacity of the observer to observe accurately' (*Sunday Telegraph*, 9 June 1996), and concluded, 'With the greatest of respect and kindness I will rename her book "The Art of Being Mrs (sic) Alexander".' Rather less 'kindly', a piece by author Caryl Phillips attacked the growth of 'Black studies' as 'dumpbins for scholars and students whose main qualification for membership is what they see in the mirror when they brush their teeth in the morning' (*Financial Times*, 1 June 1996). The caption to the photograph asks 'are they [young Black people] ill-served by 'cultural studies' from an academy unsure of its legitimate connection to the real world?'

I mention these reviews, along with a reminder of the accusation of 'irritating self-indulgence' that marks the debut of *The Asian Gang* less as an exorcism (though it is partly that, perhaps), than as an insight to the problems – one might even say, impossibility – of being 'a native researcher'. On the one hand, there are the implicit expectations that, as a Black researcher, the insights one provides will offer some 'real' and unique access to a particular community or set of issues. On the other, there are the, undoubtedly valid, queries about the relationship between researcher and researched within any given situation, and the concerns about the partiality or neutrality of the vision thus engendered. With 'native' researchers, however, there are additional twists: as, for example, the way in which the credibility of the research for *The Art of Being Black* depended less on the quality of the ethnographic data than on my authenticity, as a 'real' Black person, in conducting the research. The critique here turns on the assumption of a class difference, in which my imagined claims to authentic Blackness are revealed to be only 'skin deep', and my reach for the 'Black experience' illegitimate. Academics (unlike journalists and novelists), it seems, are not 'Black enough', by virtue of profession alone. Interestingly, in the review by Howe, there is the additional suggestion that the young men at the core of the study were also 'inauthentic' Black subjects; he comments, 'She appeared at ease with the upwardly mobile. She could not penetrate "the wild bunch".' If neither researcher nor subjects are 'Black enough', the implication is that there is a 'real' experience that remains beyond study – accessible perhaps only by gatekeepers like Howe or Phillips themselves. Which begs the question about how that experience is ever to be accessed or represented – a problem for anyone with a commitment to any kind of social analysis or social change.

Leaving aside the additional irony that these attacks by two of Britain's leading Black figures took place in the conservative press, neither paper known for their liberal views on 'race', there remains the seemingly intractable problem of how 'race' and ethnicity should be researched, and by whom. For Howe and Phillips, the process of 'writing race' necessarily carries with it a need for an imagined Black authenticity, which the position of the 'professional' researcher necessarily makes impossible and illegitimate – a methodological Catch 22. On the other hand, as the opening story about the *THES* illustrates, the position of a 'native' researcher writing about 'race' renders the writer too subjective and unreliable a witness, the writing too 'political' and therefore unacademic. Either way, the 'native researcher' is guilty of fraud, or even betrayal.

The solution for many 'native' researchers on race and ethnicity in Britain has been a simple one – to avoid the taint of empirical work and retreat to the safe abstraction of high theory. Ethnography, in particular, has long been considered the academic equivalent of high treason and the ethnographer a weapon of neo-colonial state control (Sharma *et al.* 1996: 2). This is a view not without some justification, and with which I have some sympathy. Indeed, the proliferation of 'authoritative ethnographies' and 'insider "native" accounts' (ibid.: 2) of Asian communities have wielded, and continue to wield, an important influence over understandings of race and ethnicity that have had damaging consequences for the position of these communities – consequences most recently reflected in the (mis)understandings of the 'riots' of 2001. Nevertheless, to abandon ethnography as an epistemological tool, as irredeemably flawed and necessarily complicit, seems to be in danger of abandoning the empirical 'field' – and its claims to state-sponsored, ESRC- funded 'truths' – to those researchers with nothing to lose and no impetus for change.

The targeting of 'native' ethnographers and the role of 'experts' marks a provocative challenge to research on race and ethnicity, signalling both change and continuity in the ethics of the research process. It is worth noting, for example, that the most stringent criticisms come from other 'natives' within, or connected to, the academy. This points, perhaps, to the emergence of a stratum of 'native' academics and researchers with at once the confidence to challenge the narrowly prescribed roles of the 'house' researcher, and the institutional insecurities of an arena where the personal and political stakes are high, and the opportunities limited. However, it also suggests a continuing unease from the broader White establishment in dealing with the complexities of racial and ethnic difference, preferring to fall back on established notions of racial sameness and essentialist claims-staking than a more fraught political and ethical field. The critique of 'native' research thus challenges a foundational myth concerning the role of same-race researchers (Andersen 1993), which was a response to criticisms of earlier eras of White 'pathology sociology'. The ideology of 'racial matching' in research pivots on the assumption that 'native' researchers occupy an innate 'insider' status that places them apart from the oppressive regimes embodied by mainstream White, middle-class, male 'professional' academics and guarantees access to the hidden 'Truth' of experience.[9] Interestingly, this perspective also finds sympathy with the emergence of Black 'identity politics' within and outside the academy from the late 1970s (Lawrence 1982).

Black or 'native' researchers are thus constructed as necessarily 'innocent' within the research process,[10] and are wielded both as a solution to White racism and as middlemen for the continued second-hand attentions of the academic mainstream.

What once constituted a radical critique of 'White sociology' as method and epistemology has now passed uncritically into the common-sense lore of methodological research. The consequences for Black researchers are, however, problematic in a number of ways. First, there is an unquestioning assumption of the homogeneous nature of group experience and of the separation into discrete communities of difference. The implication is that not only does a researcher of colour have unproblematic and unmediated existential access to her own community, but also that this 'experience' is unique to that community. Second, there is the unquestioned assumption of the absolute parity of experience between researcher and researched, that this link is 'natural' rather than political, and the related idea that this is somehow a desirable guarantee of authenticity. Third, there is the reinscription of ideologies of absolute 'insider' and absolute 'outsider' status, which writes across divisions, or commonalities, of gender, class, religion, political standpoint and so on. This places Black researchers in the uncomfortable, and impossible, position of 'speaking for' their community and having to defend their right to do so. Fourth, the logical conclusion is that Black researchers can, and should, work only on issues of race and ethnicity, and only on the Black communities of which they are 'members'. In writing this, I have in mind the White professor in Birmingham who told me, when I was planning my doctoral research, that I was the wrong race, class and gender to study African Caribbean youth, and that maybe I should consider doing research on Asian women. Black researchers are therefore denied a freedom of choice allowed to most White researchers who, despite these arguments, have continued to research whomsoever they like, with the wielding of a reflexivity get-out-of-jail-free clause. Fifth, Black researchers are perceived as politically motivated and therefore professionally suspect, at the margins of an arena already marginalised within the Academy.[11] Indeed, a recent survey of ethnic minority lecturers in British universities noted that the few that exist are overwhelmingly concentrated in new universities, in lower positions and on temporary or part-time contracts. Even more worrying is the rise in the use of 'native' research assistants or students by established White academics as means of gaining access to minority communities and as an alibi for their work – what Sandra Wallman has referred to as 'Ethnography by Proxy' (1980), but I think of more as 'ethnography by stealth'.

While a number of Black researchers have written of the contingent and problematic nature of racial identification in research (Song and Parker 1995; Twine and Warren 2000), the problems of theorising 'native research' have come to the fore, ironically, in the recent emergence of research on Whiteness. The growth of empirical work on White ethnicities has led researchers to confront the implications of their own Whiteness in ways that previous work 'across' race did not. As 'native researchers', however, the over-riding concern has been to establish difference from the 'natives' under research; to highlight issues around class, gender, ethnicity, nationality, age, political persuasion, sexuality and so on as mediators of a simple racial identity (Gallagher 2000). Paradoxically, this has been an important strategy for those White researchers wishing to revalidate researching minority communities, through the reclamation of a minority ethnic identity for themselves.[12]

As Les Back (2002) has persuasively argued, however, the process of reflexive distancing amounts to a denial of commonality and complicity in the research process – in this case, of a shared racial privilege. Building on a tradition of dialogic research on Whiteness that negotiates the terrain of difference and similarity (Frankenberg 1993; Blee 2000), Back's work on far right groups opens up new – and fraught – debates about the problems of identification and recognition in research in 'the Grey Zone'. Specifically, his work challenges the emotional, psychological and political neutrality of researching race, and asserts its 'ethical ambivalence' (2002: 57) as a necessary and productive tension. Marcus has similarly argued that complicity in research demands the entry of the ethnographic project into a broader, undetermined moral and cognitive space, which recognises both the mutuality of the research encounter and that its significance is 'somehow tied into what is happening *elsewhere*' (1998: 119).[13] The process of writing 'race' then becomes a mediation of an always already compromised field with an undetermined and unknowable matrix of consequences.

That being said, a recognition of the impossibility of ethnography does not deny its necessity, though it does demand a reckoning with its dangers. As I have already argued, to refuse an engagement with the empirical heartland of the ethnographic enterprise is to cede the field to empiricist culture collectors. What I am arguing is that research needs to be placed within the context of wider power relations, while simultaneously acknowledging the unfinished and indeterminate nature of this encounter. This requires the insistence not simply on a *truly* reflexive and explicit acknowledgement of the 'relations of production' (Clifford and Marcus 1986) of research and textual creation, but on the wider, always already racialised discourses into which these texts enter. Michael Keith has argued that the privileging of the notion of reflexive textual creation in the idea of 'fiction' is in danger of 'Writing culture and forgetting the audience' (1992: 556). Ethnographies of 'race' and ethnicity do not enter into a neutral institutional or epistemological arena: what is said, or not said, is taken up, silenced, edited, reinterpreted or dismissed according to the (admittedly fragmented) demands of the academy or wider society.

The role of the 'native' researcher is a particularly invidious one within this wider arena. On the one hand, there is the danger of being simply invisible, dismissed as 'too subjective' or 'too political'. Winddance Twine has thus noted that 'Race, of course, greatly affects one's authority to make certain knowledge claims' (2000: 22). On the other, there is the danger of incorporation, or co-optation, where the attribution of authenticity enables the, sometimes opportunistic, claiming of 'insider' knowledge as incontestable 'Truths'. I would argue strongly that, within this wider arena, reflexivity is important as a strategy for the refusal of the attribution of 'authenticity', a refusal to be made to 'speak for your community'. However, this refusal has to carry with it a recognition of the ways in which even partial truths can be used to reinscribe or dislocate dominant forms of knowledge.

What this requires, perhaps, is a more political sensibility in ethnographic production. By this I mean not a return to an earlier idealistic illusion of the transformative potential of ethnographic research (cf. Willis 1977), but a more cynical strategy of 'damage limitation', with an eye to the uses and abuses of ethnographic practice and production (Stacey 1988). The notion of 'fictive' ethnography needs to be carried through, not as an exercise in authentication, but as a fully dialogic process that challenges the notion of 'cultural' truths at its very heart. Within this process, self-reflexivity should serve a dual function: first, to undermine the notion of the ethnographer's authority and reveal explicitly the partiality of her 'truths' within the production of an ethnographic text. Second, reflexivity should look outwards, at the wider relationships and inequalities that generate research interests and structure its reception. This requires, particularly of the 'native' ethnographer, a refusal to be placed as a gatekeeper or representative or expert, but also a recognition of the potential complicity of the research within the wider arena, whatever the ethnographic intention. There is, of course, a tension within these two objectives – a refusal of authenticity for the 'native' researcher, particularly, runs the risk of being ignored (too subjective, too political, too 'White') or dismissed. At the same time, a focus on 'partial truths' can lead to accusations of *naïveté* and the material, often violent, 'Truths' of discrimination – of privileging postmodern technique over 'reality'.[14]

Writing race – constructing *The Asian Gang*

If I am honest, there were times after the publication of *The Art of Being Black* that I could not help thinking that somewhere I *had* missed the point. Several years on, I think that, in my eagerness to challenge the negative images surrounding young Black men in Britain, I had over-compensated, playing down the structuring forces on the formation of racialised identities and their negative consequences. I had also under-estimated the public interest in the research and the ways in which aspects I assumed would be implicitly understood by an audience (such as the use of humour and irony) were turned into the reinscription of dominant negative attitudes (around sexism, for example).

With *The Asian Gang*, I was determined to avoid these mistakes. In writing the book, I was determined to make the process of the research explicit; to explore the ways in which ethnicity, gender, class and age mediated access and the material I obtained. My aim was not to lay claim to the privileged insights of experience, nor to authenticate my role as a 'native' through the claiming of a conveniently reconstituted Asian/Bengali identity, but to disrupt the distinction between 'native' and 'non-native', 'participant' and 'observer', positionality and personality. While I would acknowledge that my identification as 'Asian' facilitated my access initially, it was neither a sufficient nor simple foundation for the relationships that emerged later. Nor were these relationships based on ideas of shared 'culture', but on a less tangible set of alliances and hard-won mutual trust and affection. In recognition of this, I wanted to make visible the participation of the young men themselves in the creative process – in the use of interview material, in their choice of their own names, in the returning of their 'voices' on the tapes at the end of the project – most of all in the writing up, through their involvement in the reading and editing process. I also wanted to make explicit the development of these personal and emotional relationships within the research, and explore the interweaving of autobiography and ethnographic narration – to humanise and demystify both the subjects and process of research.

At the same time as this 'internal' dialogue was taking place, however, I was also consciously mediating an 'external' representation – the entrance of the finished text into a broader set of institutional and discursive structures. Some of these are clearly visible in the book itself – the engagement with representations in the media, with the police and courts, in the school and youth service. Though I had not intended it at the outset of the research, the symbol of 'the gang' was not something that I could ignore – it had everyday practical, material and ideological consequences. It was clearly not adequate to see these representations as simply wrong and easily put right through my ethnographic 'truth': rather I had to explore the intersection of representation and experience as mutually, if unequally, implicated in identity formation.

There are, however, less visible debates that structure the work. The first comprises the institutional strictures that surround research on 'race'. This is clearly apparent in the process of finding a publisher for the work (but could be applied equally to issues of funding). One sociology editor in a major publishing house told me that readers were 'not interested' in Asian youth, because they were 'too dull'. However subsequent events may have altered her perception, the reaction was interesting because it reflects an overarching idea that research on 'race' had to be about problems, about threat, about visible and specific 'Otherness', to be commercially viable. Research by an Asian woman on young Asian men simply wasn't sexy enough, which says something additional, I think, about the differential weightings given to different marginal groups within a racialised academic landscape – about whose experience matters, in what ways and under what circumstances, and recounted by whom. The editor at Berg, which is a much smaller publishing house specialising in ethnographic monographs, liked the book but insisted on the current title, *The Asian Gang*, despite my repeated appeal that the title completely misrepresented the contents. Actually, with the addition of a Preface that deals with this issue, the title grew on me, if only because it set up a series of expectations and discourses that the book hoped to challenge. Nevertheless, in reviews so far, the title is what seems to bother readers most. Ruggiero (2001), for example, castigates the book for ignoring criminological work on 'gangs' and for overlooking the formative role of 'drugs' in gang identities; again a telling example of the ways in which racialised youth identities are given a predetermined and self-fulfilling sociological reality, while texts that challenge this representation are dismissed as 'peripheral', unacademic, unrealistic and 'self-indulgent'.

Second, while not wishing to defend my choice in *not* writing the book that this reviewer, or others, wanted me to write, it is perhaps worth reflecting on why I chose to ignore certain 'realities' in *The Asian Gang*. This also reveals invisible processes of selection and silencing within the work, and in particular, my own personal perception of the obligations of the ethnographer. The absence of a fuller discussion of drugs, for example, was three-fold: first, the issue of drugs did not arise as a focal point of concern during the period of my research. This is not to deny that drugs formed part of the landscape and activities of the young men, but it was a minor element in a context where other issues were more foregrounded and significant. Second, the role of drugs simply did not interest me – it told me nothing about identity formation and contestation that marked out young Asian men; it was simply an activity that is almost ubiquitous amongst young men of all ethnicities and backgrounds within an inner-city environment (and beyond). Smoking cigarettes, on the other hand, was a very central and revealing way of exploring issues of respect and authority within the group. Third, I did not want to add to an already distorted external representation of young Asian men that focused on cultural breakdown and crisis, and that would allow what, for me, were more important issues to be ignored in favour of a sensationalist and inflated exposé of drugs and criminality. It was, put starkly, not a tradition with which I was prepared, either for myself or for the young men, to be associated with or implicated in. This is not to admit that I sought to project a uniformly positive and uncritical picture – but it is to admit my choice and responsibility in selecting issues for consideration, and also to insist that negative elements are present only when they can be fully explored and contextualised (as for example in the discussion of violence), rather than to fuel someone else's fantasies of gangland 'reality'. Whether this renders the text more or less valid, more or less 'true', good or bad ethnography, is for the reader to decide.

Conclusion: on the impossibility and necessity of ethnography in 'writing race'

Despite appearances to the contrary, my aim in acknowledging the dilemmas and contradictions of 'native ethnography' is not to provide a handy stick with which to beat either ethnography-as-practice or the 'native researcher'. Both have been a focus of their fair share of scrutiny, and have engendered important critical insights into the process and claims of research more generally. Rather, the purpose of this chapter has been to explore the necessary vicissitudes of an ethnographic approach to 'writing race', and to challenge residual claims to 'Knowledge' and 'Truth' in race research in Britain.

While the literary turn in ethnographic writing has irrevocably deconstructed the ways in which ethnography is *thought*, the ways in which ethnography is *done* have proved more resilient to change. Fictions of 'truth' continue to form the foundation for fictions of innocence in research practice – the researcher becomes the modern embodiment of the career explorer, discovering hidden and exotic 'tribes' within the Metropole. Within this paradigm, what constitutes very real issues of power inequality in research too easily become transformed into practical issues of access – methodology becomes separated from wider issues of theory and epistemology. The danger for the 'native' researcher is to reinforce these fictions of unassailable difference, by design or default, through the misrepresentation of a political field for a 'purely' cultural one. Ironically, for 'native' researchers, even more than 'non-native', the dangers lie in the claiming of a specialist knowledge or access – of 'going native' or, indeed, '*being* (made) native'.

These dilemmas are not specific to ethnography; they are perhaps even more apparent and urgent in the uncontested disciplinary 'neutralities' of other arenas of empirical or theoretical research. No research on race and ethnicity is either accidental or apolitical in its inception, practice or dissemination, in its inclusions and exclusions, its visibilities or its silences: no research is about 'Truth' in any unmediated or pure imagination. Michael Keith (1995) has argued for the importance of 'radical contextualisation' in the formation of academic knowledge and political action – of the historical, geographical and temporal spaces within which 'truths' are asserted, action taken and knowledges produced.

'Writing race' can, then, be argued to be impossible (and unethical) – bound up with 'partial truths' and implicated in political process. To acknowledge this, however, is to run the risk of losing ground to those who still assert the purity of cultural authenticity and their untrammelled access to it. These more simple portraits are undoubtedly easier to turn into policy documents and media soundbites, and they carry with them all the power of self-fulfilling prophecies. It is in the face of this alternative – the handy heat-and-serve culturalist packages – that ethnography, however impossible, also becomes a necessity.

Philippe Bourgois thus argues, 'Ethnographic method allows the pawns of larger structural forces to emerge as real human beings who shape their own future' (2000: 208). Ethnography carries with it the potential to explore the textured and contradictory space between 'structure' and 'agency' that is either occluded or rendered completely distinct in other methods of research and writing. Bourgois writes:

> Methodologically, it is only by establishing lasting relationships based on mutual respect that one can begin to ask provocative personal questions, and can expect to engage in substantive conversation about the complex experience of extreme social marginalisation….The traditional quantitative survey methodologies of upper middle class sociology or criminology collected via hit-and-run parachute visits behind apartheid lines tend to collect fabrications.
>
> (ibid.: 205)

I would broaden Bourgois's targets to include all qualitative research methods and also the evasions of high theory, which asserts – as a colleague recently did at a workshop on the 'riots' of 2001 – that what people themselves think 'doesn't matter' in the face of its purer theoretical and historical insights.

The ability of ethnography to provide *'some kind of voice'* (Willis and Trondman 2000) socially and corporeally embedded, and otherwise silent, is an important, even precious, one, but one that demands a critical and political sensibility to avoid becoming either exotica or 'pornography'. The balance lies not only in the conduct of research and the production of text, but also in the contingencies of reading – and perhaps it is here that both the fallacies and the urgencies of 'Writing race' lie.

Acknowledgements

Love and thanks to Les Back, Ko Banerjea, Wendy Bottero, Jane Franklin, Caroline Knowles, John Solomos, Miri Song and France Winddance Twine for their comments on earlier drafts of thischapter. I would also like to thank all those who attended the Research Seminar at South Bank University, the Critical Ethnography seminar class at UC Santa Barbara and the Department of Sociology at City University where versions of this chapter were presented and discussed.

Notes

1   For Visweswaran, 'fieldwork' involves a critical confrontation with 'home' – the intersections of personal location (race, gender, class, sexuality, etc.) with the research process.
2   Both in terms of the fragmented knowledges and subjective involvements that lie at the heart of the ethnographic project.
3   Marcus Banks (1996) has noted that early ethnographic work in the 'race relations school' was undertaken by anthropologists with field experience in the former colonies, and it

remains the case that many anthropologists working on ethnicity in Britain have continued this tradition (cf. Werbner 1996; Watson 1977).

4   Cf. Errol Lawrence's (1982) attack on 'sociology and Black pathology', which lambasts 'White sociology' for its 'blame the victim' focus on cultural difference at the expense of structural disadvantage and racism.

5   Cf. Malinowski's vision of the goal of ethnography as 'to grasp the native's point of view, his relation to life, to realise his vision of the world' (1922: 25).

6   A good example of this is Roger Ballard's (1994) edited collection, *Desh Pardesh*. In the preface, Ballard writes, 'Our objective has been to make the accounts we present *as authentic and as objective* as possible' (1994: x, my emphasis).

7   See for example Rosaldo's (1989) account of the myth of the 'Lone Ethnographer'.

8   Back's 1996, 2002 work is an exception.

9   Cf. Blauner and Wellman, 'There are certain aspects of racial phenomena....That are particularly difficult, if not impossible, for a member of the oppressing group to grasp empirically and formulate conceptually. These barriers are *existential and methodological as well as political and ethical*. We refer here to nuances of culture and group ethos; to the meaning of oppression and *especially psychic relations;* to what is called the Black, the Mexican-American, the Asian and the Indian experience' (cited in Andersen 1993: 40, my emphasis).

10   Cf. Pnina Werbner's defence of anthropology in Britain (1996) 'Most ethnographic monographs on ethnic minorities in Britain were written by *members of the communities themselves, or by incorporated members*...by anthropologists with *long-term field experience* in Africa, Asia or the West Indies, and by recent immigrants from the Middle East and Africa' (1996: 74, my emphasis).

11   I mention here the senior White academic who complImented me on how well written *The Art of Being Black* was, and added 'you must have had a very good editor', and the professor who recently asked me if *The Asian Gang* was 'a real book'.

12   What Ko Banerjea has termed the claim to 'secondary Whiteness' (personal communication, 13 September 2002).

13   What Douglas Holmes has termed 'illicit discourse' (in Marcus 1998).

14   What has been characterised as 'the death and furniture' critique of postmodernism.

10 Race, a word too much?

The French dilemma

Sophie Body-Gendrot

Despite different historical and ideological constructions, and although the identities of the established and of the outsiders vary as well as the latter's strategies and tools to address problems of 'otherness' and of racism, the societal processes of integration/exclusion are remarkably similar throughout developed countries.

My first awareness of 'similarities' relative to the actors I was studying, that is, populations differing by their numbers, codes of references and ideologies from the majorities in the societies they lived in, came when I completed my Ph.D. dissertation in 1983 at the Institute of Political Science in Paris. I had done fieldwork in New York for several years, looking at local conflicts involving actors with different ethnic and racial identities, but the controversies over public schools, jobs and housing had also class and ideological components. As I was about to complete this 800-page dissertation, I became aware of the similarities in the claims made by different types of have-nots in France, i.e. youth of postcolonial origin, instrumentalizing violence to become visible in the eyes of policy-makers and to influence local decisions concerning their marginalized neighborhoods, their future and the racism they said they were the victims of.

The African-Americans I had interviewed in Ocean-Hill-Brownsville in Brooklyn or the Puerto Ricans on the Lower East Side in Manhattan were regarded as newcomers in the cities where they lived. So were these French youth, although their fathers had usually settled in France in the 1960s or sometimes before. They lived in segregated public housing projects at the periphery of cities and, economically, they were at the bottom of the ladder. They had no political clout and as a tool of last resort, it seemed to me, they used intimidation and the 'culture of riot' to reverse a situation of powerlessness and boredom, and the obstacles they faced when they tried to express their 'voices' in the public space as any French person would. In return, as soon as their mobilizations gained some visibility, their opponents socially constructed their 'race' or rather their ethnicity as a visible marker of their 'difference' and of their incapacity to melt into the mainstream. But besides a nationalist posture, the stakes of the opposition also concerned class and power. Were the established majorities ready to share some of their power and to open their ranks to these violent youngsters who were poor, with a different origin yet with French nationality, according to democratic ideals of equal treatment for all? It seemed to me that the processes of exclusion leading to urban violence could be compared.

In the case of the African-Americans of Ocean Hill, the local teachers' union (United Federation of Teachers, UFT), composed mostly of Jewish members, would not let a phenomenon of ethnic succession take place via public jobs in New York, as historically had been the case for every new wave of immigrants (Body-Gendrot 1993a). Instead, they attempted to 'enlarge the scope of the conflict' and find allies within the established New York population thanks to a larger conflict that displaced the smaller ones (Schattschneider 1960: 67). Soon, anti-Semitism versus racism pitted the contenders against each other, and the liberal political elites around Mayor John Lindsay and the Ford Foundation paid a hard price for their siding with the racial minorities, as the middle classes would not hear appeals to social justice but defended their hard-won historical victories.

The same phenomenon repeated itself, 10 years later, on the Lower East Side under the Koch mayoralty: whereas the Puerto Ricans were in their legal right to get preferential treatment in the new public housing units, after a program of urban renewal had destroyed their former integrated neighborhood, the lower-middle-class Hasidic Jews used their class allies to prevent this group of inferior social status moving in, a group that would threaten the value of the area's property, according to them. But this rhetoric hardly hid the fact that race was also at stake here. Then ideology was used to enlarge the scope of the conflict: anti-Semitism versus racism (the Puerto Ricans lost), lower middle classes versus the marginalized (Body-Gendrot 1993a).

In the case of France, a similar process took place when immigrant and French youth from public housing projects were seen on television, joy-riding in stolen cars, and fighting the police. The larger audience could not possibly identify with their struggle and, rather, they were represented as barbarians by journalists who lived elsewhere and who did not try to explain to their readers the identity crisis these youth went through. What was at stake and unsaid was the general hostility of French society towards immi-grant populations living in public housing at the periphery of cities. That foreign families had settled for good and that some of their male children, most frequently French, were suffering from racism and social exclusion, and using intimidation to get some respect, was ignored.

However, I faced several obstacles in drawing my comparisons: first, research in political science at the beginning of the 1980s, emphasizing the similarity of processes triggering the mobilization of minority actors, both in France and in the USA, was odd. It was not a 'noble' topic, compared with state sovereignty or the political parties, for instance. The few French sociologists who took some interest in the mobilizations of those youth in France perceived them as a possible social movement. They did not interpret them as a reaction to racial exclusion in the field of inter-ethnic relations (Body-Gendrot and Duprez 2002). Then for ideological reasons, at a time when Marxism still strongly influenced the French social sciences, there was a strong reluctance to include the USA, the capitalist country *par excellence*, in comparative work. Methodologically, how could a comparison be developed on ethnic and racial conflicts in large cities when, at the very same time, researchers in political science suggested suppression of the term *race* in the vocabulary of social sciences, claiming that it was devoid of meaning? (See Israel and Bonnafous 1992.) I will come back to this point later . To sum up, three elements made international comparisons on this topic most difficult at the time: the official ignorance of ethnic and racial discriminations that French citizens of postcolonial origin experienced and the lack of statistics concerning race and ethnicity; the amnesia relative to the Algerian War, unlike the awareness of the legacy of slavery in the USA; the refusal of incorporating into cross-national analyses 'the Trojan horse' embodied by the USA and the illegitimacy of comparing two vastly different societies. In this chapter, I will attempt to show that difficulties for comparative research on race and racism in cities arise from a deviant construction of the problem of racism in France; then from inadequate tools; then from divisions among researchers.

A deviant construction of the problem

The French choice: emphasizing the struggle against socio-economic inequalities

At the beginning of the twentieth century, when foreigners settled in French areas, they were not perceived as foreigners in spaces that were themselves fractioned into tiny enclosures. Before the First World War, more than a dozen different languages were spoken in the territory (Schnapper 1991: 108). Denizens' migration to cities was incorporated within the global exodus of the French peasantry and they became marginalized just as other regional components of the working class were. They were perceived as tramps or vagrants and 'unassimilable' by the urban middle classes. Most of them experienced the same fate and commonalities. The boundaries were established on the class factor and externality was not linked then to nationality (Gallissot 1988). Between the current discourse on marginalization/exclusion and the label given to the dangerous classes of the past, the difference comes from the awareness that all the working class was externalized then, whereas the current working class of postcolonial origin is ethnicized today. But the two processes are the same in terms of the essentialization of the subjects under study.

Ira Katznelson, in his seminal work, *City Trenches*, demonstrated that the mobilization of the US working class of immigrant origin had been dual (Katznelson 1981). Workers mobilized in a unitary way against their employers in the working place and attempted to organize strikes to improve their working conditions and mobility into the mainstream. However, on their way home from the plant, they became Poles, Jews, Italians and Irish again and, in the neighborhoods where they lived, they were organized by political machines as ethnic residents. The Irish boss would try to get hold of the Irish vote for the local political machine, for instance, and would redistribute favors to the Irish community of the ward he was in charge of. Community organizations, settlement houses and ethnic networks would provide defense and care to these immigrants on an ethnic basis.

To that extent, the French response to immigrants in terms of social policies and hard-core urban problems was different from that of other industrial countries. In a comparative work called 'Migration and the Racialization of the Postmodern City in France', based on 2-hour-long, in-depth tape-recorded interviews conducted throughout 1988 among Muslim organizations in large French cities, I pointed out that it was significant that the French referred to '*immigré*', a word with a passive and labor-linked meaning, in opposition to the actively connoted term of 'immigrant' and that they also used 'identity' and 'culture' rather than 'ethnicity', 'communities' and 'minorities' (Body-Gendrot 1993c: 78, 1993b). This was not by accident. The French rely on a 'fictitious ethnicity' implying that, in the history of workplaces, working classes, family, social housing or remedial education, the impact of foreign-born populations who later became French citizens is ignored. No one knows how these immigrants' children helped to mold the French nation and imprint their marks. This is in contrast with the 'nation of nations' ritually celebrating her immigrants, encouraging research about them, changing the census now and then to make room for new groups, yet until the 1960s considering African-Americans and Native Americans as second-rank citizens, so central is biological race in the US imaginary (Omi and Winant 1994).

By contrast, unique historical and institutional factors molded the French perception of the nation, of the way immigrants are and should be assimilated into society. The Duke of Clermont-Tonnerre's famous assertion during the Revolution that 'All should be given to Jews as individuals and all should be refused to Jews as a nation' (then meaning a social group) impregnated the nation's ideology based on *the equal treatment of individuals*. The same assertion was repeated at the end of the nineteenth century in the National Assembly regarding Italians settled in France: the constitution of 'communities' is considered as a threat and the individual assimilation of second generations is emphasized. Even with a retrospective outlook, because of this prevailing ideology and the lack of statistics, the workers' ethnic identity remained confined to the private sphere and the mobility experienced by Italian, Polish and Hungarian immigrants via political parties, unions and the Church was not acknowledged as a mobility of immigrants or of ethnic groups within a diverse French society, but as a mobility of segments of the working-class community.

As shown by G. Noiriel, who studied several generations of *immigrés* in Longwy, a mining area of Lorraine: during the first half of the twentieth century, foreign miners of Polish and Italian origins were part of the proletariat. They were not immune from xenophobia, but they gradually moved up. Later, they denied any form of social and political succession to miners from North Africa, exerting as recently incorporated French the same forms of xenophobia and discriminations as their predecessors (Noiriel 1988). Class solidarity was forgotten and the Party and the Church's integrative function declined. Blocking succession looks very similar to the one experienced by African-American and Latino principals and teachers in New York in the 1960s: they were prevented from incorporating into teaching professions by the UFT the local teachers union, who kept such jobs for those of their white ethnic members who had difficulties moving up in other sectors (Body-Gendrot 1993a). Yet, methodologically, it is difficult to compare ethnic conflicts that are historically taken for granted as a natural historical process, due, first, to the acknowledged pluralism of local politics in the USA and conflicts of the same type officially denied and not studied as such in France. In other words, the contexts of a differentialist society and of an assimilationist society could not be more different.

The Algerian trauma

When comparing forms of internal and racial exclusion, that is, the legacy of slavery in the USA and the postcolonial situation in France, one of the problems came from the very particular historical situations they emanate from: on the one hand, the centrality of race permeates social relations in the USA and, on the other, the ethnicization of social relations in France is not openly acknowledged. The term *ethnic* is itself negatively connoted to the Holocaust in France and the Jewish case is always used as a proof ethnic differences should not be marked. Whereas African-Americans have fought and continue to do so to make the injustice of their fate known over and over to the rest of the world, and whereas they have accepted and demanded this racial definition also found in the census, in France the consequences of the Algerian War, which today still makes the identity of *immigrés'* children so confusing for them, have been obfuscated.

Historian Benjamin Stora sums up why this trauma still impacts today on French society in terms of racism and exclusion. In 1962, 1 million French people suffered from the independence given to Algeria, a French territory. The French people have always felt that they were betrayed by their home country (when I speak publicly about the racism immigrants' children experience, in the south of France Pieds-Noirs ask me 'Why don't you speak of us, instead of them?) and they tend to vote heavily for the far right. Why is that so?' 'The more the Algerian War fades away, the more this repressed history haunts French society' (Stora 2002: 20). Further, some Harkis – Algerians who sided with France and were tortured and massacred by the

Liberation Front (FLN) in Algeria – escaped and came to live in France. They were ignored by the government and placed in hastily established army camps for decades (Body-Gendrot 1995: 573). These two populations in exile keep the painful issue of the colonial war alive, along with the *immigrés* and their children, that is, on the whole, 5 or 6 million people out of 60 million, who have their own views of the colonial episode.

Algerian independence marked the end of a strong French nationalism with an imperialist vision component, and this is another element making this history so singular. At first, the French were not aware that two centuries of their colonial adventure had ended and that, if nationalism was just reduced to the French territory, it would undergo a trauma. The defeat indeed caused a deep narcissistic wound, Stora adds, and it was De Gaulle's genius to immediately attract the French people's attention to the necessity of reforming institutions, modernizing the economy, preparing Europe – in other words, forget the South.

> It is difficult, though, to forget such a wide cataclysm and the irruption of memories can be dangerous....With the refusal of analyzing the war and drawing consequences, the new Republique which was created in 1958 was unable to fight the extreme right which interpreted the colonial war within a racial paradigm and with a violent aversion for multiculturalism.
>
> (Stora 2002: 20)

In Algeria, colonization was based on a hierarchy ranking the French colons and the unmeltable Muslims at the bottom. Today, the same differentialist racism is spread by Le Pen and his followers in France. Forty per cent of French people who carry representations inherited from the past, and who feel their status is threatened, admit that they feel close to some of his ideas, and the first round of the presidential elections in 2002 showed that, despite its protest meaning, the nativist vote in most social categories (youth, elderly, farmers, white-collar workers, blue-collar workers, the unemployed, etc.) had progressed. This vote is likely to be visible again in regional and European elections when the proportional representation of parties interferes.

After the civil rights movement and Black Power revolution, African-Americans and other minorities succeeded in gaining affirmative action and welfare measures from white law-makers, not to mention the Great Society programs that acted as channels of political integration for some of the activists. This is why one may speak of an 'ethnicization of minorities'. Race was mobilized for political, economic and symbolic struggles and blurred the previous working-class/ethnic divisions (Katznelson 1981). But, in France, anti-racist movements have not gone forward to change the school-books and include more objective perspectives on the colonial periods, or to mark anniversaries and memorials for the French-Algerian casualties. The resistance of those who never accepted the retreat of France from Algeria and the historical hostility to Islam as a religion may explain this political prudence from the various governments. To take an example, when, after months of negotiation, the new Mayor of Paris, Bertrand Delanoe, arranged to put a plate on a bridge in Paris, reminding the public that in 1961, 40 years before, hundreds of Algerians had been drowned in the Seine by the French police, not only were ranks of policemen so thick that guests could not approach the plate, but (facing the Police Prefecture) has since already been removed several times by anonymous hands.

The continuing tensions within French society related to the Algerian War are evoked here to explain the difference between French cultural racism and US racism. Racism in France is not based on the cult of blood or on a mystical *Volkgeist* but on cultural distinctions (Weil 2002; Taguieff 2001; Guillaumin 1992). Most Algerian *immigrés'* children do not master the complexity of this history. They have binary fantasies about the French defeat and the power of Algeria, and construct a memory with the few stories their parents told them and what they see on television. They feel neither comfortable with the French colonialist history nor with the violent Algerian history, and this confusion prevents them from grasping what is going on on either side of the Mediterranean Sea. This loss of bearings may foster their violence as a means of expression and of visibility.

Despite very different trajectories, what can be compared cross-nationally nevertheless is the confinement, the exclusion and the stigmatization experienced by visible minorities who are poor and socially segregated in the USA, the UK and in France. The latter country, however, has changed considerably in the last 20 years. Ten years ago, anticipating the expansion of social exclusion with ethnic connotations, A. Touraine remarked that, formerly,

> French society based on classes carried with it conflicts and inequality. The laissez faire society that France is currently becoming carries ghettos within it....As a consequence, a 'social' logic...gives a meaning to new identities based on the collective experience of exclusion.
>
> (Touraine 1991)

But whereas negotiations could put an end to labor conflicts, the ethnicization of social relations hardens fundamentalist oppositions and tensions over identities, which become essentialized and fundamentalist oppositions.

Inadequate tools

What are the tools French researchers can use in international comparisons on race and racism? They face four obstacles, it seems: first, the terms race and ethnicity do not cover the same meaning here and there. Then there has been a demonization in France of statistical approaches linked to the category *ethnicity* possibly leading to communitarianism. After the controversy on quantitative issues taking ethnicity into account, it now appears that this approach is jammed, all the more as researchers are themselves divided.

Defining 'race'

British and US research on race relations acknowledges the existence of races, of identifiable skin markers and of biological differences. The analysis of this form of universal racism is linked to institutional mechanisms and to the interests of minority groups. The issue of the autonomy of racism as an ideology has fostered many controversies that will not be evoked here but, among others, the necessity not to forget class, gender, age distinctions and 'the exploited of the excluded' within race (Ware 1992; Body-Gendrot 1998).

The French stand has been notably different. First, there has been a question mark concerning the fuzziness of the term race. Races are seen as abstract and dangerous constructions. Charles Murray's universal approach in *The Bell Curve* (Murray and Hernstein 1994) or the racial categorizations of the US census are strongly rejected by the French scientific community. In other words, the idea is that while racism is real, races are not. Terms that appear similar to *race* do, fact in each country cover different histories and structures, they belong to diverse semantic spaces and traditions, and they cannot be translated as if they were alike.

Second, when in other countries anti-racists claim the right to live in unity respecting differences, a large proportion of the French agrees that one should indeed respect the differences of those who cannot assimilate and that there should be no hybridization (Todd 1994). The anti-racist postures mirror the differentialist racist ones and lead to a 'Nazification' of the enemy, Taguieff claims, essentializing it. The denunciator becomes the very category of its denunciation (Taguieff 1996).

For such reasons, the struggle against racism has remained thwarted in France. The condemnation of racism might have been more visible had the socio-economic crisis of the two last decades not also served to weaken or distort cultural movements (Wieviorka 2000). A French survey among immigrant associations incorporating first and second generations in the 1990s revealed that, for community leaders, social stakes were seen as more important than cultural ones and that citizenship and communitarianism were hardly quoted, not even such issues as the 'scarf' or multi-culturalism (Withold de Wenden 1992: 39). Most of all, the elder spokesmen of post-colonial origin are well aware of the ethnic biases of the French universalist system and of the non-receptivity of the political system to ethnic lobbying but, as they need the help of the state for their individual integration, they play the national and local cards of integration and keep a low profile in terms of cultural assertion (Withold de Wenden and Leveau 2000: 154). I remember playing a tape for my students in which Nejma, a Jamaican woman from the Bronx, talked with Rose, a woman of Algerian origin living in a working-class 'Red Belt' area, Genevilliers, in the Parisian region, and compared their lives. What was most striking was the vindictive and militant tone of Nejma, and her frustration with the racism of white US society, which she denounced on and on, whereas Rosa would complain about the marginalization of her neighborhood in socio-economic terms, yet say how attached she remained to the place where she grew up. Nejma was impatient with Rose for not sharing her view that whites were racists while the latter expressed concerns of a different type.

The demonization of communitarianism and of differentialism

In an editorial titled 'Communitarianism, This is the Enemy', R. Grossmann, the president of the urban community and deputy mayor of Strasbourg, after the attempted arson of a synagogue during the spring of 2002, gave his point of view in a widely circulated magazine:

> Communitarianism substitutes disastrous (*funestes*) allegiances to citizenship. It is likely to bring back a state of war on national soil. It is also able to launch extreme forms of violence that would tear the French apart. It negates individual rights, jeers at the Republique and supports terrorism over the democratic debate. Now has come the time of tribes, and civil peace and Republican citizenship are threatened....There is a thin difference between Sarajevo, a city where communities killed each other, and our French cities.
>
> (2002: 36)

These views reflect the excesses with which communitarianism is demonized in France. There is very little tolerance for the expression of collective visible markers in the public space and for those 'whose recruiting is based on the membership in a group with a prescribed status' (Leca 1985: 11). It is as if the famous assertion of the Higher Council to Integration had not evolved since 1991: 'The French conception of integration should obey a logic of equality and not a logic of minorities. The principle of identity and equality...impregnate our conception...to the exclusion of an institutional recognition of minorities' (Haut Conseil à l'Intégration 1991: 10). As recently as June 1999, France refused to sign the European Charter on Regional or Minority Languages because of the mention of the term *minority*. Such iron ideology makes problematic the position of researchers tempted to denounce the failures of the model of integration for French citizens of post-colonial origin, who, despite their merit, experience many forms of exclusion. Few authors have studied the consequences of racism and of institutional racism, and those who have been violently accused of being communitarians or saboteurs of the French Republic (Wieviorka 2000: 13).

No adequate statistics

The major obstacle to pursuing comparisons on this theme comes from the lack of statistics relative to French immigrants or to the so-called second generation. The moment they are French, they are lost for statisticians. How many Algerians with French nationality are in jail? How many ethnic entrepreneurs are Jewish? How many Africans are denied decent housing? No one knows to what extent 'the national preference' hampers their trajectories. A major quantitative study was undertaken by a demographer, M. Tribalat, and her team in 1994. The survey offered a new conceptual frame allowing the in-depth analysis of the trajectories of immigrants once they were settled in France. New explanations for the integrative process were offered. Methodologically, ethnicity (language, religion...) and national origins were used as central concepts to analyze the diversity of groups' trajectories (Tribalat 1995). This survey caused a huge controversy as it was violating a taboo and, scientifically, the study was discarded as faulty by institutionalized demographers (Blum 1998). Although, with this survey, interesting international comparisons could be launched, the bitterness of the attacks currently prevents further surveys of this kind taking place in France and no private foundation exists to provide alternative funding. Isolated monographs show nevertheless that racism and racial discrimination hamper the mobility of French males of postcolonial origin who are segregated in poor neighborhoods with deficient public services (Debarbieux 1998; Body-Gendrot and Duprez 2002). More and more public agents say openly at the individual level that the universalistic treatment of public services produces discriminations. But there is no systematic data, no large-scale quantitative survey, so that no one knows the extent of the phenomenon (Simon 1999).

The community of researchers still divided

There is an awareness among French researchers that the data gathered on an ethnic basis could jeopardize the gains of a 'model' of individual integration that has its own merits, not essentializing identities and allowing many immigrant children to experience forms of mobility close to those of the French of European origin. This is specifically the case for immigrant girls who are better students and tend to participate in all economic sectors, who interact with all kinds of actors and who take advantage of the plural sources forming their identity. Whereas mixed marriages in Germany amount to 5 per cent for second generations, the figure was over 40 per cent in France in 1996 (Claude 2002). The term 'mixed' may be misleading however: such marriages may occur within the same community between someone with French nationality and someone without. It is nevertheless categorized as a 'mixed' marriage.

Not being obsessed with differences, or encapsulated in politics of collective identities but rather concerned with melting in may also have advantages, as the Tribalat survey showed at the time: in terms of school trajectories, housing mobility, inter-marriages, religious practices, many stereotypes of the French concerning postcolonial immigrants proved to be wrong. To be able to play with one's multiple social identities as one wishes, to distanciate oneself from the group of belonging and to cast the dice according to the subjective interpretation of one's environment may be an asset. Commonalities are too often lost in the patrolling of identity groups' borders, which also happens in France, at the territorial level, among peer groups in deprived neighborhoods and less often when the international situation produces an 'interiorization of the exterior' according to the evolution of the Middle East and of Muslim countries (Body-Gendrot 1993b; 2000). For his part, the president of *SOS Racisme*, Malek Boutih, refuses to see immigrants' children amalgamated with 'five thousand youngsters who terrorize their community, collectively rape the girls, appease their younger brothers by knocking them out, arm themselves with military weapons and exert tortures in the basements of public housing' (Claude 2002: 15). The culture of excuse (or of victimization) is over, which may put an end to the structural analysis that prevailed for 40 years among left researchers, excusing these youth but setting them apart at the same time as if they were not 'us'.

The question French social scientists concerned with inter-ethnic relations ask themselves nowadays concerns the kind of classification that could be clear, coherent and comprehensive, if social justice is to lift privileges granted to majorities and to grant protections and rights to 'Others' (de Rudder *et al.* 2000: 22; Simon 1999: 4; Wieviorka 2000: 97–8). How could such a classification avoid hierarchies and symbolic devalorization of particular categories? Can differences be thought without hierarchical connotations (Tabboni 2001: 73; Body-Gendrot 2004: 381)? Then were such a classification found, would it be accepted by the wider population?

Our own experience with the lack of political will to redress institutional racism within the police in France indicates that the road leading to adequate comparisons on race and racism will be long (de Wenden and Body-Gendrot, forthcoming). In 10 years, only two cases on race and two on gender have successfully been prosecuted: the victim in France still has to prove intentional discrimination to the criminal law judge (Lanquetin 2000).

Conclusion

Twenty years of 'soft' anti-racist pedagogy or of violent denunciations have not broken the rampant trend of nativism, which was so strongly revealed during the first round of presidential elections in France in 2002. The left has obviously not had the political will to create a Commission on Racial Equality as the president of the Higher Council on Integration, S. Weil, had suggested. In 1999, the creation of a National Commission to study and fight discriminations, and the green number meant to receive grievances relative to racial and ethnic discriminations, were a symbolic way to gain time and not to hurt a majority that is still largely xenophobic. No databank allows researchers in this National Commission to measure the extent of discrimination. The decentralized councils meant to treat the grievances received through the green number did not implement noteworthy changes in practices. The left has simply not decided to act on this complex issue. It never passed voting rights for long-settled immigrants who pay taxes and are not represented. It ignored the 7 million public and private jobs that are closed to non-Europeans and the sentencing that consists in sending back to the country of origin delinquents who never lived there.

Yet, to be fair, there are now more measures taken to exert surveillance on the color-blind distribution of public housing units, on the assignment of immigrant pupils to vocational tracks and in the access to discotheques. An elite school, the Institute of Political Science, has opened its ranks to seventeen students from deprived neighborhoods on a quota basis (out of 5,000) and the controversy is gradually fading away. However, this example has not been followed by other elite schools. In a hypermarket of Marseilles, a form of territorial affirmative action has been launched, using the category 'local resident' to offer jobs in priority to postcolonial families heavily segregated in the housing projects nearby (Body-Gendrot 2000). But it is unlikely this operation will be repeated.

As for political representation, the example of women shows that the representation of French of immigrant origin will probably have to be done forcefully through a quota system. Entrenched political machinery at the local level and the lack of involvement by citizens on issues of racism (except sporadically) indicate that French political parties will not automatically open ranks to conform to their democratic ideals. To restrict the space of racism and allow more bottom-up action, French democracy needs to pay attention to minority demands, however discreet they are.

11 A life of sad, but justified, choices

Interviewing across (too) many divides

Michèle Lamont

My book *The Dignity of Working Men: Morality and the Boundaries of Race, Class, and Immigrant* (Lamont 2000) draws on 150 interviews conducted with people who are very much unlike myself. All (or a large fraction) of my respondents were (1) male (I am female); (2) working-class people (I am a professional); (3) people of color (I am white); (4) from developing nations (I am a North American); (5) Muslims (I am Christian); (6) members of former colonial empires (I am French Canadian); (7) older (I was in my thirties when I conducted the interviews). The book analyzed how black and white working-class men living in the New York suburbs, and white and North African men living in the Paris suburbs, define 'us' and 'them.' To get at this question, I asked them to describe in concrete and abstract terms whom they feel similar to and different from, inferior and superior to, close to and distant from, at work, in their neighborhood, and in their communities. I found that perceived moral comparisons largely drove their responses, and that they mobilized moral criteria of evaluation to draw boundaries against various categories of people (for instance, against immigrants and members of other classes and racial groups).

The book revealed that the various populations I studied perceived different groups as most 'other:' Euro-American workers drew the strongest boundaries toward blacks and the poor, but they were relatively accepting of immigrants who were perceived as pursuing the American dream. Although they envied the money and resources of the middle and upper-middle class, they were on average quite critical of their values, and particularly of their perceived weak interpersonal morality. The African-American workers I talked to shared these orientations, although they were less critical of the poor. In France, in contrast, the poor and blacks were considered 'part of us' by French workers, in the name of the republican and socialist ideals, whereas immigrants, subsumed under 'North African immigrants,' were often presumed to be fundamentally different and immoral. French workers also drew stronger boundaries between themselves and members of the middle and upper-middle class, associating them with exploitation and domination. For their part, the North African immigrants also used morality as a key principle for making distinctions, but they emphasized aspects of morality different from those of the other groups of respondents. Particularly crucial to them were taking responsibility for one's family members and showing warmth toward other human beings. In this respect, they resembled African-Americans who, in defining who is worthy, put more emphasis on the 'caring self' than on the 'disciplined self' most valued by white workers. In fact, much of the book consists in comparing the kinds of moral arguments that the four groups of men I interviewed mobilize to draw boundaries against other groups.

The Dignity of Working Men was preceded by *Money, Morals, and Manners: The Culture of the French and the American Upper-Middle Class* (Lamont 1992), in which I used a similar approach to get 160 American and French professionals and managers to describe their own categorization system and their definitions of 'us' and 'them.' The book compared residents of 'cultural centers' (Paris and New York) and those of 'cultural periphery' (Indianapolis and Clermont-Ferrand) to assess the centrality of cultural capital, as opposed to that of moral and socio economic status, in upper-middle class culture.

In the methodological appendix of *MMM* (as it came to be known), I described my research strategy as follows: I considered the interview situation as an experiment of sorts, where the participants are presented with the same stimulus (myself) and asked to describe how they recognize a worthy person, and what they define as high-status signals (or signals of moral/cultural/socio economic worth). I had no illusion that the artificiality of the interview situation would get them to offer a specific 'presentation of self' that would reflect only one of their potentially numerous putative 'authentic selves' – I was convinced, as I still am, that recognizing the artificiality of the conditions under which social science data are collected (even in naturalistic experiments) is an essential dimension of the production of sound research in the social sciences. In *The Dignity of Working Men* (or *DWM*), I pursued a similar strategy, while recognizing that my own identity would be 'read' very differently by the four populations of working men whom I was interviewing, in part because their own social position, socio-demographic characteristics, and social origins gave them greater distance from me than the white professionals and managers I had interviewed for *MMM*.

In *MMM* as in *DWM*, I attempted to present myself as having a blurred identity to the extent that it was possible. I could not 'fudge' my gender identity very much, and indeed, in many cases, their responses expressed clear gender norms in relation to which the men were hoping that I would take a position. My national identity and professional status, however, were somewhat fungible.

To begin with my national identity: I had lived in the USA for almost 10 years at the time I did the interviews for *DWM* (and four years for *MMM*). I had also lived for 4 years in France and spent considerable time in and around Paris over the years. I had a great deal of familiarity with these two societies, although I am French Canadian and can still claim the status of outsider to the two national contexts. This status allowed me to ask the simplest questions of both professionals and workers, as they were unclear about how much I knew and did not know about their societies. Moreover, my accent (in English and in French) could signal clearly to respondents that I was an outsider to the social fabric in which these men lived. I believe my outsider status was particularly crucial in interviews with North African immigrants to France and African-Americans, because I was able (to some extent) to position myself as a foreigner with a sympathetic ear, as opposed to a guilty member of the national polity. I can think of a number of instances where this 'definition of self' on my part facilitated openness on their part. Because they could not be entirely sure whom they were talking to (i.e. how much I knew about their world), I also like to think that they could not offer as tightly controlled a presentation of self as they would have to a French or an American interviewer. To sustain this blurring, I tried to maintain a certain vagueness in my responses to their questions concerning my own life, adopting a kind of psychoanalytical non-interventionist pose throughout the interviews, and I resisted opening up until after the interview/experiment had ended, to the extent that it was possible.

Blurring surrounded my professional identity as well. For both *MMM* and *DWM*, respondents were contacted by letter, written on Princeton University stationery and signed by me. Their names had been found through phone books, after we had identified towns located within census tracts that included individuals presenting the class or racial characteristics that we were looking for. The letter described me as an assistant professor (for *MMM*) and associate professor (for *DWM*) of sociology, and explained that I wanted to interview them about how they select their friends at work and in their community, and about their leisure activities, with the purpose of writing a book on the topic. A research assistant would follow up with a short phone interview to explore whether they were willing to participate in the study, and to verify that their age and occupation qualified them for the study. If they agreed to participate, I would meet them at a place and time they chose, most often in a restaurant or in a public place, but sometimes at home.

Upon meeting me, they were often confused about whether I was the assistant to whom they had talked over the phone, or 'the professor' (I was perhaps too young and too female to fit the bill). Although many of the professionals were attuned to the status categories within the academic system, and would ask me questions about my position in it (including questions about Princeton University), the workers were often much vaguer and frequently had only the faintest idea of what the interview was for (although it was spelled out in my letter). I would clarify the situation if asked, but I would also do what I could to downplay my occupational status. Indeed, my intended presentation of self was that of the 'girl next door' who demonstrated an uncomplicated and straightforward demeanor and made people comfortable (by avoiding academic jargon, for instance). In the interviews, my goal was to make participants forget who I was, and to lead them to talk to me without taking into consideration my own identity.

I am not naïve concerning the extent to which it is possible to have a participant bracket the interviewer's identity. Too much has been written about, for instance, the race-of-interviewer effect to allow me to revel in this illusion (Sanders 1995). Nevertheless, I am convinced that the craft of interviewing involves the ability to put oneself into parentheses, at least to some extent. The interview is not about oneself. It is about the other, and about presenting oneself as a template against which the other can bounce his identity and world view. The interviewee will of course respond to the identity of the interviewer, but first and foremost, she or he should be entering into an exchange where she or he becomes intimately engaged with a stranger, even if it is to respond to the stimuli presented by the stranger's identity.

The fact that the participant knows that she or he will never see the stranger again can facilitate this process: it provides reassurance that the interview is not the beginning of a relationship, but a micro-episode unnaturally isolated from everyday life. The hope is that what would be gained through multiple interactions and repeated interviews, or from doing intensive fieldwork, is in the interview situation compensated for, and replaced by, an artificial intimacy created by the possibility of opening oneself to a stranger for a short but intense period of time, with the certainty that the person will not be part of one's life. The intimacy emerges as the questions move from the most general and innocuous to the most personal and challenging – for instance, ones having to do with racial and class identity, and feelings of lack of adequacy, recognition, or honor. The tone of the questions and their pace can signal to the participant that this is an experiment of sorts, which authorizes them to think aloud and try various scenarios or responses for the interviewer's benefit. For the interviewer, thinking of the interviewee as providing an instantiation of working- or upper-middle-class discourse (without denying their humanity and singularity) is certainly helpful in generating the appropriately conducive experimental mood.

In this context, the interview situation is understood (at least by me) as the meeting of two subjectivities with the goal of producing a somewhat original narrative on the subjectivity of one of the two parties. This narrative cannot be equated with the interviewee's 'authentic subjectivity' (which, in any case, would be the addition of all of the aspects of the person's subjectivities in real life and in the interview situation, and which therefore cannot be captured by social science research and is outside the relational process through which subjectivity is defined (Somers 1994; Jenkins 1996) – hence the necessity of resigning ourselves to working on 'snippets' or samples of subjectivity, and hence the title of this paper). Given my understanding of the nature of the data, it makes sense to collect information on participants' responses to a comparable stimulus (myself), even if they come from very different national and social backgrounds, beyond their similar occupations and age brackets (as is the case for the populations studied in *MMM* and *DWM*).

The data consist of four samples of discourses produced by respondents in similar situations, collected for the sake of comparing them with one another. Again, these four samples (of professionals in the case of *MMM* and of workers in the case of *DWM*) respond to a similar stimulus if the interviewer remains the same across populations. In this context, it is crucial *not* to match interviewees and respondents by race, ethnicity, gender, etc.: That different respondents read the stimuli represented by an interviewer differently is part of the data on the 'us/them' boundary and should not be edited out of the interview situation. Undoubtedly, a woman talks differently about womanhood to a woman and to a man. But one discourse is not necessarily less real than the other. They are different aspects of the woman's narrative about her identity.

Of course, again, 'it' does not always work. But in my view, the art and science of interviewing consists in having the ability to create a delicate balance between setting the agenda for an interview, and bracketing one's identity. The bracketing works only if the participant perceives the interviewer as having a sympathetic ear, even if the interviewee is describing the most horrific racist, ethnocentric, Darwinist representations of the world. When it works, trust, and a great interview, are the outcome.

Against this backdrop, I can easily point to a number of instances where in the interview, where participants responded directly to what they perceived to be my own identity. They made me part of their script, and used my identity as a prop to define who they are, by opposition or otherwise. More specifically:

Interviewing across gender

The professionals and the workers I talked to often live in a world that is much more gendered than the one I live in. Whereas my husband (who is also an academic) and I have a minimally gendered division of labor, many of these men have wives who are homemakers, and they themselves take very seriously their responsibilities as providers (a central element in their definition of what makes a moral person). This aspect of their identity was made salient in the differences they imputed between me and their spouses, knowing that I was a professional woman. Several workers, in particular, made sly comments about the importance of raising one's children oneself. Their own ability to 'keep their wives at home' is a source of pride, and they made clear that they believe their choice was better than mine. I interpreted their pointing to my working-mom status as an attempt to increase their control of the situation by making our gender status salient (on the basis of which they came out on top) while downplaying the class dimension (on which I came out on top). I certainly did nothing to weaken their control of the situation and suffered in silence, for the greater good of scientific progress!

A few participants also made my gender salient by making veiled (and not so veiled) sexual advances. In the case of workers, their attempts could be viewed as another strategy for empowering themselves, by making my sexuality relevant to our exchange, while downplaying our unequal occupational status and inverting the power dynamic. Of course, one cannot exclude the possibility that their intent was much more straightforward (i.e. getting laid). Advances also occurred when I was interviewing professionals, but they did not, at least in my view, carry the same intent of inversion. In all cases, I dealt with advances by playing dumb, i.e. by pretending not to understand what they meant (there again, being a non-native English speaker came in very handy).

Interviewing across and within classes

Several workers tried to explain to me what the life of working-class people is like, perhaps presuming that I had had little exposure to other classes than my own. They described with pride the meaning they attach to their struggle for survival and the resilience that it requires, contrasting these to my imputed easier life. The numerous boundaries they drew between themselves and the upper-middle class were perhaps sometimes implicitly directed at me as, for instance, when one of them told me that middle-class people are not very street smart. This interviewee, who works in a recycling plant, also chastised me for interviewing Paterson residents in their homes, pointing to the many dangers that lurk in this town (Paterson neighbors the infamous Newark (New Jersey)), the site of notorious racial riots and a city known for its high crime rate). This was undoubtedly an occasion for performing (as opposed to describing) boundary work, as he signified to me that I was naïve and lacked common sense (a profound failing in the working-class world view).

The upper-middle-class interviewees, for their part, sometimes engaged in a smug *entre-nous*, presuming that I shared much of their world view concerning the importance of money, or the moral and cultural failings of the non-college-educated, for instance. Some of them were also very taken by my association with Princeton University and wanted to know more about this venerable, if rather conservative, institution. They were very flattered by the opportunity to be interviewed by a Princeton professor, even though my presentation of self did not suggest the level of self-importance that they may have anticipated.

This discrepancy reflects perhaps a distinctively sociological irony, that is, the fact that as interviewers sociologists do not necessarily behave according to expectations. Our knowledge provides us with a distance from social roles that most citizens lack. We can easily be at odds with others, both in the context of conducting research, and as human beings. But this comes with the territory, especially if one studies subjectivities across social settings.

Interviewing across and within races

As expected, many blacks presumed that I knew little about the lives and cultures of African-Americans, and they took the opportunity of the interview to explain it all to me (in fact, I suspect that black respondents who were willing to be interviewed were in general relatively opened to whites and willing to engage, and that the refusal rate was higher among the angrier, more secessionist types). Their expectations about my low familiarity reflected the generally low level of contacts between whites and blacks, as documented by Massey and Denton (1994). Much of what they did was to explain to me what black people are like, and what racism is like and feels like, which is exactly what I was hoping for. For instance, a short and overweight respondent explained that one of his co-workers believes he looks like Arsenio Hall (who is tall and skinny), simply because he is black. In explaining what racism is like, other respondents presumed that I was on their side and were very candid about how they were dealing with their prejudiced co-workers.

A similar imputed positioning was salient when I was interviewing whites: although some presumed that I shared their racist views on blacks, others presumed that I did not. For instance, a warehouse worker, anticipating that I did not share his views, stated that people who live in rich 'lily-white' communities like Princeton don't know what black people are really like, and that it is much easier to be tolerant when your lawn is an acre wide and you live miles away from blacks. In his view, money is the best buffer in the world, and he is sorry that he does not have more. He would use it to protect himself from 'the element.'

Interviewing across the modern/traditional and Christian/Muslim divides

Interviewing North African immigrants living in Paris was a very intense experience. I had had very little contact with this population before working on *DWM*, although I had lived in Paris for 4 years and spent considerable time there at various points in my life. Discovering their lives, their world views, their families, and their houses was a challenging and a powerful experience for me and, often, for them. A great many of them had had very little experience interacting with European women before our encounter. Indeed, one of them even confessed that our exchange was the first opportunity of this sort he had ever had, although he had been living in France for more than 20 years. Our cultural distance was generally so vast that little mutual adjustment was possible. In general, the Princeton stationery had no meaning for them (if they could read at all), and several of them were very unclear about whether and how I was connected with the French government or the immigration inspection services. A few even came with their visas in hand to demonstrate that they were legally in the country.

Some of their responses to my questions were shaped by their anticipation that I wanted to know about their possible involvement in Islamic movements or by their reactions to the Le Pen ascendancy of the previous years (I conducted these interviews in 1992–3). That many of them were adamant in describing themselves as apolitical and as following 'the straight path' was reflective of this concern. Their insecurity was obviously accentuated by the fact that they did not have the framework needed to understand what an interview was about. Some asked if and when the interview would be broadcast on the radio. I felt guilty and embarrassed for not having anticipated that being asked to participate in a study would generate anxiety for them. But it was too late and I had to move on, while doing my best to respect the standard protocol of Princeton's Human Subjects Institutional Review Panel.

My own identity as North American was made salient by some of the North African immigrants in the interview situation, in that they often lumped me together with Americans and described me as belonging to a 'civilization without quality.' One of the most intense interviews was conducted with a pro-Islamist Tunisian who described the downside of modernity and what we, of the advanced industrial world, had lost as a result of our technology and cultural blinders. He mostly pointed to the warmth that in his view characterizes North African societies and is absent in modern societies. He also contrasted what he perceived to be the selfishness of the French with the hospitality and generosity of Muslims. These statements were prompted in part by my own presence, as I was lumped together with the other members of the developed societies against which he was vituperating. At the same time, the experience of being given an opportunity to exchange about such emotionally charged issues produced a high level of basic human connectivity (an emotional dimension whose role in the interview should be acknowledged) that was probably as surprising to me as it was to them.

Interviewing across and within the colonial divide

As I am a French Canadian sociologist teaching in one of the most prestigious universities, my relationship with respondents was pulled in many different directions. As I stated above, my association with Princeton University was appealing to some of the professionals, and probably prompted them to agree to participate in the study. This association did not impress French professionals as much, because many of them did not know of the university or of its position in the Great Academic Pecking Order of America. In any case, my occupation and employer certainly served as a signal of high status for professionals and, although perhaps more ambiguously, for workers.

This high-status signal may have been complicated by my status as a Québecoise. Indeed, I saw that some French respondents were torn (and in a few cases not so torn) between their understanding of my professional status and an impulse to approach me as a *'cousine du Québec,'* which I perceived both as friendly and as reflecting an over-familiar, and slightly paternalistic, colonial stance. Americans may not have as clear a view of the scripts guiding their relationship with Québecois as the French, but a few of them alluded to what they perceived as my Québec accent, presuming that they were in a position to distinguish between 'real French' and the 'non-French' spoken by Québecois. I was surprised to discover how easily, as Americans, they bought into a logic that would have classified them as non-English speakers, if applied to a British English/American English contrast. In any event, very few Québecois are university professors in the USA, and some were unclear about how these two statuses go together, which should trump the other, and how to navigate the confusion.

I believe my subjective identification with anti-colonial movements and my identity as a Québecoise (and as a Québecoise who grew up in an inde-pendentist, anti-imperialist family) facilitated conducting interviews with African-Americans and North African immigrants. The narratives on Québec national identity are replete with tales of domination that resemble in many ways those found in the progressive discourse about the identity of these two groups. Although I did not share their historical experiences or their lives, I did share their identity as a member of a group that has been discriminated against and is fighting for recognition. This kinship, I believe, encouraged blacks to talk to me about their experience with racism, and encouraged North Africans to talk to me about the cultural imperialism and the 'arrogance of the French.' The facts that I am not a native English speaker and that I have a (controllable) Québec accent in French also encour-aged their openness. This is not to say that in interviews they spoke to me the way they would have spoken to members of their own group, or that the cultural colonialism that the French exercise toward Morocco or Algeria compares to the one they exercise toward Québec. In any case, stressing that I was not French, and not American, certainly generated a bond, which I believe was conducive to better interviews.

To bring this chapter to a close, it could be useful to draw conclusions from *MMM* and *DWM* for some of the intense debates that have animated the social sciences in the USA, and anthropology in particular, over the last 20 years. Clifford and Marcus's now classic *Writing Culture* (1986) (re)opened a lasting dialogue about the relationship between the social scientist and the 'object,' about how the scholar's identity defines his or her understanding of the object, and about whether his or her description of the object is in fact an extension of the scholar's narrative about his or her own subjectivity (see for instance Fox 1991; Parkin *et al.* 2000; and Willis and Trondman 2000). This debate has been hailed as a high point in anthropological discourse, and has also been damned as the ultimate expression of its self-absorbing and self-destructive propensity.

I purposefully avoided opening this Pandora's box in the preceding pages, choosing instead to frame my contribution to this volume as a reflection on the many sad but justifiable choices I have made in my own scholarship. I did so because I am not sure that the debate has been a productive one, or that I have anything to add to it. If asked to take a position, I would agree with Paul Rabinow (1991) that the whole 'writing culture' moment was ultimately about cohort replacement within anthropology, i.e. a *'querelle des anciens et des modernes'* about the proper way of doing the craft of anthropology (and of marginalizing the Geertzian legacy).

I feel somewhat fortunate that my own discipline, sociology, has not been taken over by this hand-wringing tidal wave *qua* collective experiment. My position is that social life cannot be studied 'whole,' and that knowledge production requires cutting into it with a scalpel that often does violence to it. But I personally, and unfashionably, must confess that I have no qualm doing so. The hermeneutic circle is here to stay, and we cannot escape our own subjectivity and that of our respondents any more than they can theirs and ours. Our respective awareness has to be managed and is necessarily factored into our conclusions, *coûte que coûte*!

Acknowledgement

This paper was completed while the author was a Fellow at the Center for Advanced Study in the Behavioral Sciences. I am grateful for the financial support provided by the Andrew W. Mellon Foundation (Grant # 29800639).

12 Racial hierarchies in the USA and Britain

Investigating a politically sensitive issue

Miri Song

Opposing views on hierarchy

As a US sociologist based in Britain since 1991, I have followed scholarship and debates concerning race, racism, and ethnic identity in both the USA and Britain. While the concept of racial hierarchy has been used liberally in many US studies of race, it is less commonly used in Britain. I became especially interested in this concept as I followed recent British debates about whether or not assertions of racial hierarchy were legitimate or untenable 'hierarchies of oppression'.

The question of whether some groups are worse off than others is highly pertinent at a time when there is growing recognition of multiple forms of racisms and racial oppression. What makes the concept of racial hierarchy so compelling is that it is suggestive of an *overall* picture of how different groups fare in multi-ethnic societies. There is little doubt that racial inequalities exist in Britain and the USA, but with a few notable exceptions (see Twine 1998; Kim 1999; Bonilla-Silva 1999; Feagin 2000), there is little discussion of what, exactly, are racial hierarchies, and how they operate. 'Social dominance theory' has been influential in arguing that the means by which group-based hierarchies, including racial and ethnic hierarchies, are established and maintained are similar across social systems (Sidanius and Pratto 1999). Nevertheless, there is no one definition or conception of racial hierarchy that is used consistently in either the USA or Britain.

Systems of ethnic and racial stratification have differed historically, not only in terms of the groups involved, but also the complexity and the magnitude of the distinctions made between groups (see Shibutani and Kwan 1965; Loewen 1971; Almaguer 1994; Twine 1998). The workings of formal institutionalized systems of racial stratification, as existed in South Africa prior to 1990, or under slavery and Jim Crow in the USA, were relatively transparent. In the former South Africa (though this is only the most paradigmatic and contemporary historical example of racial hierarchy), Black people were deemed inferior to both 'coloureds' and Whites, and they lived in segregated 'townships' as lesser beings. In all aspects of their lives – economically, politically, and socially – Whites were indisputably at the top,

Black people at the bottom, and the 'coloured' population comprised a formal intermediate category (Spickard 1989).

Although forms of both overt and covert discrimination and prejudice are still all too prevalent in the USA and Europe, and 'race' continues to play a significant role in shaping overall life chances and experiences, the USA and Britain are no longer characterized by rigid socio-political constraints, but rather by a gradual modification of the social and economic parameters dividing White and non-White peoples (Kilson 1975: 255), and by ideologies and seemingly legitimate discourses that enable dominant groups to maintain their hegemonic position over subordinate groups (Sidanius and Pratto 1999).

While there is considerable agreement about the persistence of White power, privilege, and racism (see Sears *et al.* 2000), the question of which groups do and do not constitute disadvantaged ethnic minority groups is now more contested and less clear, in comparison with the past. Groups themselves, including White Americans and Britons, are contesting dominant narratives about the existing racial order.

Although the USA and Britain share in common the shifting ways in which ideas of 'race' and racial oppression feature in these societies, as well as the emergence of a 'White backlash', British debates about racial inequality and disadvantage differ from those in the USA. One aspect of the British debate that especially interested me was the assertion by some British analysts that an over-arching racial hierarchy, in which groups are placed in a top-down fashion to indicate their relative degree of privilege or disadvantage, was intellectually and politically unacceptable. A key implication of such an argument was that White ethnic minorities such as Jewish and Irish people were not necessarily more privileged or less disadvantaged than non-White ethnic minorities such as African Caribbean and South Asian Britons. One would be hard pressed to find a US sociologist who would make such a claim about the status of White ethnic minorities in the USA. The contrasting ways in which arguments about racial oppression are articulated in the two countries got me thinking about some of the difficulties involved in arguments made about racial hierarchies more generally.

A comparison of the USA and Britain engendered many questions about the nature and clarity of arguments concerning racial hierarchies: For instance, on what bases or criteria do analysts claim that racial hierarchies exist? How are racial hierarchies said to be formed around specific cultural, social, political, and economic circumstances in the USA and Britain? How and why do racial hierarchies still matter? These questions are also complicated by the fact that distinctive yet simultaneous hierarchies can occur along various dimensions of experience, whether these be based upon race, class, or gender locations.

While I cannot provide a comprehensive historical comparison of the two countries here (or a systematic discussion of all groups in these countries), I briefly discuss the dominant thinking and debates concerning racial oppression and hierarchies in the USA and Britain. Contemporary debates about racial hierarchies, including discourses about how we conceptualize the racial disadvantage and oppression of specific groups, have taken rather different forms in the two countries – not least because of their distinctive histories and their disparate ethnic and racial compositions.

In addition to the fact that there is no one definition or understanding of what racial hierarchies are across the two countries, or the fact that arguments about hierarchy make reference to many different domains of experience, I found that many arguments about racial disadvantage are highly charged and politically sensitive. Furthermore understanding and assessment of British and US debates were mediated by my own status as an Asian American woman who has lived in Britain since 1991.

The USA: a recognized racial hierarchy

In the USA, there appears to be a fairly widespread view, at least among many academics, that White Americans are at the top of a racial hierarchy, African Americans at the bottom (with sporadic reference to Native Americans as an equally oppressed group), and groups such as Asian Americans and Latinos somewhere in between.[1] For example, Vilna Bashi and Antonio McDaniel state: 'The very idea of race assumes a hierarchy of racial groups. Within this hierarchy, Africans were [and still are] on the bottom and Europeans on top' (1997: 671). One of the few analysts who has studied the Black experience in both the USA and Britain, Stephen Small, has observed: 'Black people continue to face problems which no non-Black people ever face....As people of African descent, our culture, institutions, values and history still remain the most vilified of all racialised groups' (1994b: 197).

Many analysts in the USA believe that the historical legacy of slavery is fundamental in explaining the relatively disadvantaged status of many African Americans today (see Dawson 1994; Collins 2001; Ogbu 1990). Joe Feagin, in *Racist America*, notes the 'high level of white effort and energy put into maintaining antiblack racism' as one of the many reasons why African Americans are at the bottom of the racial hierarchy (2000: 207). In other words, White Americans have simply expended much less time and energy in exploiting and oppressing other groups such as Asian Americans and Latino Americans. Both in the past and in the present, each new non-European immigrant group in the USA is 'placed, principally by the dominant whites, somewhere on a *white-to-black status continuum*, the commonplace measuring stick of social acceptability' (Feagin 2000: 210, emphasis original). Feagin also argues that, viewed historically, African Americans 'have been oppressed much longer by whites than any other group except Native Americans' (2000: 206). Given the extraordinary history of enslavement and Jim Crow laws (Woodward 1966), such an experience of racial oppression and struggle is historically distinct from the kinds of racial subordination and disadvantage suffered by other groups (ibid.).

In addition to arguments about their distinctive historical treatment and experiences, African Americans have fared badly according to various socio-economic indicators (see Bonilla-Silva 1999). The following aggregate statistics illustrate how stark the disparities are in the quality of life between Black and White Americans: on average, Black families earn about 60 per cent of what White families earn, and survive on roughly 12 per cent of the wealth of average White families. As individuals, their life spans are 6 to 7 years shorter than Whites (Feagin 2000: 202).

Both in the past and in the present, African Americans have often been the victims of horrific racial attacks, and this is reflected in the media attention devoted to events such as the beating of Rodney King by Los Angeles policemen in 1992, or the heinous murder of James Byrd, who was tortured and dismembered by White supremacists in the South. There is also research in the USA which suggests that White Americans' 'anti-black orientation' is deep, and filled with fear and loathing, and that they feel less distance and hostility in relation to other Americans of color (Frankenberg 1993; Feagin 2000; Shih 2002).

So where are other minority groups positioned, in relation to White and African Americans? Various analysts suggest that Asian Americans are an intermediate group, between Whites at the top and Blacks at the bottom of a racial hierarchy (see Feagin 2000; Gans 1999; Kibria 1998; Matsuda 1993; Okihiro 1994).[2] In fact, Vijay Prashad (2000) suggests that South Asian Americans are effectively honorary Whites. Claire Kim (1999) argues that Asian Americans have been 'racially triangulated' in relation to Black and White Americans: Whites valorize Asian Americans in comparison with Blacks on cultural and racial grounds, enabling Whites to refute the legitimate claims and grievances of African Americans. At the same time, Whites engage in 'civic ostracism' by constructing Asian Americans as alien and unassimilable. As such, White Americans manage to retain their dominant, privileged positions in society. Latinos, too, who comprise a very heterogeneous group (Nelson and Tienda 1988), are sometimes said to occupy an intermediate position, between White and Black Americans – though there is less consensus about their placement on a hierarchy, not least because there are Black, Brown, and White Latinos.

While anti-Arab and anti-Muslim prejudice is not new in the USA, post-September 11th, there has been heightened awareness of racial hatred and prejudice against people deemed Arab or Muslim. Nevertheless, the Middle Eastern and Arab populations in the USA are very small, and the evidence of 'Islamophobia' is not likely to challenge fundamentally (at least for the foreseeable future) the widespread consensus that there is a racial hierarchy in the USA, with Whites at the top and African Americans at the bottom.

Britain: a 'hierarchy of oppression'?

In Britain, unlike the USA, most research has (until recently) stressed the *commonality* of experience of ethnic minorities in relation to the White majority, based upon a disadvantaged status in relation to the housing and labor markets, racial abuse, and certain forms of social exclusion and marginalization. Most British analysts do not conceive of ethnic minority experiences in terms of a top-down hierarchy. This may be because, in Britain, many South Asians and African Caribbeans have shared in common the history of British colonialism in the Indian sub-continent, the Caribbean, Africa, and South Asia (though the experiences of these populations have been clearly distinct in each of these places). Although slavery did reach the shores of England during the second half of the sixteenth century, and slavery itself ended as late as 1838 (only 30 years before its abolition in the USA), slavery in the USA was more widespread and integral in economic and social terms (see Walvin 1985; Shyllon 1974).

In Britain, the stress has been on the shared experiences of many non-White immigrants, who were former colonial subjects, coming to Britain in the postwar period to work in predominantly unskilled or semi-skilled jobs as disadvantaged minorities (see Solomos 2003; Miles 1989; Sivanandan 1982).

The stress on commonality, however, has not precluded the emergence of distinctive representations of these groups. For instance, some South Asian people, especially post-*The Satanic Verses* and September 11th, encounter racial epithets concerning their putative foreignness, which stress, among other things, their distinctive religious beliefs and their wearing of saris, turbans, and salwaar kameez. Tariq Modood (1994, 1996) has pointed to the importance of understanding the dynamics of 'cultural racism', which is said to be targeted at certain groups that are seen as being assertively different from the wider society, such as South Asians – though he does not mention the visibility of Hasidic Jews.

In recent years, British Muslims have increasingly been defined in terms of negativity and alienation, drawing on notions of an emergent Pakistani and Bangladeshi underclass (Alexander 2000: 6–7). Mainstream media reports have tended to whip up fears about Middle Eastern and South Asian people (and especially young men), depicting them as fanatical and dangerous religious zealots in our midst. This negative depiction of Asians had been preceded by their former representation as foreign, but law abiding and unproblematic – especially in comparison with the representation of African Caribbeans as muggers and Rastafarian drug dealers (Alexander 2000).

While the recognition of Islamophobia has helped to transcend the commonly criticized Black–White binary and to broaden the frameworks for theorizing racism in Britain (Silverman and Yuval-Davis 1999), it has also engendered heated debate about racial hierarchies. Tariq Modood has notably claimed, 'I think it is already the case in Britain now, as it has been in Europe for some time, that the extra-European origin group that suffers the worst prejudice and exclusion are working-class Muslims' (1996: 12) – a view that may or may not be upheld by Asian Muslims themselves. Arguing along similar lines, Muhammad Anwar states that:

> it is clear that they [Asians] face double discrimination, racial and reli-gious. It appears that white people express more prejudice against Asians and Muslims than against [Black] Caribbeans. Recent examples include Muslim girls being refused jobs because of their dress and Sikh pupils refused school admission because of their turbans.
>
> (1998: 186)

To suggest that one ethnic minority group suffers the worst prejudice and exclusion has been unacceptable to many British analysts, both on intellec-tual and political grounds. Tariq Modood has been accused of positing a 'hierarchy of oppression', which tends to deny the prejudicial experiences of White minorities, such as Jewish and Irish people in Britain (see Walter 1998). According to Mary Hickman, 'When disadvantages experienced by Irish people are acknowledged this is usually accompanied by the notion of a "hierarchy of oppression" based on the idea that no white group could expe-rience the level of racism which a black group can' (1998: 289).

One point that a number of scholars in Britain has made is that many kinds of signifiers of both phenotypical and cultural differences have been used in relation to both 'visible minorities' (Ballard 1996) and White ethnics over time (Anthias and Yuval-Davis 1992; Mac an Ghaill 1999). So claims that it is people of color who *exclusively* suffer certain forms of racial-ization, based upon their non-White physical appearance, are contested. For instance, in relation to the signifiers attributed to Semitic features (see Gilman 1985), Phil Cohen (1996) suggests that Jewish people have been racialized, and he refutes the suggestion that Asian Muslims suffer more or worse racial prejudice than Jewish and Irish people, based on the presump-tion that being White in Britain has shielded them from racial discrimination and prejudice.

In contrast to the US situation (in which a predominantly anti-Black conception of racism is employed), it is much more common in Britain for analysts to identify a variety of racisms that are flourishing in contemporary Europe, including anti-Jewish, anti-Muslim, anti-Arab, anti-Turk, anti-African and anti-Gypsy racism (Brah 1996: 167) – despite the view by some, such as Bronwen Walter (1998), that racism suffered by Irish and Jewish people is yet to be seriously acknowledged. While many British analysts acknowledge that each of these racisms has its own specific history and characteristic features, the implication of such a wide-ranging list of racisms, discussed together, is that they are somehow equivalent and compa-rable. By comparison, the coupling of anti-Jewish and anti-African racisms would rarely appear in US studies, for the dominant understanding there is that such disparate forms of racisms are not equivalent.[3]

Although many British analysts are sympathetic about putting Asian experiences on the map, and about conceding that 'race' is more than about Black and White (an understanding that is regarded as reductive in its emphasis upon color-based racism), they resist what they perceive to be a model of racial victimology that renders invisible the disadvantages experienced by White minorities in Britain. Another reason why some British analysts refute Modood's argument is that, in addition to privileging and valorizing the oppressed status of Asian Muslims, it appears to disregard the notion of racial solidarity or shared problems, in its pursuit of an essentialized category (Alexander, forthcoming).

Difficulties with assertions of racial hierarchy

My characterization of the debates in the USA and Britain are clearly generalized, but in comparison with the USA, there is more contentiousness about whether or not it makes sense to conceive of Britain's ethnic minority experiences in terms of a racial hierarchy, or, if you will, a 'hierarchy of oppression'. The general consensus in Britain appears to be that the concept of hierarchy is not appropriate in describing the British ethnic/racial landscape. A further argument made by some is that it is politically unacceptable to assert such a 'hierarchy of oppression'. By comparison, in the USA, there is a fairly robust consensus that there is a racial hierarchy (with Whites on top, Blacks on the bottom, and Asians and Latinos somewhere in between). So while arguments about racial hierarchy in Britain are still relatively recent and considered to be very controversial, the belief that a stable and tenacious racial hierarchy exists is almost a truism in the USA.

In reviewing the US and British writings on 'race', I found myself dissatisfied with the dominant perspectives on racial hierarchy in *both* countries. While I will focus primarily on the problems with US thinking on a racial hierarchy, I do not think that British debates on this issue are unproblematic either. I found that there is often little discussion in both US and British literatures about the bases or criteria underlying the assertion of racial hierarchies.

It doesn't help that the concept of racial oppression is so murky and so vast. For example, in comparison with measures of racial attacks, how relevant are factors such as a group's average family income, or the nature of their representation in the popular media, for the overall assessment of how a group fares? There are many and different (though in many ways related) dimensions of a group's status and experience.

Turning to examples from the USA, while a group (such as African Americans) is disadvantaged across many socio-economic domains, it is possible that it may be in a relatively privileged position along other areas of social experience. Conversely, a group (such as Asian Americans) that fares relatively well, according to a number of socio-economic indicators, may be relatively disadvantaged according to other criteria. Most analysts do recognize that groups' experiences can differ across various domains, but in many studies of 'race' and racial inequality, the concept of a top-down hierarchy is often used as a short-hand to convey an overall ranking or positioning of groups, so that specific experiences along particular axes or domains of experience tend to be obscured by this broad and static ranking of groups.

There is evidence that, along many socio-economic indicators, African Americans, Native Americans, and Latino Americans fare worse than Asian Americans and White Americans (Feagin 2000; Sidanius and Pratto 1999). Despite the fact that most US analysts (either implicitly or explicitly) point to African Americans as the most racially oppressed group, some data concerning African Americans, Native Americans, and Latino Americans do not always bear out this view.

In comparison with numerically small groups such as Native Americans, who constitute only 1 per cent of the population (US Census 1990), African Americans comprise 12 per cent of the population and their experiences are regarded as paradigmatic of racial oppression in the USA. However, when compared with some other minority groups, African Americans fare better than some Latino sub-groups and Native Americans on certain socio-economic indicators. For instance, according to the 1990 US Census, Puerto Ricans' poverty rate was 38 per cent (African Americans 32 per cent), their percentage obtaining a university degree was 10 per cent (African Americans 12 per cent), and their home ownership rate was 23 per cent (African Americans 31 per cent).

Another key issue that arises in US discussions about racial hierarchy is the differential historical treatment of groups. It can be difficult, if not impossible, to compare the historical experiences and treatment of certain groups. How do we compare the genocide of Native Americans with the enslavement of African Americans? Native Americans are still an extremely disadvantaged group. Native Americans' indicators for median family income and poverty rate are almost identical to those of African Americans, but their percentage obtaining a university degree was only 9 per cent (African Americans 12 per cent) (US Census 1990). In many parts of the USA, it is literally possible to forget about Native Americans as a disadvantaged group because they suffer from post-genocide invisibility. Yet it would be unsustainable to argue that Native Americans have been *more* racially oppressed than African Americans, and the recognition of Native American genocide does not derogate the severity of slavery and Jim Crow. Such a comparison is akin to comparing apples and oranges. Furthermore, if we are to consider the historical treatment of disparate groups, how should understandings of racial hierarchy include and conceive of the status and experiences of asylum seekers and other disadvantaged migrants who are recently arrived?

The US literature on racial inequality (rightly) puts a heavy emphasis upon socio-economic criteria in assertions about the location of groups along a racial hierarchy. While socio-economic data regarding various groups is crucial for assessing a group's overall experience, some measures of socio-economic well-being, in isolation from other criteria, can also obscure the multifaceted experiences of different groups. Although it is undeniably important, socio-economic well-being does not translate simply and directly into social and political forms of power and prestige (Song 2003).

Many studies have argued that Asian Americans occupy an intermediate status in the US racial landscape. While there is certainly some basis for this argument, as an Asian American myself, I feel that this broad categorization of Asian Americans eclipses the great heterogeneity of Asian American experience, by class, ethnicity, and histories of settlement. Much specific information can be lost, for instance, by grouping together poor, working-class Laotians, Korean immigrant store owners, and professional third-generation Chinese Americans. Conversely, while African Americans are socio-economically disadvantaged as a whole, there is a significant sector of African Americans who are middle class, and much more privileged than their poor, inner-city, and rural co-ethnics (Grant *et al.* 1996; Landry 1987).

In the USA, although Asian Americans are relatively privileged according to socio-economic indicators:

> Asian-Americans as a group do not own the major corporations of banks which control access to capital. They do not own massive amounts of real estate, control the courts or city government, have ownership of the mainstream media, dominate police forces, or set urban policies.
>
> (Marable 1995: 199)

In fact, they are relatively under-represented in politics and public life more generally (Lien 1997). Asian Americans are explicitly targeted by jokes and physical intimidation in the mass media and public spaces (Tuan 1998). By comparison, it is considered politically incorrect to make racist jokes about Blacks or Latinos.

Some of my skepticism about generalized arguments concerning the privileged status of Asian Americans stems from personal experiences of racial harassment and social exclusion in addition to feelings of invisibility in wider US culture and politics (Song 2001). I have always found the 'model minority' stereotype to be quite double-edged, and not a straightforwardly positive resource (Wong *et al.* 1998; Kibria 1998).

While there is significant empirical evidence of structured, institutionalized forms of inequality and subordination in relation to African Americans, some recent studies also suggest the need to explore the various forms of cultural and social capital possessed by Black Americans (see Young 1999; Carter 2000). While Black Americans have endured severe discrimination, they also have access to numerous co-ethnic institutions, such as colleges, churches, and powerful political associations, such as the National Association for the Advancement of Colored People (NAACP). In contrast, many Asians and Latinos may be subject to less segregation and discrimination, but they are still largely culturally and institutionally invisible in the USA – though their presence and power are subject to regional variations in the size of these groups.

The notion of racial hierarchy in the USA has relied upon a rather unitary (i.e. anti-Black) understanding of racism and racial disadvantage. This is now changing, with the growth of Asian and Latino scholars, who are documenting the many and diverse experiences of sub-groups contained within the categories of Asian and Latino (see Nieman-Flores 1999). In recent years, social psychologists researching the effects of racism have also begun to question whether models of racial identity based on the experiences of African Americans (the group most studied regarding the effects of racial prejudice in the USA) are adequate to understand the racial and ethnic identities of other groups, such as Latino and Asian Americans (see Murrell 1998: 194; Crocker and Quinn 1998).

It is important that generalized assertions of hierarchy, which provide an important macro-picture of how groups fare, do not obscure or overlook the specificities of group experiences. Comparisons of the disparate experiences of groups, and their location along a hierarchy, are bound to be difficult and complicated, given the many dimensions of group experience, some of which are not directly or easily comparable.

In defense of racial hierarchy

Turning to Britain, I find myself quite ambivalent about certain aspects of the British debate (which, I realize, is not totally unified). On the one hand, I welcome the emphasis upon pluralistic and inclusive understandings of racialized experiences, so that, for example, anti-Semitism, anti-Romany, anti-Celtic, and anti-Irish racisms are recognized. On the other hand, if my reading of the British debate is accurate, I am not entirely comfortable with one implication of this debate – that to question the equivalence of these disparate racisms is automatically divisive and suspect.

Despite the difficulties I have identified in US arguments made about racial hierarchies – namely (1) the lack of clarity and consensus about which criteria we should consider in assessing the existence of racial hierarchies and (2) the privileging of socio-economic indicators at the expense of other domains of experience – I do not necessarily object to the idea of a racial hierarchy *per se*, in which the *nature and intensity* of groups' racialized experiences are assessed and compared. I would, however, like to see a less rigid and monolithic theorizing of racial hierarchies, which is based upon the experiences of a wide range of groups, and which can register more sensitively the various and sometimes contradictory domains of experience.

I disagree with Modood's argument – not because he has considered how the experiences of Asian Muslims may be distinct from those of other minority groups in Britain, but because I do not think that he has substantiated his claim that Asian Muslims are in fact the most racially oppressed group in Britain. Even now, in Britain, the recognition that Muslims are the object of racial attacks, especially post-September 11th, in no way means that African Caribbeans or Jews will experience less severe or fewer incidents of racism. Unfortunately, articulations of racisms are not a zero-sum pie.

Our necessarily subjective perceptions of the nature and degree of racial prejudice – however important and relevant they may be – cannot be the basis for claims that a particular group suffers more or worse racial prejudice and discrimination than another. This also applies to my argument about disaggregating and questioning the privileged-status Asian Americans, as my argument is undeniably based upon my subjective experiences as an Asian American. While such perceptions cannot stand on their own, they can be the starting point for a careful, empirically based study of particular groups' experiences.

Despite the difficulties in actually documenting or measuring such differences, we should not overlook the possibility that some groups experience *particular or distinctive* forms of racial abuse or disadvantage more frequently or more intensely than other groups. Regional differences in the treatment and experiences of groups are also possible – as suggested in Larry Ray and David Smith's (2000) study in the Manchester area about White male racists' attitudes toward Asians, as opposed to African Caribbeans. The recognition of multiple forms of racism as experienced by many different groups should not preclude an empirically based exploration of the variable impact and intensity of racisms and racial oppression across disparate groups.

Investigating the nature and intensity of many different kinds of racialized experiences should not be dismissed as merely fanning the flames of identity politics, even if there are potentially divisive implications in doing so. Even if we dismiss the argument that Muslims (or, for that matter, any other group) are the most oppressed group in Britain, as having no empirical basis, it is important that we do not operate in a climate in which analysts feel unable to ask questions about the differential experiences of groups – despite the recognition that ethnic and racial alliances must be fostered and that there is much that is still commonly shared among racialized minorities in both Britain and the USA.

(Unintentionally) rocking the boat

Critical discussions concerning arguments about racial hierarchies are further complicated by the fact that it is difficult to divorce the personal and political investments of groups (and analysts) from debates about racial hierarchy. One reason why Tariq Modood's claims about the ultra-oppressed position of Asian Muslims in Britain has been treated with not only dismay, but also suspicion, is that some British analysts believe that he is shamelessly supporting his own team. It is understandable that who we are as people – in terms of gender, class, ethnicity, and nationality – fundamentally frames not only our everyday perceptions but also the research questions that engage and fascinate us (Twine 2000). But one danger that accompanies our awareness of our personal backgrounds and issues is that our particular interests and experiences may limit, as well as enhance, our ability to critically assess debates that concern the groups to which we belong.

As an Asian American woman, I could (reasonably) be assumed to be personally invested in debates about exactly where Asian Americans fit into the US racial landscape, because I grew up in the USA, and I call myself an Asian American. By challenging what I believed to be (1) an overly generalized depiction of African Americans as uniformly disadvantaged across all spheres of social life and (2) an overly generalized characterization of Asian Americans as a privileged, 'intermediate' group in the racial hierarchy, is my perspective influenced by the fact that I am Asian American? Absolutely. My own perceptions and experiences of what it means to be Asian American have been encapsulated within my racial assignment as an Asian American woman and, while I am sensitive to the racialized experiences of other groups, I am most attuned to the particularities of my own experiences. However, this realization does not in itself invalidate the necessarily partial perspective I offer here.

In raising questions about racial hierarchy, I worried that I would be met by some hostile readings of both my intentions and thoughts, especially in the USA. Because of the strength of feeling about the special status of African Americans (which, understandably, may be in need of protection, given the on-going tide of 'White backlash'), I felt like I was going out on a limb, by querying what felt like a long-standing academic orthodoxy about the racial order in the USA. Over the years, I have felt that certain lines of inquiry are implicitly 'no go areas', and I have bristled against the sense of being intellectually straitjacketed.

I was especially worried that African American scholars and students might perceive my intervention as somehow belittling or denying the racial oppression they have suffered and continue to suffer in the USA. I have no intention of questioning the severity of African American oppression, either in the past or the present. Politicos keen to deny the continuing reality of African American oppression could, conceivably, employ such a view to argue that African Americans are not particularly disadvantaged any longer. I have no wish to bolster such an agenda. The very fact that I feel the need to justify my critical interest in racial hierarchy reveals how worried I have been about offending American, and especially African American, scholars.

Having lived in Britain for over a decade, another concern of mine was that I was out of touch with events and the political climate in the USA. While this is possible, I think that my location outside the USA has given me some degree of intellectual space and freedom to query dominant modes of thinking from a different perspective – one admittedly shaped by a very different social and political history and context.

The writing of this paper has entailed a different set of worries concerning a British audience.

As discussed earlier, I am rather uneasy with one implication of a pluralistic and seemingly equalizing 'cartography of racism' in Britain – that to make any direct comparisons about the varying nature and intensities of racisms and racialized experiences (whether between different 'visible' minorities or between White and 'visible' minorities) would be frowned upon. But in espousing this position, I was concerned that I would be seen as a 'typical' American imposing yet one more American paradigm onto the case of Britain. In recent years, analysts such as Bourdieu and Wacquant have complained of the imperialistic tendencies of North American intellectual argument: 'so today numerous topics directly issuing from the intellectual confrontations relating to the social particularity of American society and of its universities have been imposed, in apparently de-historicized form, upon the whole planet' (1999: 41). While wholesale impositions of American theory and paradigms (including an imposition of the US racial hierarchy model) onto Britain (or elsewhere) would clearly be inappropriate and unjustifiable, I would argue that an outright dismissal of the idea of a racial hierarchy in Britain (as seems to be suggested by some analysts) may not be desirable either; perhaps we can consider the utility of an adapted and less rigid understanding of hierarchy in relation to Britain.

Conclusion

The discussion of racial hierarchy in relation to Britain and the USA has illustrated that the conceptualization of groups' disparate experiences along a racial hierarchy is specific to national contexts, and is fundamentally shaped by the differing populations, histories, and political climates of each country. The notion of racial hierarchy appears to make more sense in relation to the contemporary USA than Britain, where the histories and experiences of diverse formerly colonized people – African Caribbeans, Asians, and the Chinese – are more similar than are the distinct modes of incorporation of US ethnic minority groups. However, the recognition that the concept of racial hierarchy may fit the USA better than Britain does not mean that (1) we should not compare the racialized experiences of disparate groups, or (2) automatically dismiss arguments which suggest that some groups may be, in *some* respect, more racially oppressed than others.

A willingness by US analysts to be more pluralistic in their conceptions of racialized experiences would result in a more dynamic and less monolithic understanding of racial hierarchy in the USA, just as the willingness of British analysts to seriously consider claims about the potentially different nature and intensity of racialized experiences would open up British debates.

It is evident that discussion about racial hierarchy can be politically sensitive and fraught. Assertions about racial hierarchy can entail invidious comparisons between groups and can thus contribute to inter-ethnic tensions and divisiveness. Groups are invested in particular narratives about their experiences and positions in relation to others (Blumer 1958), and there is a real political stake underlying discussions about racial hierarchy. This is why debates about racial hierarchy tend to be charged with a tenor of group competition. Amidst the scramble for scarce group resources, and against a backdrop in which disparate groups may know very little about each other, there can be little room for empathy.

Racial inequalities continue to exist in both the USA and Britain, and their intersection with other forms of inequality and disadvantage is complex. I believe that the concept of racial hierarchy can be helpful – however flawed the arguments about hierarchy may be – in investigations of racialized experiences across groups. However, this framework needs to be adapted to take into account the many different axes or domains of social experience and, as discussed earlier, there is no consensus about which criteria are the most fundamental in the operation of racial hierarchies.

We must be aware that the collective positioning of increasingly diverse groups within an over-arching racial hierarchy may obscure important forms of internal variation within groups and complex forms of stratification inter-weaving class, gender, and race. Studies addressing the concept of racial hierarchy also need to pay more attention to complex inter-ethnic relations, and to contested narratives about the particular experiences of different groups. The growing intermingling of groups, and the fact that it is increasingly common to possess a 'mixed' heritage, also attests to the significant racial complexity of both the US and British populations. Furthermore, the claims made by diasporic communities, migrants, and asylum seekers for both equality and inclusion in society, as well as claims to difference, should also inform our understandings of disadvantaged or excluded groups (see Schuster and Solomos 2002).

In our explorations of groups' racialized experiences, we also need to achieve a balance between the recognition of differential group trajectories and histories, and the fact that various processes of racialization are often mutually constitutive of one another. We need to know more about how racial hierarchies are formed around specific social, economic, political, and cultural circumstances in the USA and Britain.

Notes

1   However, some analysts eschew a top-down hierarchy framework. Michael Omi and Howard Winant (1994) delineate the historically variable processes of racialization of different minority groups, pointing to the genocide suffered by Native Americans, African American slavery, the colonization of Mexicans, and the exclusion of Asian Americans (see Kim 1999: 105).

2   For a historical example of how the Chinese in Mississippi actively worked at occupying an intermediate position between White and Black Americans, see Loewen (1971).

3   In Britain, Whiteness is increasingly problematized in terms of class differences between working and middle-class White Britons, and in terms of ethnic and religious differences between Jewish, Welsh, Scottish, Irish Catholics, and White English Protestants (Jenkins

1997). By comparison much of the discourse around Whiteness in the USA concerns the gradual consolidation of groups known as White (or 'honorary' Whites) and the many privileges assumed to be associated with Whiteness (see Waters 1990; Frankenberg 1993; Dyer 1997).

13 Experiences in ethnographic interviewing about race

The inside and outside of it

Alford A. Young, Jr

A common feature of qualitative research endeavors is the quest to establish intimate or sustained interaction with research subjects in presumably 'natural' settings. In essence, the researcher steps into, and to varying degrees shares in, the social worlds of the individuals under study. Scholars who engage this form of research are forced to continuously reflect upon and account for the depth and quality of their relationships to the individuals, situations, and conditions comprising their research agenda. In fact, in the past 30 years there has been a period of rich dialogue about these matters. That dialogue is commonly referred to as the insider and outsider debate (Andersen 1993; Baca Zinn 1979; DeVault 1995; Merton 1972; Naples 1996; Stanfield 1993; Wilson 1974).

At stake in this debate is an understanding of the extent to which being socially distant or dissimilar to the kinds of people under study affects both the richness or accuracy of the data being collected and the subsequent analysis that unfolds. An initial underlying presumption in this debate was that researchers who share membership in the same social categories as their respondents (the most common being race, gender, and class) were best suited to uncover ideas, arguments, and opinions about issues and concerns related to those people or to those social categories (Merton 1972). A corollary presumption was that those researchers who do not share such membership either had to work especially hard to acquire the trust and confidence of respondents, or else accept that their scholarly analysis and interpretation may not reflect the veracity, depth, or subtlety that emerges from so-called 'insider' research. In reacting to these presumptions, qualitative field researchers strove to address whether and, if so, how greater ease, comfort, comprehension, and transparency could be established in the course of research, especially if such researchers occupied extreme outsider statuses. These efforts led field researchers to explore more critically the epistemological implications of either working to further their insider statuses or to confront the problems resulting from their outsider statuses (Andersen 1993; Baca Zinn 1979; De Andrade 2000; DeVault 1995; Ladner 1998; Naples 1996; Venkatesh 2002; Wilson 1974).

As most of these discussions centered on exploring the possibilities for increasing, maintaining, or reconciling the difficulties of securing insider status, an implicit value was placed upon the insider position as the location that is most conducive for data collection.[1] The belief was that functioning from this position would enable the researcher to acquire the most meaningful, accurate, and honest data. Outsider positions were taken to be less constructive, if not all together detrimental, for conducting qualitative research. This chapter problematizes that notion. I argue here that it is not always the case that occupying outsider positions necessarily inhibits a researcher from acquiring rich and insightful qualitative data. As a challenge to the problematically narrow preoccupation with increasing insiderness, my objective in this chapter is to promote a reconsideration of outsider statuses. In doing so, I explore how the maintenance of rapport in the field can be threatened, if not altogether ruptured, by certain kinds of insider statuses.

My argument is rooted in my experience as a qualitative researcher of people who share my race, gender, and age statuses, and who were reared, as I was, in an urban, low-income social environment. Consequently, my claims about the virtues of being on the outside come from my occupying a position of extreme insiderness as a researcher and, therefore, suffering through the tensions that I will discuss later in this chapter. In making my case, I first briefly explore how the insider–outsider debate has unfolded around research on race in US sociology, the sub-field in which my work is most directly situated. I then provide accounts from my own fieldwork experiences to call attention to some virtues of the outsider position. I conclude by situating my experiences in some recent arguments about the significance, utility, and power of outsider statuses in sociological theory, and in qualitative field research in the area of race and ethnicity.

Race and the insider–outsider debate in US sociology

Qualitative research on race and ethnicity has been a central point of emphasis in the insider–outsider debate. In large part, this is due to the fact that, as a principle mechanism of structuration and social division, race occupies a particular place of importance in US social and societal relations. It is used to demarcate who is allowed entry into various social arenas and settings, more so by informal or non-legally sanctioned practice today in the USA rather than by means of the Jim Crow segregation policies of earlier times. Thus, race factors into the creation of multiple sites for insider–outsider divisions to emerge. Accordingly, field research initiatives on matters of race and race relations have been the site for myriad deliberations and debates about the insider and outsider statuses of the researcher. In terms of social scientific scholarship explorations of race in the USA, one needs to turn back no further than to the 1960s to discover why and how the issue of the insider–outsider debate became an overwhelming preoccupation in sociology.

At the end of the 1960s, US sociology was subjected to a strong critique by a new generation of African American sociologists who challenged the discipline's potential to provide intimate and in-depth analyses of the African American social experience (Ladner 1998). It was not incidental that this debate began to unfold at the end of the decade in which many highly publicized and well-read studies of African Americans, particularly ethnographic accounts, were produced by non-African American scholars (Hannerz 1970; Liebow 1967; Moynihan 1965; Rainwater 1970; Schutz 1969; Stack 1974). Prior to the 1960s, sociological research on African Americans was largely carried out by African American scholars (the most prominent of whom include Horace Cayton, St Claire Drake, W.E.B. Du Bois, E. Franklin Frazier, and Charles S. Johnson) who stepped into highly racially segregated communities to conduct their work. The legally enforced extreme segregation that many African Americans were subjected to prior to the 1960s meant that African American sociologists of that time rarely experienced the kind of social or geographic distance that would have made them appear as outsiders in any critical way to the black Americans that they studied. Undoubtedly, in some cases there were extreme class differences between these scholars and those in their research populations, but the segregation experienced by even the most privileged African Americans meant that the majority of black Americans were forced to occupy a social world of their own that often made them mutually familiar, if not intimately connected, across class lines. However, the social transformations in the 1960s ruptured these relations.

The civil rights movement, a rapid rise in urban unrest, and a domestic policy agenda centered on the reduction of poverty resulted in the African American community becoming a major preoccupation for many in mainstream America (Katz 1989; O'Connor 2001). This attention led to a private and publicly funded docket of research on black Americans, mostly in urban communities. Many non-African American sociologists and other social scientists poured into these communities to conduct this research. This development soon led to deep reflection on and consideration of the extent to which non-African American scholars could appropriately immerse themselves into African American communities in order to uncover and interpret their social and cultural dynamics.

It was in the midst of these developments that African American scholars and conscientious lay people argued that strong commitments to cultural awareness, understanding, and sensitivity were crucial for the crafting of legitimate scholarly forays into African American communities.[2] For these and other black Americans in the 1960s, the pejorative implications of the culture of poverty argument necessitated that only African Americans pursue cultural analyses of black America. This was because the arguments associated with the culture of poverty thesis centered on profligate cultural traits and characteristics, and this became a pervasive ideological framework for assessing African American life during that time. While this perspective was disseminating, a counter-argument emerged. It claimed that only African American scholars could discern the intricacies and complexities of African American culture and social organization in ways that put black Americans on equal footing with others in American life.[3]

Since the 1960s-era debates on this matter, a range of developments, including the turn toward the epistemological implications of reflexivity and subjectivity in social analysis, promoted a commitment by social scientists not only to critically evaluate their relationships to the people that they studied, but also to position these considerations more directly at the center of their research. More specifically, this initiative involved researchers' effort to document both the extent to which they developed intimate or substantive ties to the people in their studies and the enduring difficulties in trying to secure and maintain such ties in the effort to make substantive arguments about these people. These developments were not directly spawned by researchers of the African American community, but rather impacted qualitative sociological studies of black Americans by carving out a space for detailed discussion of how researchers grappled with the impediments and tensions involved with the intimate study of this constituency. Hence, this unfolding has led to the rethinking of the insider–outsider dichotomy in social research.

Rethinking the insider–outside dichotomy

Contemporarily, the insider–outsider debate has reached a point where the rigid dichotomization of insider and outsider positions has been called into question. It has been argued more recently that the biases and shortcomings associated with a researcher's occupation of an outsider status can sometimes be overcome or managed by the researcher's explicit acknowledgment of the existence of social distance or categorical dissimilarities between him or her and the individuals under study. Indeed, more thorough assessments of a researcher's distance or dissimilarity to the people under study, coupled with the researcher's declaration that no attempt was made to artificially or simplistically reduce or resolve these circumstances, have been woven into many of the contemporary qualitative studies that involve extending beyond racial and ethnic boundaries (Bourgois 2003; Lamont 2002; Venkatesh 2000; Waters 1999). Moreover, it has become customary to include an appendix or a preface that illustrates exactly how the researcher engaged the field and established rapport with the individuals who were the central points of concern in the research. Indeed, in some cases attention was drawn to these issues throughout the body of the work itself. The point of this effort was to demonstrate to audiences how much researchers were aware of biases or shortcomings in their approach to field sites, which then conveyed a sense of legitimacy about their resulting work.[4]

The effort to more explicitly and provocatively explore how insider–outsider categories apply to researchers is a key advance over early claims that any extreme outsider status threatens the validity of the research. Accordingly, another key advance in research over the past three decades has been to open up considerations of how outsider status factors in the field-work experience, particularly in the development of ties to informants and the cultivation of respondents. One such consideration is the researcher's documentation of how one or more of their outsider characteristics become relevant points of reference in the fieldwork experience. For example, one scholarly commentary (Naples 1996) documents how respondents who initially took the researcher to be an inside member of the community some-times self-defined as outsiders because they felt themselves to adhere to different cultural practices and ways of thinking in comparison to other community members. Although not concerned with any outsider statuses maintained by the researcher, this work provided an important analytical space for rethinking whether and how outsiderness plays into the data collection process in constructive ways.

Another commentary on ethnic identity focused on respondents' inability to immediately discern whether the researcher occupied an ethnic insider status relevant to the research agenda (De Andrade 2000). That inability became a crucial factor for creating conversations in the field about this identity, which ultimately led to what the researcher found to be a rich and insightful pool of data for her project. The author interviewed people of her own nationality (Cape Verdian) about their ethnic consciousness. However, in most of the interviews the respondents made it clear that they were not immediately sure that De Andrade was, herself, of that nationality. In analyzing her experiences, De Andrade offered that the insider position is not static and durable, but is instead dynamic. It is continually recreated throughout the course of one's fieldwork. Her interviews, then, were serial experiences in working to establish and continually maintain an insider status throughout the conversations.

A third commentary (Reinharz 1997) asserts that one or more of a researcher's multiple selves may become relevant in the interactive dynamics of fieldwork. These multiple selves include a researcher's race, gender, or class status, as well as varied aspects of their personality or personal experi-ences. If they do not appear at first sight, any of them could become visible to respondents and informants during the course of fieldwork. More impor-tantly, respondents and informants may react to any of these in ways that foster, hinder, or dramatically affect conversations with the researcher. In essence, respondents and informants may use these features and characteris-tics to determine the ways in which that researcher is an outsider or insider, and adjust their interaction with the researcher accordingly throughout an interview or fieldwork encounter.

These and other investigations have led to the contemporary assertion that there is no singular insider or outsider position that researchers occupy during the course of fieldwork, but rather myriad positions and statuses that can be viewed by respondents either as insider or outsider depending on the social circumstances or conditions affecting the research endeavor (De Andrade 2000; Jackson 2001; Naples 1996; Reinharz 1997). Accordingly, the distinction between insider and outsider status should best be thought of as an analytical rather than experiential divide. Moreover, it has now been accepted that insider and outsider positions are fluid as they are continually restructured, retained, and abandoned during the course of interaction between researchers and respondents (De Andrade 2000; Naples 1996; Reinharz 1997; Riessman 1987; Song and Parker 1995). These more recent commentators have demonstrated that insider status, though crucial for the ultimate advance of field research, is neither easily attainable nor consistently maintainable. Thus, although researchers continue to strive to maximize their insider status, in fact they stand experientially in the midst of ever-shifting configurations of both positions.

We are now at a moment when contemporary social science inquiry has accepted that outsider status not only cannot be fully erased in the course of research, but that it also plays a role in the production of data. Some of these conversations have been about how respondents define themselves as outsiders to distinguish aspects of their identities and experiences, or how respondents' designation of the researcher as an outsider promotes conversation that informs the researcher about certain attitudes, opinions, or world views maintained by these respondents. Despite these advances and transformations, an enduring value is still placed upon the insider status as the privileged position from which to converse with respondents. By this I mean that researchers ultimately aim to increase their insiderness even if they know that they must contend with the various issues concerning outsiderness. Consequently, there is a lack of more critical exploration of how insider status may, in fact, inhibit conversation during specific moments in fieldwork.[5]

Reflections on an insider's dilemma and the outsider possibilities

I claim that outsider status must be given more attention because in certain cases it serves as a causal factor for stimulating important and revealing conversations in the field. In what may seem utterly ironic, I make my case by assessing my experiences in a long-standing engagement in what immediately appears to be extreme insider-situated research. My experiences with qualitative inquiry have largely been centered on studying African American men (a group in which I hold membership) of an age group in which I just recently exited (20–35), and who, like myself, were born and reared in urban, low-income communities.[6] The source of my remarks are my years of intensive fieldwork with low-income African American men in Chicago, all of which culminate in my book *The Minds of Black Men: Making Sense of Mobility, Opportunity, and Future Life Chances* and a manuscript-in-progress tentatively entitled 'American Dreams against the American Dilemma: How Upwardly Mobile Black Men Confront Race' (forthcoming).

Both works reflect my long-standing interest in how young African American men think about mobility processes in US society. Each explores not only how these men contemplate their personal prospects for mobility, but also how those ideas are situated within their understandings of how mobility unfolds for others in US society. *The Minds of Black Men* takes up the case of young men who were born into socio-economic despair and seemingly have extremely limited mobility options. 'American Dreams...' focuses on men who were born in similar circumstances, but who have experienced somewhere between moderate to extreme mobility as young adults. The data for both projects were produced through intensive interviews in the Chicago communities in which these men reside. My experiences in both projects forced me to reconcile with the issues and concerns associated with the insider–outsider debate.

My connection to most of these men began with my having established relationships with two field contacts who worked with residents of two of Chicago's major public housing developments. As my initial field contacts told me some time after I began my work, the insider elements that helped them decide to put me in contact with these men were that, as a black male reared in an impoverished urban community, they accepted my interest in avoiding the hackneyed, voyeuristic accounts that often predominate in explorations of the struggles of poor black men engaged by researchers, journalists, and other investigators. Eventually, many of the men explained to me that they were motivated to share their views with me because my research agenda was focused upon issues far removed from the kinds usually brought to them, and that I was a black male delivering these new agenda issues to them.

When talking with these men, rather than asking about their roles in violent activities or about the histories of failure or frustrations in trying to get ahead, I presented them with a set of seemingly more mundane questions. I wanted to know how they thought that other kinds of people in US society got ahead or what held them back. I also wanted to know what they thought to be good jobs in US society, how they could be found, and what they thought it took to get them. In essence, I wanted to know how some aspects of everyday thought unfolded for these men despite whatever more exotic, fantastic, or tragic circumstances were a part of their life stories. It turned out that some of the more extreme accounts emerged as they told their stories, but only in the midst of my inquiring about the less glamorous concerns that constituted my agenda. Much of the discussion with the more mobile men, which involved talking about how they learned to overcome obstacles and barriers, supplemented the comments about the matters provided by the first set of men. My situations with them, at least in my view, took the form of our conversing about a social world that we generally understood in the same way, but with some caveats and differences in points of view.

From a basic categorical standpoint, I appear to have been an extreme insider in the course of this work. However, the truth of the matter is that at certain moments this experience has been riddled with moments of bewilderment, confusion, and tension, all of which resulted from assumptions that some of these men made about me on the basis of assumed insider connections. In the course of my fieldwork and in the years that followed, I have been drawn to think about the sometimes crippling effects of insider status and the benefits that may come from being a compassionate outsider. That effect is the rupturing of rapport with those individuals whom I studied.

Rapport is immediately assumed to be a product of interaction predicated upon two principal features associated with insider status: intimacy and trustworthiness. The comfort or familiarity that comes with insider status can also promote impatience or confusion when one or more of the interacting parties does not seem to follow the implicit rules of dialogue for people who are familiar with each other.[7] Put more specifically, one may feel that he or she should not have to say certain things to familiar others because those others should already be 'in the know.' Being asked to say something about those things can rupture or at least disturb rapport. A number of encounters that I experienced in my fieldwork demonstrated this fact. I now turn to some cases.

On a hot summer day in 1994 I was in the course of interviewing a 24-year-old man about his views on mobility and opportunity in US society. This gentleman, whom I will call Ken, is a former gang member and ex-convict who was working full time in a small factory and seemingly on his way to moderate socio-economic security and a basic sense of well-being. Much of our initial discussion was about how Ken had moved from gang membership, vice activities, and periodic involvements with violence to an early adulthood of marriage and parenting while still residing in the West Side community where he was reared. While life seemed better at present than it had been in the past, Ken spoke about how precarious his situation was, given that he was only recently in a good job and also quite close (in both social and geographic senses) to the very environment that launched him into gang membership and ultimately a term in prison.

In the midst of conversing about a range of issues associated with the social situations and mobility prospects of African Americans, Ken shared with me his perspective of how black Americans deal with each other over mobility prospects. He expressed disgust with what he believed was the consistent effort of many black Americans to label high-achieving African Americans as universally uncaring about the well-being of poorer African Americans. Ken said:

> First of all for us to become equal we got to sit there and start treating each other, you know, as equals, you know. 'Cause now you got brothers out there now, you dig, with that Goddamn oreo shit, you know. You

know, I know you see it. And then when you tell them 'That's what I hate, every time I see a brother getting over he an oreo.' No, you can tell when a motherfucker is an oreo, you know. It's, man, listen.

Upon uttering his last words, 'It's, man, listen,' he paused and waved his hand as if I had heard enough about a situation that would be familiar to me as an African American. Indeed, I was quite familiar with the expression 'oreo' – a reference to black Americans who are regarded as behaving as if they were white but, due to phenotype, appear quite clearly to be black (thus playing off of the image of the Oreo cookie, constructed from two dark chocolate cookies connected by a white cream filling). I encouraged Ken to continue his narrative but, rather than saying anything more, he looked at me as if he was confused about my request. He finally shrugged his shoulders as if to convey, 'What's more to be said?'

Clearly, I did get Ken's point. In the course of a few years of fieldwork in this neighborhood, I had heard a few men talk about their sense of the problems black Americans have in dealing with each other. I also heard a few black men talk about the lack of support that black men sometimes show for each other. My exposure to these exchanges came about not only in the midst of doing research, but also over many years of participating in street-corner banter in the urban community in which I was raised. My objective in trying to get Ken to speak was not to rectify my ignorance, but to provide me with more data in the form of a more detailed opinion I could record on audio-tape.

I mentioned in my notes that day that, following a second attempt to get Ken to expand on the topic, he looked at me in a puzzled way before shaking his head and appearing to dismiss my efforts. The fact that he not only did not say anything more, but also expressed some mild agitation over my encouraging him to do so, is a minor but crucial example of the detriments of occupying, at least for the portion of our conversation concerning how black Americans feel about each other, the insider position.

This case is an illustration of what a respondent believed need not have been said because, taking into account who he was talking to, he believed the point to have been made. Moreover, this situation demonstrates how impossible it is to know exactly what or how much individuals do not say at certain junctures in an interview because they believe that they are in conversation with someone who fully understands their views. In thinking about this aspect of my conversation with Ken, I was drawn to ponder how much was unsaid amidst the hundreds of hours of dialogues that I had with Chicago-based African American men because they may have felt that this information simply went without saying for someone like myself.

Another critical moment in an unfinished discussion occurred while I was interviewing 'Kwesi,' a 24-year-old gang leader. Kwesi explained to me that, after a few years of active gang involvement during his adolescence, he went on to serve in the Air Force (resulting from a court adjudication following his arrest for involvement in a gang-related incident). The four years that he served put him in contact with a broad range of people, places, and institutions in comparison to his early years as a resident of the impoverished Near West Side community area of Chicago. This exposure, together with involvement in gang-related and vice activity, provided him with a rich repertoire of personal situations and circumstances to draw from in order to explain why he felt that race and class were pivotal factors in determining how people got ahead in life and which people reaped the larger share of societal rewards.

Kwesi made it clear in the course of our first lengthy discussion that he felt as though I shared his general disposition about race and black–white relations in the USA. While he had never been to college, he had encountered enough of the world to figure out that my being an urban-reared, African American male and coming from a university setting implied that I had seen at least a bit of the same social worlds as him. I felt that our previous exchanges allowed him to surmise that I reacted to those social worlds much like he did. His sense of connection with me on these issues was nearly suspended shortly after I asked him the following question, 'Do you agree or disagree that America is a land of opportunity where everybody can get ahead, and everybody gets what they deserve?'

This was a standard question that I asked every man to respond to in each of my studies. While I had some idea that most men would reply in a similarly critical fashion to the question, my interest was in any differences in the precise content and extent of each response. Without hesitation Kwesi responded, 'Oh wow, it was great until you put the last part.' He then broke out in laughter before repeating back to himself the last part of my question, 'Everybody gets what they deserve.' He then continued, 'That last line kind of changed the whole answer right there!' He broke out into more laughter. After taking a minute to scale down his laughter to a slight chuckle, he said, 'But we're going to say "yes."' Almost immediately he then blurted out, 'Strike the last line 'cause black men do not get what they deserve!'

I took it that the 'yes' was a response to the first part of my question, about the USA being a land of opportunity. Having felt as if I had achieved a base level of clarity about his sentiments I continued, with my common follow-up question: 'And what makes you feel that way?' Kwesi leaned back, twisted his face, and then said to me, 'Come on. We need – you just need to juice. You just need to juice, you know.'

The follow-up question seemingly struck him as ridiculous. He did not appear to be very angry, just somewhat bewildered by my asking it. My notes from that day's encounter, taken shortly after our conversation, divulged that Kwesi appeared to be struggling to work out what more I could possibly want of him on this matter – as if I was asking him to fill in a blank when no such blank existed. As it turned out, after having told me to 'juice' (African American vernacular for asking someone to discontinue an activity) he said nothing more, leaned back again, and waited for the next question.

While familiarity did not necessarily breed contempt in the foregoing exchanges between myself and each of these men, it did foster a sense of closure at certain moments in our conversations because neither of them felt obligated to elaborate upon that which they regarded as perfectly understandable to me. In neither case did the interaction seem to involve significant risks or threats to the overall research endeavor, yet each provided a moment to critically reflect upon how a rupturing of rapport can result from an apparent insider's denial of what should be taken as implicit understandings. More importantly, each case serves as a site for considering some deeper questions of the problematics associated with insider status in qualitative research.

To press the case even further, one could simply imagine the situation if I had not been an African American male involved in asking these men to talk about societal rewards as they pertain to mobility and opportunity in US life. The problems that a so-called outsider (in this case, a researcher of a different racial and/or class category) might have in maintaining conversations with these men certainly are not withstanding. These include a lack of trust or comfort between researchers and the people under study, researchers' inability to understand of the terminology or vernacular, or perceived lack of appropriate respect, sensitivity, or appreciation of the cultural attributes of the people under study. However, after taking all of this into account, it is also quite possible that men in my studies might have been prepared to explain more fully or further elucidate their views to an outsider such that a broader and more expansive narrative could have emerged around the topics that we discussed. Thus, a different, and in some ways potentially more comprehensive, insight into how these men take stock of themselves as social actors might have been produced from their having to speak to people who they construed as outsiders to their experiences and social environments. Instead, in these cases my insider status averted rather than extended the conversation.

The point of providing these examples is to extend consideration of the less-recognized virtues of outsiderness and the question of how insider and outsider statuses function together in fieldwork, especially how both operate as providers of possibilities and problems in the field. The critical review of the foregoing examples indicates that different kinds of data can be acquired when the outsider position is taken as a legitimate point of entry into fieldwork. With that understanding in mind, we now turn to this chapter's final statement, which concerns how researchers may think more deeply about their locations along the outsider–insider continua and how this affects their potential to best answer the research questions that drew them into the field. After all, it may often be the case that a researcher wants to know something about intimate matters concerning race and ethnicity that a respondent chooses not to submit for for public commentary, thus making the outsiderness of the researcher particularly problematic. However, it may also be the case that respondents want to communicate something to a researcher that comes from, and thereby represents, a world far from that which is familiar to the respondent, thus making researcher outsiderness an advantage. Either objective can be advanced by researchers who are intensely mindful of where they think they stand between the ends of insiderness and outsiderness, and how they think that respondents are locating them.[8] In the case of my own work, considerations of the virtues and drawbacks of insider status have led me to think about how one of my outsider statuses (university student) allowed the men to see me as a conduit to a world far beyond their own. They understood that I was going to take their messages, after embedding them in a discursive style suited for academia, to audiences that they would probably never access by themselves. Many of these men made my outsider status as a university student instrumental for their purposes in talking to me. Accordingly, this provided one context whereby I was enabled to think of my outsiderness as a virtue rather than a hindrance.

Tools for coming to terms with the inside and outside of researching race

Academic discussions of race are often replete with the same tensions, anxieties, pitfalls, and *faux pas*. As such, they are no different from other public discussions on the topic. This underscores why the insider–outsider debate around race has emerged and endured as long as it has in the world of scholarship. The preceding argument about the under-recognized virtues of outsider status calls for researchers to strike a balance in thinking about how insider and outsider statuses function in the qualitative research enterprise. The goal in advancing the virtues of outsider statuses, then, is to do so while preserving a place for insiderness, given all that has rightfully and necessarily been argued about it. That is, it remains crucial to keep in mind the virtues of outsider status without disregarding the socio-political ramifications of neglecting the insider dimension.

Being on the inside means that the researcher can maintain a shared sense of comfort and ease in interacting in the field, and that the researcher is sensitive and responsive to the cultural and social distinctiveness of the people under study. The overwhelming social dynamic that race continues to be in US life dictates that one should not ignore what the discussion about insiderness means for the ultimate production of research that reflects integrity and responsibility while dealing with such a volatile topic. Rather than engaging a fierce and narrowly focused quest to increase insiderness, what field researchers must take seriously is their mutual positioning in outsider and insider statuses. This means researchers' taking Reinharz's notion of multiple selves and using it to think about the capacity for these selves to be connected to a range of insider or outsider positionings. While researchers cannot be in full control of how they are located by the people whom they study, they can think about the fieldwork experience as involving an amalgamation of insider and outsider positionings that come together to open up as well as restrict access to data. The challenge, then, is for researchers to strive to maintain a critical reflexivity about this as they work to negotiate the ever-shifting terrain of relating to respondents in field research.

As a step toward advancing this end, we turn to the ideas of two recent commentators on insider and outsider statuses. Both have shed some new light on the outsider position in ways that highlight its utility rather than suggest that it should be avoided or minimized. The first, Patricia Hill Collins (1998), discusses what she calls the 'outsider-within' circumstances affecting the lives of upwardly mobile African American women. Collins employed this term to document that African American women are no longer strictly excluded from the symbolic and institutional domains of social power and influence (one need only think of President George Bush's incorporation of Condoleeza Rice into a primary leadership position in US politics). Rather, Collins argues that they face situations whereby their presence near the nucleus of power and influence also increases the surveillance, and subsequent social control, to which they are subjected. Thus, while they become insiders to a certain extent, the fact that they become subjected to critical observation (for instance, on matters such as style of dress, bodily comportment, manner of public interaction) highlights the extent to which they are still outsiders in the social spheres.

In contrast, the insider-without positioning captures those moments when black women have entry and access to privileged information because they serve as subordinates to powerful people (think, for instance, of house cleaners or home care workers who stand, quite literally, in the private domain of the society's most privileged people and thus garner some unique and exclusive insight into how these people function). These women are insiders-without because they are not equal partners in these domains, but they do have special access to them. Anyone who occupies outsider-within or insider-without positions, then, stands in places altogether different from those who are either more fully on the inside (and who have access to the most intimate details and dimensions of others' lives) or the outside (who have no such access, nor the means to adequately interpret whatever information they happen to acquire).

Turning Collins's notion around slightly, one can think of outsider-within and insider-without positions as more accurate depictions of the situation of qualitative researchers. Each depiction weaves together the two analytical ends of how scholars may relate to their respondents, in part as a result of how respondents react to the researchers. Like Collins's upwardly mobile African American women, qualitative researchers must assess the particular way or ways in which insider and outsider status come together for them. In order to reap the benefits of each position while engaged in the field, they must give some attention to how these interweavings vary across each research endeavor, as well as how the arrangements of costs and benefits differ in association with these variations.

Another statement about the insider–outsider dichotomy, provided by Sudhir Venkatesh (2002), addresses the research-related shortcomings and advantages of low-income African American community residents' inability to precisely, consistently, or accurately locate him in terms of his own racial and ethnic classifications. Venkatesh stresses that his informants' confusion about his ethnicity does not so much illustrate a unique problem in the course of conducting fieldwork as much as it reflects a slightly more extreme version of an experience that every field researcher encounters. He argues that all field researchers come upon research sites not solely to socially immerse themselves into them like the people under study, but to observe, interpret, and deliver to others a message about them, thus inevitably placing these researchers firmly in some form of outsider status. Hence, researchers have a stake in social settings that is different from regular or everyday participants because they are there to make critical observations about these settings. In doing so they function in at least one critical way as outsiders.

Although the discussion of his outsider status as a researcher is not necessarily an original claim, Venkatesh more importantly posits that a careful consideration of the complex and multiple ways in which residents respond to researchers as outsiders provides crucial information about how these residents make sense of who they are and how they represent themselves as members of a community. Implicit in this argument is that good qualitative research is not produced simply by 'getting in' or by achieving extreme immersion into the everydayness of a community. Rather, good research may be achieved in part by the researcher committing to sincere reflexive thought about how and why the researcher may be regarded as an outsider by the people under study.

Conclusion

Collins and Venkatesh provide vital conceptual and experiential support for thinking about how to maneuver in outsider positions. An implication of their work and my own is that researchers must avoid and thereby losing track of other issues and cirmcstances devoting exclusive attention to affirming insider status. Of course, researchers must always acknowledge and assert the cultural complexity of the people whom they study, and they must strive to capture and represent the voices of these people to their best ability, given that they are the ultimate creators of the statements being made about them. However, researchers must develop a keen appreciation and preparedness to make use of what being on the outside can do to cultivate discussion rather than hinder it. In part, this comes out of sincere consideration of the status that one occupies as a researcher. Through such functioning, one is already indelibly grounded in a particular outsider kind of status; that of being an individual who enters a social setting not simply to engage it like other participants might, but to analyze and document something about it for audiences often far removed from it.

The quest to enhance one's insider status as well as contend with outsider status is essentially an effort to create, develop, and sustain conversations in the field. Hence, the aim of the researcher must be to work toward maintaining the values and perspectives that are associated with insiderness while being conscientious about and appreciative of what being on the outside means for advancing conversations with people. This is especially the case for the often idiosyncratic, but sometimes turbulent and virulent, circumstances pertaining to race and race relations in the USA. Taking into account the case examples and arguments raised here, it is crucial to think about how the insider status can sometimes work against that goal.

Notes

1   Venkatesh is a notable exception in that he emphasizes how an outsider status can advance the process of data collection. His argument will be considered more directly later in this chapter.
2   An excellent summation of the aims and claims of the 1960s-era insider–outsider debate concerning sociological research on African Americans is provided by William Julius Wilson (1974).
3   The mindset of African Americans about 1960s-era cultural inquiry about them, and its role in facilitating the anxiety and mistrust that led to the African American-centered debates about insider and outsider statuses, has been documented and explored in a series of intellectual and social histories of urban poverty research in the USA (Katz 1989; O'Connor 2001; Patterson 2000; Valentine 1968).
4   In some cases, scholars chose to explain their work in this tradition by affirming how it concerns people, issues, or circumstances that are intimately associated with or a part of the researcher's own life experiences. One example of such an effort is Patillo-McCoy (1999), an African American ethnographer who studied the social dynamics of a class sector of the African American community in which she also holds membership. Another is by a white American anthropologist, Carol Stack (1974), who studied the family dynamics of low-income African American mothers while she, herself, was a young mother.
5   While Naples (1996) has effectively problematized the notion of the insider status as the most relevant position for data collection, her commentary does not comprehensively explore outsider statuses that apply to the researcher. Her point about outsider status concerns how respondents identify with that position. Furthermore, while De Andrade argues that insider status is neither immediately presumed nor static in fieldwork on racial and ethnic concerns, her commentary implicitly validates the vision of the insider perspective as the ideal for qualitative inquiry. She does so by affirming that working toward increased insider status is the ultimate goal, and she does so at the expense of exploring how that effort might be a hindrance for data collection. The challenge remains to better situate the outsider status as a powerful position by which to explore social phenomena such as racial consciousness and race relations.
6   I consistently make it a point to assert that, although I was born and reared in a community with poverty and urban blight, I was a product of a solid middle-class African American family. Unlike a significant number of such families that achieved extreme mobility by the early 1970s, my parents neither located to the suburbs nor to a more privileged urban neighborhood. They (but more so my father than my mother) chose to remain and, through years of civic involvement and community-based initiatives, 'fight

the good fight' on the behalf of African Americans much less well-off than they were. While this may appear to be a small point of clarification relative to the larger argument of this chapter, I believe that it does serve the purposes of helping to make clear how I situate myself in the course of my fieldwork in urban communities (i.e. a more privileged, and consequently more lucky, individual than the people that I study) and disavowing the legitimacy of any claim that men such as the people that I study should be doing better with their lives because someone like myself presumably made 'it out of the ghetto.' The odds stand against such men significantly more than they did for me.

7   The sub-field of sociology known as ethnomethodology developed out of a scholarly preoccupation with the latent rules of social exchange and social discourse, and, thus, established an understanding of the degree to which everyday social action and social order is predicated upon people following these rules (Garfinkel 1967).

8   Indeed, some of the most insightful findings from ethnographies of black Americans that were conducted by non-African Americans were predicated on the authors' making explicit mention of their initial lack of understanding or profound curiosity about some aspect of African American culture (even if such explication was presented in an apologetic or discerning tone). Ulf Hannerz's *Soulside* (1969) is replete with numerous testimonies from the author about how unfamiliar or intrigued he was with certain events or phenomena unfolding around him as he studied a poor-to-working-class African American street in 1960s-era Washington, DC. It remains the case that many classic and contemporary ethnographies of poor black Americans done by non-African Americans rarely dwell in great detail upon the revelations brought to the author by his or her outsider status.

14 Writing in and against time

Les Back

It is easy to forget that sociologists are writers and that we need to think about our craft from this point of view. As our discipline has become ever more elaborate and theoretically complex, the impulse to communicate has been eclipsed by the desire for epistemological sophistication and theoretical elegance. Sociologist C. Wright Mills wrote in the late 1950s 'to overcome academic prose you have first to overcome the academic pose' (1959: 219). Mills's career was committed to challenging the academic status quo and is worth revisiting in the current climate. He died in 1962 at the young age of 45. He was a prolific writer but wordcraft did not come easily to him. His daughters have edited a collection of his letters. In them we find a desperate pursuit of the right language. In a communiqué to his friend William Miller he expresses his dissatisfaction with the early drafts of what was to become his classic book *White Collar*. 'I can't write it right. I can't get what I want to say about America in it. What I want to say is what you say to an intimate friend when you are discouraged about how it all is' (Mills 2000: 136). His aspiration is noble and extraordinary given the state of academic writing today. Could you imagine anything worse than reading a sample of turgid academic prose – I am thinking particularly of my own – to a desperate friend?

The reason why I am drawn to these questions is connected to a similar kind of moment of truth. When the reader's comments came back for my last book entitled *Out of Whiteness* (with Vron Ware, University of Chicago Press, 2002), my father was mortally ill. Like many men of his class and generation, he had a terrible fear of hospitals. George Orwell (1970c) once wrote that the working-class fear of hospitals can be traced to their disciplinary nature. In the mind of a worker, hospitals were little more than a medical version of the Poor House. I didn't want him to die amongst strangers so I stayed with him through long nights. I took my manuscript with me and read it at his bedside. It was a haunting experience. As I read my attempts to write, I heard the sound of his rattling chest and diminishing breaths. In those moments and through the many nights I spent in Mayday Hospital, Croydon – the same hospital that I was born in – I changed my view about the value and importance of the kinds of work we do.

Søren Kierkegaard wrote in his book *Philosophical Fragments* that thinking is like a dance. 'Then the dance goes merrily,' wrote Kierkegaard, 'for my partner is the thought of Death, and [it] is indeed a nimble dancer' (1936: 7; see also Phillips 1999: 65). For him thinking need not involve engagement with others or listening to their voices. Continuing with the dance metaphor, he concluded 'every human being, on the other hand, is too heavy for me' (ibid.). But, those who have looked into the face of death, really looked, will know that Kierkegaard's words furnish a profound lie. The thought of death should not be embraced like a dance-floor intimate. We would be in a bad state of affairs if we lived with the sound of diminishing breaths ringing in our ears. As the great Peruvian poet Cesar Vallejo commented, 'nothing is possible in death except on top of what is left in life' (1980: 15). It is in this sense that I've started to view the importance of sociology as part of an embrace with and connection to the dance of life with all its heavy and cumbersome steps. It is an aspiration to hold the experience of others in your arms while recognizing that what we touch is always moving, unpredictable, irreducible and mysteriously opaque. As a consequence of this, we are always writing in and against time.

This might seem a long way from the issues of method at the heart of this book and the question of researching race and ethnic relations. The first point to stress is that research is a literary activity as well as a set of investigative procedures. What is at stake in these issues of style and rhetoric is not merely the matter of process. The notion of 'writing up' research seems to imply some kind of automatic transcription. Yet, every budding researcher knows there is nothing automatic about the craft of written argument and social representation. What follows is an attempt to sketch some of the issues that I've found myself thinking about in relation to practical scholarship. Also, it aims to discuss the role that sociology and social research might play in the discussion of race and ethnic relations. The intention is not to offer a balanced review. Rather, it is an attempt to provide individual and perhaps idiosyncratic answers to a set of deceptively simple questions. What is social research needed for? What are we doing as we sit down to write surrounded by piles of tapes and transcripts?

Dialogue and displacement

Renato Rosaldo in his book *Culture and Truth* (1989) demolishes the idea that we can write about societies as if they hold still while we sketch them. What anthropologists call the 'ethnographic present' (i.e. the idea that eternal assertions can be made like Nuer religion is…, middle-class culture is…) simply seems absurd when you think about it. The idea that we are writing in time, at a particular moment, which is partial and positioned and in place, is a major advance. I think we are also writing against time, trying to capture an outline of an existence that is fleeting. We cannot know the soul of a person we have listened to but we can know the traces that they leave 'on top of life', to use Vallejo's phrase.

I've come to think that this is what I am trying to do as I sit down at the computer with interview transcripts or ethnographic descriptions at my side. The fact that those traces of life are opaque and that the person who made them is always to an extent unknowable doesn't mean that all is lost. In fact, I have become tired of reading elegant pronouncements on the unknowability of culture and social life; there is no compensation in these bold statements of defeat for me any more. I think this realization has put a distance between me – intellectually at least – and some of my closest friends. Part of the after-shock of poststructuralist critiques of social science is a turning away from the kinds of encounters that I want to argue for. This critique has been centred around the meaning and status of writing.

Roland Barthes argued that writing is not a means to reflect the world. Rather, 'to write' is an intransitive verb with the result that writing is reified as a thing in itself almost regardless of content (Barthes 1970: 142). Writing here is an act of language rather than a means of recording a sense of reality beyond it. In short, when we write we are drawn into a series of patterned communicative formulae that are already available. This material web of discourses or representations means that our message is already subverted by The Word and the structure of language itself. These arguments have a long historical lineage and go back to Plato and Socrates, who both argued against the adequacy of written speech as a poor transcription of 'spoken truths'. Jacques Derrida is critical too of the way Western philosophy makes speech, and by extension writing, the original site of truth. The notion of 'logocentrism' here attempts to name this dependence on language. It is derived from the Greek '*logos*', meaning the origin that structures and orders the nature of truth. Derrida's notion of deconstruction is aimed at a critique of logocentrism and language – both written and spoken.

Part of Derrida's critique is an argument for a broader notion of inscription that would include photography, music, embodiment and sculpture as forms of writing. While one might accept aspects of this line of argument, the effect of deconstruction on the research agenda of the last decade has been a turning away from the project of empirical enquiry. In Britain at least, the impact of the critique of 'writing culture' associated with the work of anthropologist James Clifford has led to an anxiety with regard to the epistemological mooring of ethnographic engagement. In a sense, these concerns about the relationship between power and knowledge have come to eclipse a long-standing critique – albeit from a different angle – of the abuses of sociological knowledge. Here the epistemological challenge to sociological authority was based on the political consequences of the work of white sociologists for minority communities. Information gathering and the scrutiny of racialised migrant communities becomes synonymous with a 'note-taking' hand that is little more than an extension of the political arm of a racist state (Centre for Contemporary Cultural Studies 1982; Ladner 1998). Sociological writing was complicit in producing, circulating and legitimising cultural pathologies about minority communities. On a more mundane level, as Errol Lawrence pointed out, the white sociological accounts of the cultural life of black and minority communities were boring travesties in which the sociologist was analogous to a dry-mouth fool who remained thirsty in the midst of an abundance of water (Lawrence 1982).

At least two, perhaps unintended, consequences followed from the lines of critique outlined above. The first is a turning away from empirical research that is in part a refusal to be placed in the position of a 'data collection agent' for oppressive forces. The second consequence is that the empirical accounts that are written have the quality of 'good news stories' in which anything that is difficult or potentially damaging is filtered out. I know I have been guilty of this in my own writing. I want to return to the consequences this may have later. There may be another way to respond to both the epistemological and political critiques, particularly in the field of race, ethnicity and racism research, and this involves embracing the idea that our writing always falls short. The acceptance that the best we can hope for in writing the social world is degrees of failure (i.e. part truths) need not result in a turning away from a commitment to dialogue.

Partiality and failure do not mean that the lines in our portraits have no semblance of likeness. The oscillation between proximity and distance integral to the kind of writing I want to do means that we can never be sure about the quality of what is produced. As John Berger has commented:

> It seems to me that the whole question of where one is when writing has to do with this – it's that phrase used by Robert Capa who said something like 'agh you know, when the picture's not good enough – go closer.' And it seems to me what I've tried to do in maybe all the books I've written is to get in very close and then to try and bring something back from a starting point outside. How much I succeed, and what I am bringing back, I often don't know…maybe the actual way I work implies this displacement, this displacement of going in as close as you dare, and then finding, sometimes with difficulty, a way back.
>
> (John Berger, from an interview with Jeremy Isaacs,
> *Face to Face*, BBC 1995)

Writing is about the process of retrieval, i.e. the something that is brought back. But the quality of that something is mysterious and may be beyond the comprehension of the writer. That's what I think we need readers for – to tell us we are wrong but also when the words resonate.

Some might conclude that proximity to research participants and empirical dialogue always runs the risk of a researcher's judgement being clouded and duped through over-familiarity. Part of the politics of doing the work I've done – particularly with people who are avowed or common-sense racists – is to subject odious and pernicious views to critical evaluation, deconstruction and analysis; it is not merely a matter of reproducing them. Familiarity, rather than militating against criticism, involves the deepening of critical judgement. However, this process is precarious and more complex than it seems and cannot be compensated through political postures. Given that the divisions of power and oppression are essential to any discussion of race and ethnic relations, the field is – like it or not – deeply implicated in political issues. The quality and nature of being implicated in the politics of race is often glossed by invoking a political position, i.e. being an anti-racist researcher. I think this is particularly important for those writers who might be positioned within ethnic majorities or within privileged racialised groups. I want to explore this issue through looking at the work of George Orwell, who wrote expansively against colonialism and anti-Semitism, and the recent controversies surrounding his legacy.

Critical insight and the uses of autobiography

The diaries of Malcolm Muggeridge provide a tragic commentary on George Orwell's last few days and weeks. Muggeridge was his friend and discussant, and they shared many lunchtime debates on politics and culture in the heart of London. Orwell was just 46 when he died. The entry in Muggeridge's diaries for 26 January 1950 described the scene at Orwell's funeral. He wrote of his surprise that so many of the mourners were Jewish. 'Interesting, I thought, that George should have so attracted Jews because he was at heart strongly anti-Semitic. Felt a pang as the coffin was removed, particularly because of its length, somehow this circumstance, reflecting George's tall-ness, was poignant' (Bright-Holmes 1981: 374). Orwell wrote extensively and critically about anti-Semitism, as well as against the colour bar in Britain, racism and colonialism. Yet, the idea that Orwell was at core anti-Semitic has lingered and been reinvigorated during the discussion of the centenary of his birth and a profusion of new biographies. In 2002, prior to the publication of his Orwell biography, D.J. Taylor wrote that anti-Semitism was Orwell's 'dirty secret' (Taylor 2002). I am not going to discuss these biographies in depth (Taylor 2003; Bowker 2003; Lucas 2003). It's worth remembering that Orwell never wanted a biographer; he must have turned in his grave recently as three appeared in a single year. Like the object of my favourite literary joke, these books fill a *much needed gap* in the published record of literary Orwellia. The political controversy about Orwell and his alleged racism provides a spur to re-examine his writing on anti-Semitism. In Orwell's work, we can find interesting and important questions about the relationship between insight and culpability.

To characterise Orwell as a bigot misses the complex way in which he took his own cultural legacy as the starting point for critical reflection. In this sense, the world Orwell was born into – aspirant, imperial and petty bourgeois – was riddled with anti-Semitism. Yet, at the same time he sought to develop a political critique of anti-Semitism from the inside. He wrote in 1941:

> What vitiates nearly all that is written about anti-semitism is the assumption in the writer's mind that he himself is immune to it. 'Since I know that anti-semitism is irrational,' he argues, 'it follows that I do not share it.' He thus fails to start his investigation in the one place where he could get hold of some reliable evidence – that is, in his own mind.
>
> (Orwell 1970a: 387)

Orwell complicated any simple or comfortable separation between racism and anti-racism, and he made a case for understanding racism in terms of its warped rationalities and equally what its believers need it for. These essays seem to point towards the need for developing interpretative tools that engage with racism's pernicious and enduring power.

Central to this process is the need to grapple with the power of racist rhetoric, on the one hand, while on the other dealing with the desires and fears or the receptive yearning amongst those who find its erroneous answers appealing. For Orwell that also begins with an impulse to situate the understanding of hate within oneself. He wrote at the conclusion of his essay on anti-Semitism:

> It will be seen, therefore that the starting point for any investigation of anti-semitism should not be 'Why does this obviously irrational belief appeal to people?' but 'Why does anti-semitism appeal to me? What is there about it that I feel to be true?' If one asks this question one at least discovers one's own rationalizations, and it may be possible to find out what lies beneath them. Anti-semitism should be investigated – and I will not say by anti-semites, but at any rate by people who know that they are not immune to that kind of emotion.
>
> (Orwell 1970a: 388)

Is this an admission of a 'dirty secret'? Of course not. Does it mean that he recognised the power of anti-Semitism in himself and his work? I think the answer must be an unequivocal 'yes'. Yet at the same time he is wilfully trying to identify, interpret and transcend the culture of racism of which he is himself part. Is this transcendence total and complete? I think not, but this is true of the power of racism in our time and the contingencies in reckoning with its efficacy in the lives of whites both personally and professionally.

George Orwell wrote in 1944 that:

> the weakness of the left-wing attitude towards anti-semitism is to approach it from a rationalistic angle. Obviously the charges made against the Jews are not true. They cannot be true, partly because they cancel out, partly because no one people could have a monopoly of wickedness. But simply by pointing this out one gets no further....If a

man has the slightest disposition towards anti-semitism, such things bounce off his consciousness like peas off a steel helmet.

(1970b: 112–13)

The same can be said of what might be referred to as moral anti-racism today. Orwell's suggestion is that, rather than pointing out why racism is bad or wrong, we start from the point of view of trying to understand why racism appeals to people and what they need it for. The police cling to the stereotypes of violent black youths, and what they see as 'the truth' about the policing of black communities, because it helps them make sense of a world that confounds and shuns them. Orwell's challenge is how to get inside or proximate to the appeal and commitment to racism.

In an essay on H.G. Wells, Hitler and Totalitarianism published in 1941, he concluded: 'The people who have shown the best understanding of Fascism are either those who have suffered under it or those who have a Fascist streak in themselves' (Orwell 1970a: 172). This is perhaps a confession of sorts. One might easily supplant fascism here with 'anti-semitism' or 'racism' and the sense of Orwell's approach would be the same. I think there is something in this that also destabilises our categories of thinking and the places where we might find understanding, or tools for interpretation. In this sense, the 'racist's feeling' that, deposited in dominant social groups, can provide a tool or a resource for interpretation and critical reckoning that is both sociological and political.

I think, too, we have to allow the people about whom we write to be complex, frail, ethically ambiguous, contradictory and damaged. The tendency to write society as if it were populated by Manichaean camps of people who are good or bad, angels or devils, is a strong temptation. I know that I have done this, sometimes with the best of intentions. When one is writing about stigmatised and excluded social groups, this temptation is particularly keen. What right do we have to outline their weaknesses or failings? The danger here in creating heroic portrayals is that we make the very people whose humanity one may want to defend less than human. We don't allows them to be as complicated as we are, i.e. compounds of pride and shame, weakness and strength. Equally, when we make white racists into monsters there is a danger of organising racism into some – often very predictable white bodies – and away from others. I think sociology can play a role in opening up the false comforts achieved in such absolute moral categories.

Perhaps, I am mindful of this precisely because people I have loved have also given popular racism a voice, including my own father who I mentioned earlier. One of the paradoxes of this – and I am always compelled by the paradoxical effects of racism on our culture – is that towards the end of his life the only person who could reach through cancer and the morphine-induced haze was a black nurse. It was she who held his hand as he passed the brink of life. I want to believe that this was some kind of atonement or coming to terms. The hand has been iconic in the thinking of philosophers in relation to what it means to be human. For both Kant and Heidegger the hand was emblematic of human distinction. 'The hand reaches and extends, receives and welcomes – and not just things: the hand extends itself, and receives its own welcome in the hands of others' (Heidegger 1968: 16). But the hand too is the symbol of exclusive power: the straight arm of the Nazi salute (Derrida 1987), the open-hand halt of the racial segregationists (Gordon 1996) or the gendered exchange in the hand that is taken in patri- archal marriage (Bell 1998). Opposite the hand that separates and glorifies the racial body there is also the hand that touches and the material surfaces of connection. Touch may be a useful metaphor for a sociological ethics because, as Clifford Geertz has commented, 'foreignness does not start at the water's edge but at the skin's' (2000: 76). Indeed, the act of research might be best characterised as an attempt to establish such surfaces of connection across human experiences.

Centring the act of writing around the positioned and reflective sociolo- gist is something that I want to argue for, yet there are real risks in this as well as rewards. In short, autobiography has its misuses. Self-reflection can inhibit or pre-empt the need for dialogue and deep listening to others. I have felt this several times when working or talking with people who are writing about worlds of which they are in a direct sense a part. I recognise traces of this in my own work. The danger here is that autobiographical experience becomes the only necessary source needed to think with and write with. Listening to others becomes irrelevant because she or he already knows the culture from the inside and paradoxically the accounts of the people being listened to are muted. The role of autobiographical or experi- ential knowledge is always that of an interpretative device. In this sense subjectivity becomes a means to try and shuttle across the boundary between the writer and those about whom she or he is writing. It is not about narcis- sism and self-absorption but common likenesses and by extension contrasts. It is those likenesses and contrasts that enable the sociologist to hold accounts of the social life in the same place without folding the person one is listening to back into one's self – 'Oh, okay. You are just like me, after all!' Otherness doesn't begin at the boundaries between class or 'racial' groupings or differences of gender and sexuality but at the limit of our touch. There can be no simple appeal to the inside that does not also acknowledge the variegations within social groups.

If a writer's experience and subjectivity is useful, we need to think about what it is needed for. Here I am suggesting that these experiences are of little use if they are not put to work in service of reaching out to others. In her beautiful book *Remembered Rapture,* bell hooks comments:

A distinction must be made between that writing which enables us to hold to life even as we are clinging to old hurts and wounds and that writing which offers to us a space where we are able to confront reality in such a way that we live more fully.

(1999: 11)

Although she is not talking about sociological research, such a distinction might be applied to the misuses of autobiography outlined here. The acid test is the degree to which it enables the writer to 'confront reality' in a way that enhances insight.

Reflective engagement and *Life Passed in Living*

Theodor W. Adorno warned that 'Every debate about the ideals of education is trivial and inconsequential compared to this single ideal: never again Auschwitz. It was the barbarism all education strives against' (1998: 191). The politics of understanding the features of contemporary racism and the imitators and apologists of Nazism is dedicated to this aim. Critical thinking can play a modest part here, in the commitment to see at the inter-section of horizons and contrasting values. It involves critical judgement while remaining open to counter-intuitive possibilities that challenge both our interpretations and our political beliefs.

Hyper-political posturing is not necessarily politics. More than a few self-professed 'political intellectuals' – of all ages – indulge in pieties of this sort on the conference circuit. Such histrionics mask difficult matters of substance. As political tools books are fairly weak instruments of change, regardless of the current talk about the relationship between knowledge and power. Primo Levi once wrote that:

> It is a matter of practical observation that a book or a story, whether its intentions be good or bad, are essentially inert and innocuous objects.…Their intrinsic weakness is aggravated by the fact that today all writing is smothered in a few months by a mob of other writings which push up behind it.

(1991: 157)

Perhaps the desperate academic innovations of 'political intent' are a response to the inherent weakness identified so eloquently here. Academic 'prophets' and 'demagogues' – to cite Max Weber's telling phrase – may take comfort from playing to the colloquium gallery. I want to suggest, in contrast, that the political value of sociological work lies in being open to unsettling dialogues with humility. This is not a good way to produce a stir-ring manifesto, but it perhaps has the merit of greater honesty with regard to the truths that are touched, if not wholly grasped, through sociological endeavour.

It does not, however, follow that this means a retreat from political issues and towards detachment and neutrality. In this sense, Rojek and Turner's notion of 'engaged detachment' (Rojek and Turner 2000) is not only a literal contradiction but also confused and obfuscating. The kind of orientation I want to propose with regard to the project of understanding and political contestation might be described as reflective engagement, i.e. a political intervention that realises the limits of writing and the complexities of dialogue and listening. The urgency and speed of politics mean that the window of opportunity for making an intervention will not wait for a beautifully crafted monograph 3 years after the fact. Making public interventions and aspiring to be a public intellectual involves embracing a wide range of writing genres alongside academic forms. It includes writing letters to newspapers, journalism and essays for popular and political journals.

What does this amount to? What, if any, lessons follow from the line of argument developed here in relation to the concerns of this book. Well, the first and most fundamental point is to be careful about the risks involved when venturing into the public sphere and openly criticising groups that may have the power to harass and harm you. In the information age researchers are not the only ones with inquiring eyes: you may need protection from those who look back through the research lens at the researcher. Second, there are gains to be had from getting close in ethnographic terms to the thing one is trying to describe and understand. This encounter not only involves confronting unsettling voices, it may produce a disruption in the language and categories of our understanding and interpretation. Third, I think it is incumbent on us – where possible – to show the people we have listened to what we have written about them, even if it means having to present them with severe criticism. This also includes an account of our place in the story we are telling. Finally, there is real merit in using the invitation to sociology to enrich the stories we tell about our world, ourselves and our times. The injunction to salvage cultural fragments from the debris piled up at the feet of modernity is a central trope in anthropological writing. As Ruth Behar has pointed out, the idea of loss and of 'worlds on the brink of disappearance' is one of the things that has animated anthropologists as writers.

In the globalised world, the relationship between centre and margin are becoming more complex, patterns of suffering and uncertainty ever more terrifying. The kind of engaged listening I want to argue for may turn out to be less dispensable than it might seem on first sight. John Berger once wrote that writers, storytellers and by extension sociologists are 'death's secretaries' (1991: 31). By this I think he meant that writing is about keeping a record and producing a kind of register of life. Regardless of the epistemological melancholy and self-mutilating doubt abroad in today's social science faculties, the tradition of drawing and transcribing life passed in living is a noble one to be cherished. Ruth Behar concludes:

> One thing remains constant about our humanity – that we must never stop trying to tell stories of who we think we are. Equally, we must

never stop wanting to listen to each other's stories. If we ever stopped, it would all be over.

(2003: 37)

It is far from over. If social research is to have a future it must hold to the project of listening and speaking to people who live the consequence of the globalised world with respect and humility while maintaining critical judgement.

I am arguing for an engaged sociology of race and ethnic relations that listens actively. The paradox is that we academic scribes are not always very sociable. We cling to the library like bookish limpets that, like Kierkegaard, find real human beings too heavy to embrace. We speak a lot about society but all too often listen to the world within limited frequencies. I am proposing an approach to listening that goes beyond this, where listening is not assumed to be a self-evident faculty that needs no training. Somehow the literature produced by the grey men of methodology – and I am using this gendered phrase advisedly – do not help much with the kind of fine tuning I would like to argue for. The lacklustre prose of methodological textbooks turn the life in the research encounter into a corpse fit only for autopsy. I want to end by returning to C Wright Mills, who famously referred to sociology and scholarship as a craft.

For Mills there is nothing workaday in this notion of sociological craft because integral to it is creative thinking and expression. In Mills's view, sociology at its best is a compound of craft and imagination. He knew all too well that this involved being self-consciously committed to affecting argument and writing creatively. The danger he foresaw was that the socio-logical work might develop as its tool a technical language that turns inwards on itself. Jean Amery once observed that specialist language 'in sounding learned, strives to prove its own significance more than the value of its knowledge' (1994: 4–5). To avoid this, we have to aspire to be writers and to make research writing an art form. It may seem like an unnecessary ambition, or even burden, particularly for those at the beginning of their careers as researchers. But perhaps there is comfort in the knowledge that we cannot know the quality of what we write ourselves. This, I have always felt, is a liberation because all we can do is strive to do the best work we can. Whether we succeed or not is a matter for the reader to decide.

Acknowledgement

Thanks to Pat and Lionel Caplan.

Bibliography

Abrams, P. (1982) *Historical Sociology* near Shepton Mallet, Somerset, England: Open Books

Abu-Lughod, J.L. (1991) *Before European Hegemony: The World System A.D. 1250–1350* Oxford: Oxford University Press

Adorno, T.W. (1998) *Critical Models: Interventions and Catch Worlds* New York: Columbia University Press

Adorno, T.W., Frenkel-Brunswik, E., Levinson, D. and Sanford, R. (1950) *The Authoritarian Personality* New York: Harper

Al-Ahsan, A. (1992) *Ummah or Nation? Identity Crises in Contemporary Muslim Societies* London The Islamic Foundation

Al-Azmeh, A. (1993) *Islams and Modernities* London: Verso

Alcoff, L. (1991/92) 'The Problem of Speaking for Others' *Cultural Critique* 20: 5–32

Alexander, C. (1996) *The Art of Being Black* Oxford: Clarendon Press

——(2000) *The Asian Gang: Ethnicity, Identity, Masculinity* Oxford: Berg

——(2002) 'Beyond Black: Rethinking the Colour/Culture Divide' *Ethnic and Racial Studies* 25, 4: 552–71

——(forthcoming) 'Embodying Violence: Riot, Dis/order and the Private Lives of 'the Asian Gang' in C. Alexander and C. Knowles (eds) *Representation, Identity and Difference* Basingstoke: Palgrave Macmillan

Ali-Bey, R.A. (1996) *Louisiana Lynching: A Modern Day Legacy of an X Slave* Miami, FL: House of Ra Pub

Allen, J. (2000) *Without Sanctuary: Lynching Photography in America* Santa Fe, NM: Twin Palms

Almaguer, T. (1994) *Racial Fault Lines* Berkeley: University of California Press

Amery, J. (1994) *On Aging: Revolt and Resignation* Bloomington and Indianapolis: Indiana University Press

Ames, J.D. (1942) *Association of Southern Women for the Prevention of Lynching, and Commission on Interracial Cooperation. The Changing Character of Lynching Review of Lynching, 1931–1941, with a Discussion of Recent Developments in this Field* Atlanta, GA: Commission on Interracial Cooperation Inc.

Andersen, M. (1993) 'Studying across Difference: Race, Class and Gender in Qualitative Research' in J. H. Stanfield and R.M. Dennis (eds) *Race and Ethnicity in Research Methods* London: Sage

Anthias, F. and Yuval-Davis, N. (1992) *Racialized Boundaries* London: Routledge

Anwar, M (1998) *Between Cultures* London: Routledge

Appadurai, A. (1996) *Modernity at Large* Minneapolis: University of Minnesota Press

Augoustinos, K., Tuffin, M. and Rapley, M. (1999) 'Genocide or a Failure to Gel? Racism, History and Nationalism in Australia' *Discourse and Society* 10, 3: 351–78

Ayubi, N.N. (1991) *Political Islam: Religion and Politics in the Arab World* London: Routledge

Baca Zinn, M. (1979) 'Field Research in Minority Communities' *Social Problems* 27: 209–19

Back, L. (1996) *New Ethnicities and Urban Culture* London: UCL Press

——(2002) 'Guess Who's Coming to Dinner? The Political Morality of Investigating Whiteness in the Gray Zone' in V. Ware and L. Back *Out of Whiteness: Color, Politics and Culture* Chicago IL: University of Chicago

Back, L. and Solomos, J. (1993) 'Doing Research, Writing Politics: The Dilemmas of Political Intervention in Research on Racism' *Economy and Society* 22, 2: 178–99

Back, L., Cohen, P. and Keith, M. (1999) *Between Home and Belonging: Critical Ethnographies of Race, Place and Identity* London: Centre for New Ethnicities Research, University of East London

Back, L., Crabbe, T. and Solomos, J. (2001) *The Changing Face of Football: Racism, Identity and Multiculture in the English Game* Oxford: Berg

Balen, B.v. and Fisher, A. (eds) (1998) *De universiteit als modern mannenklooster* [The University as Modern Monastery) Amsterdam: het Spinhuis

Balibar, E. and Wallerstein, I. (1989) *Race, classe, nation. Les identités ambiguës* Paris: La Découverte

Ballard, R. (1992) 'New Clothes for the Emperor? The Conceptual Nakedness of the Race Relations Industry in Britain' *New Community* 18, 3: 481–92

——(ed.) (1994) *Desh Pardesh* London: Christopher Hurst

——(1996) 'Negotiating Race and Ethnicity' *Patterns of Prejudice* 30, 3: 3–33

Banerjea, K. (2002) 'The Tyranny of the Binary: Race, Nation and the Logic of Failing Liberalisms' *Ethnic and Racial Studies* 25, 4: 572–90

Banks, M. (1996) *Ethnicity: Anthropological Constructions* London: Routledge

Banton, M. (1973) 'The Future of Race Relations Research in Britain: The Establishment of a Multi-Disciplinary Research Unit' *Race* 15, 2: 223–9

——(1976) 'A Discussion Note on Ethnic Relations, Policy Research, and Contract Research' unpublished paper

——(1977) *The Idea of Race* London: Tavistock

——(1991) 'The Race Relations Problematic' *British Journal of Sociology* 42, 1: 115–30

Bardaglio, P. (1991) 'An Outrage upon Nature': Incest and the Law in the Nineteenth-Century South' in C. Blesser (ed.) *In Joy and in Sorrow. Women, Family, and Marriage in the Victorian South, 1830–1900* New York: Oxford University Press

Barker, M. (1981) *The New Racism: Conservatives and the Ideology of the Tribe* London: Junction Books

Barthes, R. (1970) 'To Write – an Intransitive Verb' in R. Macksey and E. Donato (eds) *The Structuralist Controversy: The Languages of Criticism and the Sciences of Man* Baltimore and London: Johns Hopkins Press

Bashi, V. and McDaniel, A. (1997) 'A Theory of Immigration and Racial Stratification' *Journal of Black Studies* 27, 5: 668–82

Bataille, P. (1997) *Le Racisme au travail* Paris: La Découverte

Batur-Vanderlippe, P. and Feagin, J.R. (1999) 'Racial and Ethnic Inequality and Struggle from the Colonial Era to the Present: Drawing the Global Color Line' in P. Batur-Vanderlippe and J.R. Feagin (eds) *The Global Color Line: Racial and Ethnic Inequality and Struggle from a Global Perspective* Stamford, CT: JAI Press

Becker, H.S. (1998) *Tricks of the Trade: How to Think about Your Research while You're Doing It* Chicago IL: University of Chicago Press

Behar, R. (2003) 'Ethnography and the Book That Was Lost' *Ethnography* 4, 1: 15–39

Bell, V. (1998) 'Taking Her Hand: Becoming, Time and the Cultural Politics of the White Wedding' *Cultural Values* 2, 4: 463–84

Benson, S. (1996) 'Asians Have Culture, West Indians Have Problems' in T. Ranger, Y. Samad and O. Stuart (eds) *Culture, Identity and Politics* Aldershot: Avebury

Berger, J. (1991) *And Our Faces, My Heart, Brief as Photos* New York: Vintage Books

Berkeley, B. (2001) *The Graves Are Not Yet Full: Race, Tribe and Power in the Heart of Africa* New York: Basic Books

Berlin, I. (1974) *Slaves without Masters: The Free Negro in the Antebellum South* Oxford: Oxford University Press

Berman, M. (1982) *All That Is Solid Melts into Air: The Experience of Modernity* London: Verso

Bhabha, H.K. (1994) *The Location of Culture* London: Routledge

Bhattacharyya, G., Gabriel, J. and Small, S. (2002) *Race and Power: Global Racism in the Twenty-First Century* London: Routledge

Billig, M. (1991) *Ideology and Opinions: Studies in Rhetorical Psychology* London: Sage

——(1999) *Freudian Repression* Cambridge: Cambridge University Press

——(2002) 'Henri Tajfel's "Cognitive Aspects of Prejudice" and the Psychology of Bigotry' *British Journal of Social Psychology* 41, 2: 171–89

Billig, M., Condor, S., Edwards, D., Gane, M., Middleton, D. and Radley, A. (1988) *Ideological Dilemmas: A Social Psychology of Everyday Thinking* London: Sage

Blackman, L. and Walkerdine, V. (2001) *Mass Hysteria: Critical Psychology and Media Studies* London: Palgrave

Blackmore, J. (1999) *Troubling Women. Feminism, Leadership and Educational Change* Buckingham: Open University Press

Blee, K. (2000) 'White on White: Interviewing Women in US White Supremacist Groups' in F.W. Twine and J.W. Warren (eds) *Racing Research, Researching Race* New York: New York University Press

Blum, A. (1998) 'Comment décrire les immigrés– A propos de quelques recherches sur l'immigration' *Population* 3

Blumer, H. (1958) 'Race Prejudice as a Sense of Group Position' *Pacific Sociological Review* 1: 3–7

Body-Gendrot, S. (1993a) 'Migration and the Racialization of the Post-Modern City in France' in M. Cross and M. Keith (eds) *Racism, the City and the State* London: Routledge

——(1993b) 'Pioneering Moslem Women in France' in R. Fisher and J. Kling (eds) *Mobilizing the Community* Newbury Park CA: Sage

——(1993c) *Ville et violence: l'irruption de nouveaux acteurs* Paris: Presses Universitaires de France

——(1995) 'Immigration, Marginality and French Social Policy' in K. McFate, R. Lawson and W.J. Wilson (eds) *Poverty, Inequality and the Future of Social Policy* New York: Russell Sage Foundation

——(1998) 'Now You See, Now You Don't: Comments on Paul Gilroy's Article' *Ethnic and Racial Studies* 21, 5: 848–58

——(2000) 'Marginalization and Political Responses in the French Context' in P. Hamel, H. Lustiger-Thaler and M. Mayer (eds) *Urban Movements in a Globalizing World* London: Routledge

——(2004) 'La Peur du communautarisme empêche-t-elle de lutter contre les discrimina-tions en France?' *Cahiers du DSU* 38, January

Body-Gendrot, S. and Duprez, D. (2002) 'Security and Prevention Policies in France in the 1990s: French Cities and Security' in P. Hebberecht and D. Duprez (eds) *The Prevention and Security Policies in Europe* Brussels: VUB Brussels University Press

Bollas, C. (1995) *Cracking Up: The Work of Unconscious Experience* New York: Hill & Wang

Bonilla-Silva, E. (1999) 'The New Racism' in P. Wong (ed.) *Race, Ethnicity, and Nationality in the United States* Boulder, CO: Westview Press

Bonnett, A. (1999) 'Constructions of 'Race', Place and Discipline: Geographies of 'Racial' Identity and Racism' in M. Bulmer and J. Solomos (eds) *Ethnic and Racial Studies Today* London: Routledge

Bourdieu, P. and Wacquant, L. (1992) *An Invitation to Reflexive Sociology* Chicago IL: University of Chicago Press

——(1998) 'Sur les ruses de la raison imperialiste' *Actes de la recherche en sciences sociales* 121–2: 109–18

——(1999) 'On the Cunning of Imperialist Reason' *Theory, Culture and Society* 16, 1: 41–58

Bourgois, P. (2000) 'Violating Apartheid in the United States: On the Streets and in Academia' in F.W. Twine and J.W. Warren (eds) *Racing Research, Researching Race* New York: New York University Press

——(2003) *In Search of Respect: Selling Crack in El Barrio* second edn, Cambridge: Cambridge University Press

Bovenkerk, F. (ed.) (1978) *Omdat zij anders zijn* [Because They Are Different] Meppel: Boom

Bowker, G. (2003) *George Orwell* London: Little, Brown & Company

Brah, A. (1996) *Cartographies of Diaspora: Contesting Identities* London: Routledge

——(1999) 'The Scent of Memory: Strangers, Our Own and Others' *Feminist Review* 61: 4–26

Brannen, J. (ed.) (1992) *Mixing Methods: Qualitative and Quantitative Research* Aldershot: Avebury

Bright-Holmes, J. (ed.) (1981) *Like It Was: The Diaries of Malcolm Muggeridge* London: Collins

Brown, M. and Miles, R. (2000) *Theory, Culture and Society* 17, 1: 171–5

Bulmer, M. (1991) 'W.E.B. Du Bois as a Social Investigator: *The Philadelphia Negro* 1899' in M. Bulmer, K. Bales and K.K. Sklar (eds) *The Social Survey in Historical Perspective 1880–1940* Cambridge: Cambridge University Press

Bulmer, M. and Solomos, J. (eds) (1999a) *Racism* Oxford: Oxford University Press

——(eds) (1999b) *Ethnic and Racial Studies Today* London: Routledge

Buttny, R. (1999) 'Discursive Constructions of Racial Boundaries and Self-Segregation on Campus' *Journal of Language and Social Psychology* 18, 3: 247–68

Canadian Press (1997) '1971 Murder under Review' p. E6 in the *Record*

——(1989a) 'Hearings into Teen's Death End Racism in 1971 Fed Cover-Up of Killing Native Probe Told' p. A9 in the *Toronto Star*

——(1989b) 'Murder Probe Meets Silence and Poor Memories' p. A9 in the *Toronto Star*

Carter, P. (2000) 'It's All in the "Act": The Substance of Black Cultural Capital among Low-income African American Youth' paper presented at the 95th annual meeting of the American Sociological Association, Washington, DC

Centre for Contemporary Cultural Studies (1982) *The Empire Strikes Back* London: Hutchinson

Clark, J. and Diani, M. (eds) (1996) *Alain Touraine* London: Falmer

Claude, P. (2002) 'Malek Boutih, le "désillusionniste"' *Le Monde* 13 June: 15

Clifford, J. (1988) *The Predicament of Culture* Cambridge, MA: Harvard University Press

Clifford, J. and Marcus, G. (eds) (1986) *Writing Culture: The Poetics and Politics of Ethnography* Berkeley: University of California Press

Clinton, C. (1982) *The Plantation Mistress. Woman's World in the Old South* New York: Pantheon Books

Cockburn, L. (1995) 'Real Life, Real Drama' p. 12 in the *Toronto Sun*

Cohen, P. (1996) 'A message from the other shore' *Patterns of Prejudice* 30, 1: 15–22

——(1997) *Rethinking the Youth Question: Education, Labour and Cultural Studies* Basingstoke: Macmillan

Coleman, D. and Salt, J. (eds) (1996) *Ethnicity in the 1991 Census, Volume 1: Demographic Characteristics of the Ethnic Minority Populations* London: HMSO

Collins, P.H. (1998) *Fighting Words: Black Women and the Search for Justice* Minneapolis: University of Minnesota Press

——(2001) 'Like One of the Family: Race, Ethnicity and the Paradox of US National Identity' *Ethnic and Racial Studies* 24, 1: 3–28

Community Relations Commission (1976) *Between Two Cultures – A Study of Relationships between Generations in the Asian Community in Britain* London: Community Relations Commission

Conkin, P. and Stromberg, R.N. (1989) *Heritage and Challenge: The History and Theory of History* Arlington Heights, IL: Forum

Connell, R. (1995) *Masculinities* Cambridge: Polity

——(2000) *The Men and the Boys* Berkeley: University of California Press

Craft, W. and Craft, E. (1999) *Running a Thousand Miles for Freedom. The Escape of William and Ellen Craft from Slavery* Athens: University of Georgia Press

Crocker, J. and Quinn, D. (1998) 'Racism and Self-Esteem' in J. Eberhardt and S. Fiske (eds) *Confronting Racism: The Problem and the Response* Newbury Park, CA: Sage

Cross, S. (2001) 'What is Strategic Essentialism?' unpublished paper

Damasio, A.R. (1994) *Descartes' Error: Emotion, Reason, and the Human Brain* New York: Putnam

D'Augelli, A. (2002) 'Foreword: The Cutting Edges of Lesbian and Gay Psychology' in A. Coyle and C. Kitzinger (eds) *Lesbian and Gay Psychology* Oxford: BPS/Blackwell

Davies, B. and Harre, R. (1990) 'Positioning: The Discursive Production of Selves' *Journal for the Theory of Social Behaviour* 20, 1: 43–63

Dawson, M. (1994) *Behind the Mule: Race and Class in African American Politics* Princeton, NJ: Princeton University Press

De Andrade, L.L. (2000) 'Negotiations from the Inside: Constructing Racial and Ethnic Identity in Qualitative Research' *Journal of Contemporary Ethnography* 29, 3: 268–90

de Jongh, R., van der Laan, M. and Rath, J. (1984) *FNVers aan het woord over buitenlandse werknemers* [FNV Members Speak out about Foreign Workers] Leiden: COMT, University of Leiden

de Rudder, V., Poiret, C. and V'Ourch, F. (2000) *L'Inégalité raciste: l'universalité républicaine à l'épreuve* Paris: Presses Universitaires de France

Debarbieux, E. (1998) 'Violence et ethnicité dans l'école française' *Revue européenne des migrations internationales* 14, 1: 77–92

Deleuze, G. (1988) *Foucault* Minneapolis: University of Minnesota Press

Derrida, J. (1987) 'Geschlecht II: Heidegger's Hand' in J. Sallis (ed.) *Deconstruction and Philosophy* Chicago, IL: University of Chicago Press

DeVault, M. (1995) 'Ethnicity and Expertise: Racial Ethnic Knowledge in Sociological Research' *Gender and Society* 9: 612–31

Dickson, D. (1870) *A Practical Treatise on Agriculture; to Which Is Added the Author's Published Letters* Macon, GA: J.W. Burke and Company

Dixon, J. and Durrheim, K. (2003) 'Contact and the Ecology of Racial Division: Some Varieties of Informal Segregation' *British Journal of Social Psychology*

Du Bois, W.E.B. (1899) [1996] *The Philadelphia Negro: A Social Study* Philadelphia: University of Pennsylvania Press [reprinted with a new introduction by Elijah Anderson]

Dummett, A. (1973) *A Portrait of English Racism* Harmondsworth: Penguin

Duneier, M. (1999) *Sidewalk* New York: Farrar, Straus, Giroux

Duprez, D. and Body-Gendrot, S. (2001) 'Les politiques de sécurité et de prévention dans les années 1990 en France' *Déviance et société* 25, 4: 377–402

Dyer, R. (1997) *White* London: Routledge

Eder, D., Evans, C.C. and Parker, S. (1995) *School Talk: Gender and Adolescent Culture* New Brunswick, NJ: Rutgers University Press

Edwards, D. (1997) *Discourse and Cognition* London: Sage

Elich, J. and Maso, B. (1984) *Discriminatie, vooroordeel en racisme in Nederland* [Discrimination, Prejudice and Racism in the Netherlands] 's-Gravenhage: ACOM, Ministerie van Binnenlandse Zaken

Ellis, S. (2001) *The Mask of Anarchy: The Destruction of Liberia and the Religious Dimension of an African Civil War* New York: New York University Press

Essed, P. (1982) 'Racisme en feminisme' [Racism and feminism] *Socialisties Feministiese Teksten* 7: 9–40

——(1987) *Academic Racism: Common Sense in the Social Sciences* working paper, Amsterdam: Centre for Race and Ethnic Studies, University of Amsterdam

——(1988) 'Understanding Verbal Accounts of Racism: Politics and Heuristics of Reality Constructions' *TEXT* 8, 1: 5–40

——(1990) *Everyday Racism: Reports from Women of Two Cultures* Alameda, CA: Hunter House

——(1991) *Understanding Everyday Racism: An Interdisciplinary Theory* Newbury Park, CA: Sage

——(1996) *Diversity: Gender, Color and Culture* Amherst: University of Massachusetts Press

——(2002) 'Cloning Cultural Homogeneity while Talking Diversity: Old Wine in New Bottles in Dutch Work Organizations?' *Transforming Anthropology* 11, 1: 2–12

Essed, P. and de Graaff, M. (2002) *De actualiteit van diversiteit. Het gemeentelijk beleid onder de loep* [The Topicality of Diversity. Municipal Policy in Focus] Utrecht: Forum and The Hague: E-Quality: Experts in Gender and Ethnicity

Essed, P. and Goldberg, D.T. (2002a) 'Cloning Cultures: The Social Injustices of Sameness' *Ethnic and Racial Studies* 25, 6: 1,066–82

——(eds) (2002b) *Race Critical Theories: Text and Context* Oxford: Blackwell

Feagin, J. and Feagin, C.Y. (2003) *Racial and Ethnic Relations*, seventh edn, Upper Saddle River, NJ: Prentice-Hall

Feagin, J.R. and Sikes, M. (1994) *Living with Racism* Boston, MA: Beacon

——(2000) *Racist America* New York: Routledge

Feagin, J.R. and Vera. H. (1995) *White Racism: The Basics* London: Routledge

——(2001) *Liberation Sociology* Boulder, CO: Westview Press

Feagin, J.R., Vera, H. and Imani, N. (1996) *The Agony of Education: Black Students at White Colleges and Universities* London: Routledge

Fox, R.G. (1991) *Recapturing Anthropology: Working in the Present*, NM: School of American Research Press

Fox-Genovese, E. (1988) *Within the Plantation Household. Black and White Women of the Old South* Chapel Hill and London: University of North Carolina Press

Frank, A.G. (1998) *Re-orient: Global Economy in the Asian Age* Berkeley: University of California Press

Frankenberg, R. (1993) *White Women, Race Matters: The Social Construction of Whiteness* London: Routledge

——(2001) 'The Mirage of an Unmarked Whiteness' in B. B. Rasmussen, E. Klinenberg, I.J. Nexica and M. Wray (eds) *The Making and Unmaking of Whiteness* Durham, NC: Duke University Press

Frosh, S. (2002) *Afterwords: The Personal in Gender, Culture and Psychotherapy* London: Palgrave

Frosh, S., Phoenix, A. and Pattman, R. (2001) *Young Masculinities* London: Palgrave

——(2003) 'Taking a Stand: Using Psychoanalysis to Explore the Positioning of Subjects in Discourse' *British Journal of Social Psychology,* 42,1:39-53

Fuss, D. (1990) *Essentially Speaking: Feminism, Nature and Difference* London: Routledge

Gallagher, C. (2000) 'White Like Me? Methods, Meaning and Manipulation in the Field of White Studies' in F.W. Twine and J.W. Warren (eds) *Racing Research, Researching Race* New York: New York University Press

Gallissot, R. (1988) *Perspective historique: histoire sociale, histoire urbaine, histoire nationale,* Colloque Rennes 2, unpublished mim.

Gans, H. (1999) 'The Possibility of a New Racial Hierarchy in the Twenty-First Century United States' in M. Lamont (ed.) *The Cultural Territories of Race* Chicago, IL: University of Chicago Press

Garfinkel, H. (1967) *Studies in Ethnomethodology* Cambridge: Polity Press

Gates, H.L. (1994) 'Goodbye Columbus? Notes on the Culture of Criticism' in D.T. Goldberg (ed.) *Multiculturalism: A Critical Reader* Oxford: Blackwell

Geertz, C. (2000) *Available Light* Princeton, NJ: Princeton University Press

Gilman, S. (1985) *Difference and Pathology* Ithaca, NY: Cornell University Press

Gilroy, P. (1987) *There Ain't No Black in the Union Jack* London: Hutchinson

——(2000) *Between Camps: Nations, Cultures and the Allure of Race* London: Allen Lane

Goldberg, D.T. (1993) *Racist Culture: Philosophy and the Politics of Meaning* Oxford: Blackwell

——(2001) *The Racial State* Malden, MA: Blackwell

Goldberg, D.T. and Solomos, J. (eds) (2002) *A Companion to Racial and Ethnic Studies* Oxford: Blackwell

Goldthorpe, J.H. (2000) *On Sociology: Numbers, Narratives and the Integration of Research and Theory* Oxford: Oxford University Press

Gordon, A. F. (1996) *Ghostly Matters: Haunting and the Sociological Imagination* London and Minneapolis: University of Minnesota Press

Gouldner, A.W. (1970) *The Coming Crisis of Western Sociology* New York: Basic Books

Grant, D., Oliver, M. and James, A. (1996) 'African Americans: Social and Economic Bifurcation' in R. Waldinger and M. Bozorgmehr (eds) *Ethnic Los Angeles* New York: Russell Sage Foundation

Griffin, L.J. (1993) 'Narrative, Event-Structure Analysis, and Causal Interpretation in Historical Sociology' *American Journal of Sociology* 98: 1,095–133

Grossberg, L. (1997) 'Cultural Studies: What's in a Name? (One More Time)' in *Bringing It All Back Home: Essays in Cultural Studies* Durham, NC: Duke University Press

Grossmann, R. (2002) 'Le communautarisme, voilà l'ennemi' *Figaro Magazine,* 15 June: 32

Guillaumin, C. (1992) 'Une société en ordre: de quelques unes des formes de l'idéologie raciste' *Sociologie et sociétés* 24, 2: 15–23

Gunaratnam, Y. (2003) *Researching Race and Ethnicity: Methods, Knowledge and Power* London: Sage

Halbwachs, M. (1992) *On Collective Memory* ed. and trans. Lewis Coser, Chicago, IL: University of Chicago Press

Hall, S. (1991) 'Old and New Identities, Old and New Ethnicities' in A.D. King (ed.) *Culture, Globalisation and the World-System* Basingstoke: Macmillan

——(1992) 'The West and the Rest' in S. Hall and B. Gieben (eds) *Formations of Modernity* Milton Keynes: Open University Press

——(1993) 'Culture, Community, Nation' *Cultural Studies* 7, 3: 349–63

——(1996) 'Introduction: Who Needs "Identity"?' in S. Hall and P. du Gay (eds) *Questions of Cultural Identity* London: Sage

——(1997) 'The Work of Representation' in S. Hall (ed.) *Representation* London: Sage

Halliday, F. (1996) *Islam and the Myth of Confrontation* London: I.B. Tauris

Harding, S. (ed.) (1987) *Feminism and Methodology* Bloomington: Indiana University Press

Harding, S. (2002) '"Strong Objectivity" a Response to the New Objectivity Question' in J.A. Kourany (ed.) *The Gender of Science* Upper Saddle River, NJ: Prentice Hall

Hannerz, U. (1969) *Soulside: Inquiries into Ghetto Culture and Community* New York: Columbia University Press

Haut Conseil à l'Intégration (1991) *Pour un modèle français d'intégration. Premier rapport annuel* Paris: La Documentation Française

Heidegger, M. (1968) *What Is Called Thinking?* New York: Harper Torchbooks

Heise, D. and Lewis, E. (1988) 'Introduction to ETHNO' Raleigh, NC: National Collegiate Software Clearing House

Hewitt, R. (1986) *White Talk Black Talk: Inter-Racial Friendships and Communication amongst Adolescents* Cambridge: Cambridge University Press

Hickman, M. (1998) 'Reconstructing Deconstructing "Race": British Discourses about the Irish in Britain' *Ethnic and Racial Studies* 21, 2: 288–307

Hollway, W. (1984) 'Gender Difference and the Production of Subjectivity' in J. Henriques, W. Hollway, C. Urwin, C. Venn and V. Walkerdine (eds) *Changing the Subject* London: Methuen

——(1989) *Subjectivity and Method in Psychology* London: Sage

Hollway, W. and Jefferson, T. (2000) *Doing Qualitative Research Differently: Free Association, Narrative and the Interview Method* London: Sage

hooks, b. (1992) 'Representing Whiteness in the Black Imagination' in L. Grossberg and P. Treichler (eds) *Cultural Studies* New York: Routledge

——(1999) *Remembered Rapture: The Writer at Work* London: The Women's Press

Howe, D. (1996) 'Black Becomes Grey' *Sunday Telegraph,* 9 June 1996

Human Rights Watch (1998) *Sierra Leone – Sowing Terror: Atrocities against Civilians in Sierra Leone* July

Hurh, W.M. and Kim, K.C. (1989) 'The "Success" Image of Asian Americans: Its Validity, and Its Practical and Theoretical Implications' *Ethnic and Racial Studies* 12, 4: 512–38

Ignatiev, N. (1997) 'Treason to Whiteness is Loyalty to Humanity' in R. Delgado and J. Stefancic (eds) *Critical White Studies: Looking behind the Mirror* Philadelphia, PA: Temple University Press

Israel, J.J. and Bonnafous. S. (1992) *Sans distinction de...race in Mots* Paris: Presses de la FNSP, vol. 18, March.

Jackson, J.L. (2001) *Harlem World: Doing Race and Class in Contemporary America* Chicago, IL: University of Chicago Press

Jenkins, R. (1996) *Social Identity* London: Routledge

——(1997) *Rethinking Ethnicity* London: Sage

Johnson, M.P. and Roark, J.L. (1984) *Black Masters. A Free Family of Color in the Old South* New York and London: W.W. Norton & Company

Jones, S. (1988) *White Youth, Black Culture: The Reggae Tradition from JA to UK* Basingstoke: Macmillan

Jordan, W. (1962) '"American Chiaroscuro": The Status and Definition of Mulattoes in the British Colonies' *William and Mary Quarterly* 14, 2: 193

——(1968) *White over Black: American Attitudes towards the Negro, 1550–1812* Chapel Hill and London: University of North Carolina Press

Karn, V. (ed.) (1997) *Ethnicity in the 1991 Census, Volume Four: Employment, Education and Housing among the Ethnic Minority Populations of Britain* London: Office of National Statistics

Katz, M.B. (1989) *The Undeserving Poor: From the War on Poverty to the War on Welfare* New York: Pantheon

Katz, M.B. and Sugrue, T.J. (eds) (1998) *W.E.B. Du Bois, Race and the City: The Philadelphia Negro and Its Legacy* Philadelphia: University of Pennsylvania Press

Katznelson, I. (1981) *City Trenches: Urban Politics and the Patterning of Class in the United States* Chicago, IL: University of Chicago Press

Keith, M. (1992) 'Angry Writing: (Re)presenting the Unethical World of the Ethnographer' *Society and Space* 10: 551–68

——(1995) 'Shouts of the Street: Identity and the Spaces of Authenticity' *Social Identities* 1, 2: 297–315

Kepel, G. (1987) *Les Banlieues de l'Islam* Paris: Le Seuil

Kibria, N. (1998) 'The contested meanings of "Asian American": Racial Dilemmas in the Contemporary US' *Ethnic and Racial Studies* 21, 5: 939–58

Kierkegaard, S. (1936) *Philosophical Fragments* Princeton, NJ: Princeton University Press

Kilson, M. (1975) 'Blacks and Neo-Ethnicity in American Political Life' in N. Glazer and D.P. Moynihan (eds) *Ethnicity: Theory and Experience* Cambridge, MA: Harvard University Press

Kim, C.J. (1999) 'The Racial Triangulation of Asian Americans' *Politics and Society* 27, 1: 105–38

Köbben, A. (1985) 'Oordeel en discriminatie' [Judgement and discrimination] *Etnische minderheden* [Ethnic Minorities] Meppel: Boom

Kourany, J.A. (ed.) (2002) *The Gender of Science* Upper Saddle River, NJ: Prentice Hall

Ladner, J.A. (ed.) (1998) [1973] *The Death of White Sociology* Baltimore, MD: Black Classics Press

Lamont, M. (1992) *Money, Morals, and Manners: The Culture of the French and the American Upper-Middle Class* Chicago. IL: University of Chicago Press

——(ed.) (1999) *The Cultural Territories of Race: Black and White Boundaries* Chicago, IL and New York: University of Chicago Press and Russell Sage Foundation

——(2000) *The Dignity of Working Men: Morality and the Boundaries of Race, Class, and Immigration and* Cambridge MA: New York and Harvard University Press: Russell Sage Foundation

——(2002) *The Dignity of Working Men* Cambridge, MA: Harvard University Press

Landry, B. (1987) *The New Black Middle Class* Los Angeles: University of California Press

Lanquetin M.T. (2000) *Le Recours au droit: la lutte contre les discriminations* Paris: GELD

Lauren, P.G. (1988) *Power and Prejudice. The Politics and Diplomacy of Racial Discrimination* Boulder, CO: Westview Press

——(1998) *The Evolution of International Human Rights. Visions Seen* Philadelphia: University of Philadelphia Press

Lawrence, E. (1982) 'In the Abundance of Water, the Fool is Thirsty: Sociology and Black Pathology' in CCCS *The Empire Strikes Back* London: Hutchinson

LBR (2002) *Racisme in Nederland. Jaar in beeld 2001* [Racism in the Netherlands. Year in Focus 2001] Rotterdam: Landelijk Bureau ter bestrijding van Rassendiscriminatie (LBR)

Leca J. (1985) 'Une capacité d'intégration défaillante' *Esprit* 6, June: 9–23

Leslie, K.A. (1995) *Woman of Color, Daughter of Privilege: Amanda America Dickson, 1849–1893* Athens: University of Georgia Press

Levi, P. (1991) *Other People's Trades* London: Abacus

Lewis, G. (2000) *'Race', Gender, Social Welfare: Encounters in a Postcolonial Society* Cambridge: Polity

Lieberson, S. (1980) *A Piece of the Pie: Blacks and White Immigrants since 1880* Berkeley: University of California Press

——(1985) *Making It Count: The Improvement of Social Research and Theory* Berkeley: University of California Press

Lieberson, S. and Waters, M. (1988) *From Many Strands: Ethnic and Racial Groups in Contemporary America* New York: Russell Sage Foundation

Liebow, E. (1967) *Tally's Corner, Washington DC: A Study of Negro Street Corner Men* London: Routledge & Kegan Paul

Lien, P.-T. (1997) *The Political Participation of Asian Americans* New York: Garland Publishing

Litwack, L.F. (2000) 'Hellhounds' in H.A. James Allen (ed.) *Without Sanctuary: Lynching Photography in America* Santa Fe, NM: Twin Palms

Loewen, J.W. (1971) *The Mississippi Chinese: Between Black and White* Cambridge, MA: Harvard University Press

Louw-Potgieter, J. (1989) 'Covert Racism: An Application of Essed's Analysis in a South African Context' *Journal of Language and Social Psychology* 8: 307–19

Lucas, S. (2003) *Orwell: Life and Times* London: Haus

Mac an Ghaill, M. (1999) *Contemporary Racisms and Ethnicities* Buckingham: Open University Press

McClaurin, I. (ed.) (2001) *Black Feminist Anthropology. Theory, Politics, Praxis, and Poetics* New Brunswick, NJ: Rutgers University Press

McDowell, L. (1999) *Gender, Identity and Place: Understanding Feminist Geographies* Cambridge: Polity

Mackenzie, R. (1998) 'The United States and the Taliban' in W. Maley (ed.) *Fundamentalism Reborn? Afghanistan and the Taliban* London: Hurst

Mama, A. (1995) *Beyond the Masks: Race, Gender and Subjectivity* London: Routledge

Marable, M. (1995) *Beyond Black and White* London: Verso

Marcus, G. (1998) *Ethnography through Thick and Thin* Princeton, NJ: Princeton University Press

Margalit, A. (1996) *The Decent Society* Cambridge, MA: Harvard University Press

Massey, D. (1994) *Space, Place and Gender* Cambridge: Polity

Massey, D. and Denton, M. (1994) *American Apartheid: Segregation and the Making of the Underclass* Cambridge, MA: Harvard University Press

Matsuda, M. (1993) 'We Will Not Be Used' *UCLA Asian American Pacific Islands Law Journal* 1: 79–84

May, R.A.B. (2001) *Talking at Trena's: Everyday Conversations at an African American Tavern* New York: New York University Press

Mellor, D., Bynon, G. *et al.* (2001) 'The Perception of Racism in Ambiguous Scenarios' *Journal of Ethnic and Migration Studies* 27, 3: 473–88

Memmi, A. (2000) *Racism* Minneapolis: University of Minnesota Press

Merton, R. (1972) 'Insiders and Outsiders: A Chapter in the Sociology of Knowledge' *American Journal of Sociology* 78: 9–47

Miles, R. (1982) *Racism and Migrant Labour* London: Routledge & Kegan Paul

——(1989) *Racism* London: Routledge

Miles, R. and Small, S. (1999) 'Racism and Ethnicity' in S. Taylor (ed.) *Sociology: Issues and Debates* Basingstoke: Macmillan

Milgram, S. (1974) *Obedience to Authority* London: Tavistock

Milner, D. (1983) *Children and Race Ten Years On* London: Ward Lock Educational

Mills, C.W. (1959) *The Sociological Imagination* London: Oxford University Press

Mills, K. (ed.) (2000) *C. Wright Mills; Letters and Autobiographical Writings* Berkeley, Los Angeles and London: University of California Press

Minard, R. (1952) 'Race Relationships in the Pocahontas Coal Field' *Journal of Social Issues* 8: 29–44

Minsky, R. (1996) *Psychoanalysis and Gender: An Introductory Reader* London: Routledge

Modood, T. (1992) *Not Easy Being British* Stoke on Trent: Trentham

——(1994) 'Political Blackness and British Asians' *Sociology* 28, 4: 859–76

——(1996) 'The Changing Context of "Race" in Britain' *Patterns of Prejudice* 30, 1: 3–13

Modood, T., Berthoud, R., Lakey, J., Nazroo, J., Smith, P., Virdee, S. and Beishon, S. (1997) *Ethnic Minorities in Britain: Diversity and Disadvantage* London: Policy Studies Institute

Mok, I. (1999) *In de ban van het ras. Aardrijkskunde tussen wetenschap en samenleving 1876–1992* [Under the Spell of Race. Geography between Science and Society 1876–1992] Amsterdam: ASCA

Moynihan, D.P. (1965) *The Negro Family: The Call for National Action* Washington, DC: US Department of Labor

Murray, C. and Herrnstein, R. (1994) *The Bell Curve* New York: The Free Press

Murrell, A. (1998) 'To Identify or Not to Identify' in J. Eberhardt and S. Fiske (eds) *Confronting Racism* Thousand Oaks, CA: Sage

Naples, N.A. (1996) 'A Feminist Revisiting of the Insider/Outsider Debate: The "Outsider Phenomenon" in Rural Iowa' *Qualitative Sociology* 19: 83–106

Nasr, S.V.R. (1994) *The Vanguard of the Islamic Revolution: The Jamaati-i-Islami of Pakistan* London: I.B. Tauris

Nayak, A. and Kehily, M. (1996) 'Playing It Straight: Masculinities, Homophobias and Schooling' *Journal of Gender Studies* 5, 2: 211–30

Nelson, C. and Tienda, M. (1988) 'The Structuring of Hispanic Ethnicity' in R. Alba (ed.) *Ethnicity and Race in the USA* New York: Routledge & Kegan Paul

Nencel, L. and Pels, P. (eds) (1991) *Constructing Knowledge. Authority and Critique in Social Science* London: Sage

Nieman-Flores, Y. (1999) 'Social Ecological Contexts of Prejudice between Hispanics and Blacks' in P. Wong (ed.) *Race, Ethnicity, and Nationality in the United States* Boulder, CO: Westview Press

Noiriel, G. (1988) *Le Creuset français* Paris: Le Seuil

Oake, G. (1989) 'Native Justice Evidence Would Make Riel Cry' the *Toronto Star*, second edn, p. D5

O'Connor, A. (2001) *Poverty Knowledge: Social Science, Social Policy, and the Poor in Twentieth-Century US History* Princeton, NJ: Princeton University Press

Ogbu, J. (1990) 'Minority Status and Literacy in Comparative Perspective' *Daedalus* 119: 141–69

Oguntoye, K., Opitz, M. and Schulz, D. (eds) (1986) *Farbe Bekennen. Afro-deutsche Frauen auf den Spuren ihrer Geschichte* [Coming out for Your Colour. Afro-German Women on the Trails of Their Histories] Berlin: Orlanda Frauenverlag

Okihiro, G. (1994) [1941] *Margins and Mainstreams: Asians in History and Culture* Seattle: University of Washington Press

Olmsted, F.L. (1863) *A Journey in the Back Country* New York: Mason Brothers

Omi, M. and Winant, H. (1994) *Racial Formation in the United States* second edn, New York: Routledge

Orwell, G. (1970a) [1941] 'Wells, Hitler and the World State' in *George Orwell: The Collected Essays, Journalism and Letters: Volume 2* London: Penguin Books

——(1970b) [1941] 'Anti-Semitism in Britain' in *George Orwell: The Collected Essays, Journalism and Letters: Volume 3* London: Penguin Books

——(1970c) [1941] 'As I Please – 11th February, 1944' in *George Orwell: The Collected Essays, Journalism and Letters: Volume 3* London: Penguin Books

——(1970d) [1941] 'How the Poor Die' in *George Orwell: The Collected Essays, Journalism and Letters: Volume 4* London: Penguin Books

Owen, C. (2001) 'Mixed Race in Official Statistics' in D. Parker and M. Song (eds) *Rethinking 'Mixed Race'* London: Pluto

Paine, L. (1851) *Six Years in a Georgia Prison: Narrative of Lewis W. Paine* New York: Printed for the Author

Palumbo-Liu, D. (1999) *Asian/American* Stanford, CT: Stanford University Press

Parekh, B. (2000) *Rethinking Multiculturalism: Cultural Diversity and Political Theory* Basingstoke: Macmillan

Parker, D. and Song, M. (2001) 'Introduction: Rethinking "Mixed Race"' in D. Parker and M. Song (eds) *Rethinking 'Mixed Race'* London: Pluto

Parkin, D., James, J.W. and Dresch, P. (eds) (2000) *Anthropologists in a Wider World: Essays on Field Research* New York: Berghahn Books

Patillo-McCoy, M. (1999) *Black Picket Fences* Chicago, IL: University of Chicago Press

Patterson, J.T. (2000) *America's Struggle against Poverty in the Twentieth Century* Cambridge, MA: Harvard University Press

Phillips, A. (1999) *Darwin's Worms* London: Faber & Faber

Phillips, C. (1996) 'Cultural References' *Financial Times* 1 June 1996

Phoenix, A. (2003) 'Review of Blacks and Britannity' *Contemporary Sociology* 32, 1: 26–7

Phoenix, A. and Owen, C. (1996) 'From Miscegenation to Hybridity: Mixed Parentage and Mixed Relationships in Context' in J. Brannen and B. Bernstein (eds) *Children, Research and Policy* London: Taylor & Francis

Pomeranz, K. (2001) *The Great Divergence: China, Europe, and the Making of the Modern World Economy* Princeton, NJ: Princeton University Press

Portes, A. and Rumbaut, R.G. (2001) *Legacies: The Story of the Immigrant Second Generation* Berkeley: University of California Press

Potter, J. and Wetherell, M. (1987) *Discourse and Social Psychology: Beyond Attitudes and Behaviour* London: Sage

Prashad, V. (2000) *The Karma of Brown Folk* Minneapolis: University of Minnesota Press

Pred, A. (2000) *Even in Sweden. Racisms, Racialized Spaces and the Popular Geographical Imagination* Berkeley: University of California Press

Prins, B. (2000) *De onschuld voorbij. Het debat over de multiculturele samenleving* [Beyond Innocence. The Debate about the Multicultural Society] Amsterdam: van Gennep

Public Inquiry into the Administration of Justice and Aboriginal People [A.C. Hamilton and C.M. Sinclair] (1991) *Report of the Aboriginal Justice Inquiry of Manitoba* Winnipeg, Man.: Public Inquiry into the Administration of Justice and Aboriginal People

Rabinow, P. (1991) 'For Hire: Resolutely Late Modern' in R.G. Fox (ed.) *Recapturing Anthropology: Working in the Present,* NM: School of American Research Press

Rainwater, L. (1970) *Behind Ghetto Walls: Negro Family Life in a Slum: Black Family Life in a Federal Slum* New York: Aldine Publishing Company

Rasmussen, B.B., Klinenberg, E., Nexica, I.J. and Wray, M. (eds) (2001) *The Making and Unmaking of Whiteness* Durham, NC: Duke University Press

Raper, A.F. and Southern Commission on the Study of Lynching (1933) *The Tragedy of Lynching* Chapel Hill and London: University of North Carolina Press

Rashid, A. (2000) *Taliban: Islam, Oil and the New Great Game in Central Asia* London: I.B. Tauris

Ratcliffe, P. (ed.) (2001) *The Politics of Social Science Research: 'Race', Ethnicity and Social Change* Basingstoke: Palgrave

Räthzel, N. (2002) 'Living differences – ethnicity and fearless girls in public places' in T. Johansson and O. Sernhede (eds) *Lifestyle, Desire and Politics: Contemporary Identities* Gothenburg: Daidalos

Rattansi, A. (1994) '"Western" Racisms, Ethnicities and Identities in a "Postmodern" Frame' in A. Rattansi and S. Westwood (eds) *Racism, Modernity and Identity* Cambridge: Polity Press

Rawick, G.P. (1972) *The American Slave: A Composite Autobiography*, Vol. 12, Georgia Narratives Parts 1 and 2, and Vol. 13, Georgia Narratives Parts 3 and 4, Westport, CT: Greenwood Press

Ray, L. and Smith, D. (2000) 'Hate Crime, Violence and Cultures of Racism' in P. Iganski (ed.) *The Hate Debate* London: Profile Books

Reinharz, S. (1997) 'Who Am I? The Need for a Variety of Selves in the Field' in *Reflexivity and Voice* Thousand Oaks, CA: Sage Publications

Rex, J. (1973) 'The Future of Race Relations Research in Britain: Sociological Research and the Politics of Racial Justice' *Race* 14, 4: 481–8

——(1979a) 'Race Relations Research in an Academic Setting: A Personal Note' *Home Office Research Bulletin* 8: 29–30

——(1979b) 'The Right Lines for Race Research' *New Society* 5 April: 14–16

——(1996) *Ethnic Minorities in the Modern Nation State* Basingstoke: Macmillan

Rich, A. (1970) 'Disloyal to Civilization: Feminism, Racism and Gynephobia' *Chrysalis* 7: 9–27

Riessman, C. (1987) 'When Gender Is Not Enough: Women Interviewing Women' *Gender and Society* 1, 2: 172–207

Rojek, C. and Turner, B. (2000) 'Decorative Sociology: Towards a Critique of the Cultural Turn' *Sociological Review* 48, 4: 629–48

Roof, J. and Wiegman, R. (eds) (1995) *Who Can Speak? Authority and Critical Identity* Urbana: University of Illinois Press

Root, M. (1992) *Racially Mixed People in America* Newbury Park, CA and London: Sage

Rosaldo, R. (1989) *Culture and Truth: The Remaking of Social Analysis* London: Routledge

Roy, O. (1994) *The Failure of Political Islam* London: I.B. Tauris

Ruggiero, V. (2001) 'New Folk Devils on Urban Landscape' *The Times Higher Education Supplement* 9 November 2001

Rútsdóttir, H. (2002) '"To Feel at Home" in a Foreign Country: Opportunities and Barriers of Immigrants in Iceland' *InDRA* Amsterdam: University of Amsterdam

Sale, K. (1990) *The Conquest of Paradise* New York: Plume

Sanders, L. (1995) 'What Is Whiteness? Race-of-Interviewer Effects when All the Interviewers Are Black' paper presented at the American Politics Workshop, University of Chicago, 4 January

Sartre, J.-P. (1963) *Search for a Method* New York: Vintage Books

Sayyid, S. (2000) 'Bad Faith: Anti-Essentialism, Universalism and Islam' in A. Brah and A.E. Coombes (eds) *Hybridity and Its Discontents* London: Routledge

Schattschneider, E.E. (1960) *The Semi-Sovereign People: A Realist's View of Democracy in America* Hindsale, IL: Dryden Press.

Schnapper, D. (1991) *La France de l'intégration* Paris: Gallimard

Schultz, D.A. (1969) *Coming up Black: Patterns of Ghetto Socialization* Englewood Cliffs, NJ: Prentice Hall

Schuster, L. and Solomos, J. (2002) 'Rights and Wrongs across European Borders' *Citizenship Studies* 6, 1: 37–53

Sears, D., Sidanius, J. and Bobo, L. (eds) (2000) *Racialized Politics: The Debate about Racism in America* Chicago, IL: University of Chicago Press

Sennett, R. (1993) *The Fall of Public Man* London: Faber

Sharma, A., Hutnyk, J. and Sharma, S. (eds) (1996) *DisOrienting Rhythms* London: Zed Press

Shibutani, T. and Kwan, K. (1965) *Ethnic Stratification* New York: Macmillan

Shih, J. (2002) '"Yeah, I Could Hire This One, but I Know It's Gonna Be a Problem": How Race, Nativity, and Gender Affect Employers' Perceptions of the Manageability of Job Seekers' *Ethnic and Racial Studies* 25, 1: 99–119

Shyllon, F. (1974) *Black Slaves in Britain* London: Oxford University Press

Sidanius, J. and Pratto, F. (1999) *Social Dominance* Cambridge, UK: Cambridge University Press

Silverman, M. and Yuval-Davis, N. (1999) 'Jews, Arabs and the Theorisation of Racism in Britain and France' in A. Brah, M. Hickman and M. Mac an Ghaill (eds) *Thinking Identities* Basingstoke: Macmillan

Simon, P. (1999) 'Le modèle français de discrimination, un nouveau défi pour l'antiracisme' *Mouvements* 4: 5–8

Sivanandan, A. (1982) *A Different Hunger* London: Pluto

Sjoberg, G., Gill, E., Williams, N. and Kuhn, K.E. (1995) 'Ethics, Human Rights and Sociological Inquiry: Genocide, Politicide and Other Issues of Organizational Power' *American Sociologist* 26: 11–13

Slack, J.D. (1996) 'The Theory and Method of Articulation in Cultural Studies' in D. Morley and Hall, S. (eds) *Critical Dialogues in Cultural Studies* New York: Routledge

Small, S. (1989) 'Racial Differentiation in the Slave Era: A Comparative Analysis of People of "Mixed-Race" in Jamaica and Georgia' unpublished Ph.D. dissertation, University of California at Berkeley

——(1991) 'Racialised Relations in Liverpool: A Contemporary Anomaly' *New Community* 11, 4: 511–37

——(1994a) 'Racial Group Boundaries and Identities: People of "Mixed-Race" in Slavery across the Americas' *Slavery and Abolition* 15: 17–37

——(1994b) *Racialised Barriers: The Black Experience in the United States and England in the 1980s* London: Routledge

——(2002) 'Racisms and Racialized Hostility at the Start of the New Millennium' in D.T. Goldberg and J. Solomos (eds) *Companion to Race and Ethnic Studies* Oxford: Blackwell

Smith, D.E. (1987) *The Everyday World as Problematic: A Feminist Sociology*. Boston, MA: Northeastern University Press

Smith, J.F. (1985) *Slavery and Rice Culture in Low Country Georgia, 1750–1860* Knoxville: University of Tennessee Press

Smith, S. (1989) *The Politics of 'Race' and Residence* Cambridge, UK: Polity

Solomos, J. (2003) *Race and Racism in Britain* third edn Basingstoke: Macmillan.

Solomos, J. and Back, L. (1995) *Race, Politics and Social Change* London: Routledge

——(1996) *Racism and Society* Basingstoke: Macmillan

Somers, M.R. (1994) 'The Narrative Constitution of Identity: A Relational and Network Approach' *Theory and Society* 23: 605–49

Song, M. (2001) 'Comparing Minorities' Ethnic Options' *Ethnicities* 1, 1: 58–82

——(2003) *Choosing Ethnic Identity* Cambridge: Polity Press

Song, M. and Parker, D. (1995) 'Commonality, Difference and the Dynamics of Disclosure' *Sociology* 29, 2: 241–56

Spickard, P. (1989) *Mixed Blood: Intermarriage and Ethnic Identity in Twentieth Century America* Madison: University of Wisconsin Press

Spivak, G.C. (1999) *A Critique of Postcolonial Reason* London: Routledge

Stacey, J. (1988) 'Can There Be a Feminist Ethnography?' *Women's Studies International Forum* 11, 1: 21–7

Stack, C. (1974) *All Our Kin: Strategies for Survival in a Black Community* New York: Harper Colophon Books

Stanfield, J.H. II (ed.) (1993) *A History of Race Relations Research: First-Generation Recollections* Newbury Park, CA: Sage

Stanfield, J.H. II and Dennis, R.M. (eds) (1993) *Race and Ethnicity in Research Methods* Newbury Park, CA: Sage

Starling, M.W. (1985) *The Slave Narrative: Its Place in American History* Washington, DC: Howard University Press

Stoler, A. (1995) *Race and the Education of Desire* London: Duke University Press

Stora, B. (2002) *Histoire de la guerre d'Algérie* Paris: La Découverte

Tabboni, S. (2001) 'Il n'y a pas de différence sans inégalité' in M. Wieviorka and J. Ohanna (eds) *La Différence culturelle* Paris: Balland

Taguieff, P.-A. (1988) *La Force du préjugé: Essai sur le racisme et ses doubles* Paris: La Découverte

——(1996) *La République menacée* Paris: Textuel

——(2001) *La Couleur et le sang: doctrines racistes à la française* Paris: Mille et Une Nuits

Taillon, J. (2000) 'Manitoba Government Apologizes to Osbornes' in *Windspeaker*, p. 2

Tajfel, H., Billig, M., Bundy, R. and Flament, C. (1971) 'Social Categorization and Intergroup Behaviour' *European Journal of Social Psychology* 1: 149–77

Tannock, S. (1999) 'Working with Insults: Discourse and Difference in an Inner-City Youth Organization' *Discourse and Society* 10, 3: 317–50

Taylor, C. (1992) *Multiculturalism and 'the Politics of Recognition'* Princeton, NJ: Princeton University Press

Taylor, D.J. (2002) 'Orwell's Dirty Secret' the *Guardian G2*, 13 August: 4–5

——(2003) *Orwell: The Life* London: Chatto & Windus

Thapar, R. (1989) 'Imagined Religious Communities? Ancient Indian History and the Modern Search for a Hindu Identity' *Modern Asian Studies* 23, 2: 209–31

Tilly, C. (1998) *Durable Inequality* Berkeley: University of California Press

Tizard, B. and Phoenix, A. (2002) *Black, White or Mixed Race? Race and Racism in the Lives of Young People of Mixed Parentage* second edn, London: Routledge

Todd, E. (1994) *Le Destin des immigrés* Paris: Le Seuil

Touraine, A. (1991) 'Face à l'exclusion' in *Citoyenneté et Urbanité*, Paris: Ed. Esprit

Touraine, A., Dubet, F., Strzelecki, J. and Wieviorka, M. (1982) *Solidarité* Paris: Fayard

Tribalat, M. (1995) *Faire France* Paris: La Découverte

Tuan, M. (1998) *Forever Foreigners or Honorary Whites?* New Brunswick, NJ: Rutgers University Press

Twine, F.W. (1998) *Racism in a Racial Democracy: The Maintenance of White Supremacy in Brazil* New Brunswick, NJ: Rutgers University Press

——(2000) 'Racial Ideologies and Racial Methodologies' in F.W. Twine and J.W. Warren (eds) *Racing Research, Researching Race: Methodological Dilemmas in Critical Race Studies* New York: New York University Press

Twine, F.W. and Warren, J.W. (eds) (2000) *Racing Research. Researching Race: Methodological Dilemmas in Critical Race Studies* New York: New York University Press

United Nations Department of Public Information (1995) *The United Nations and Human Rights, 1945–1995* New York: United Nations

US Census (1990) 'Inequality within Racial and Ethnic Groups'

Valentine, C.A. (1968) *Culture and Poverty: Critique and Counter-Proposals* Chicago, IL: University of Chicago Press

Vallejo, C. (1980) *The Complete Posthumous Poetry* Berkeley, Los Angeles and London: University of California Press

van Dijk, T. (1984) *Prejudice in Discourse* Amsterdam: Benjamins

——(1987) *Schoolvoorbeelden van racisme* [Textbook Examples of Racism] Amsterdam: SUA

——(1993a) 'Discourse and the Denial of Racism' *Discourse and Society* 3: 57–118

——(1993b) *Elite Discourse and Racism* Newbury Park, CA: Sage

Van Maanen, J. (ed.) (1988) *Tales of the Field: On Writing Ethnography* Chicago, IL: University of Chicago Press

——(1995) 'An End to Innocence: The Ethnography of Ethnography' in T. Van Maanen (ed.) *Representations in Ethnography* London: Sage

Venkatesh, S. (2000) *American Project: The Rise and Fall of a Modern Ghetto* Cambridge, MA: Harvard University Press

——(2002) 'Doing the Hustle: Constructing the Ethnographer in the American Ghetto' *Ethnography* 3: 91–111

Verkuyten, M. (1995) 'Alledaagse betekenissen van "racisme" en 'discriminatie' [Everyday Meanings of 'Racism' and 'Discrimination'] *Migrantenstudies* 11, 3: 181–202

Visweswaran, K. (1994) *Fictions of Feminist Ethnography* Minneapolis: University of Minnesota Press

Walkerdine, V., Lucey, H. and Melody, J. (2001) *Growing up Girl* London: Palgrave

Wallman, S., Dhooge, Y., Goldman, A. and Kosmin, B. (1980) 'Ethnography by Proxy: Strategies for Research in the Inner City' *Ethnos* 45, 1–2: 5–38

Walter, B. (1998) 'Challenging the Black/White Binary' *Patterns of Prejudice* 32, 2: 73–86

——(2001) *Outsiders within: Whiteness, Place and Irish Women* London: Routledge

Walvin, J. (1985) 'Freeing the Slaves: How Important Was Wilberforce?' in J. Hayward (ed.) *Out of Slavery* London: Frank Cass

Ware, V. (1992) *Beyond the Pale: White Women, Racism and History* London: Verso

Waters, M. (1990) *Ethnic Options* Berkeley: University of California Press

——(1999) *Black Identities: West Indian Immigrant Dreams and American Realities* Cambridge, MA, and New York: Harvard University Press and Russell Sage Foundation

Watson, J.L. (1997) *Between Two Cultures: Migrants and Minorities in Britain* Oxford: Blackwell

Weber, M. (1945) 'Science as a Vocation' in H.H. Gerth and C.W. Mills (eds) *From Max Weber: Essays in Sociology* London: Routledge & Kegan Paul

——(1949) *The Methodology of the Social Sciences* trans. Edward Shils, New York: The Free Press

Weil, P. (2002) *Qu'est-ce qu'un Français?* Paris: Grasset

Werbner, P. (1996) 'Essentialising the Other: A Critical Response' in T. Ranger, Y. Samad and O. Stuart (eds) *Culture, Identity and Politics* Aldershot: Avebury

Wetherell, M. (1998) 'Positioning and Interpretative Repertoires: Conversation Analysis and Post-Structuralism in Dialogue' *Discourse and Society* 9: 431–56

——(2003) 'Paranoia, Ambivalence and Discursive Practices: Concepts of Position and Positioning in Psychoanalysis and Discursive Psychology' in R. Harre and F. Moghaddam (eds) *The Self and Others: Positioning Individuals and Groups in Personal, Political and Cultural Contexts* New York: Praeger/Greenwood Publishers

Wetherell, M. and Potter, J. (1992) *Mapping the Language of Racism: Discourse and the Legitimation of Exploitation* London: Harvester Wheatsheaf

Wieviorka, M. (1984) *Les Juifs, la Pologne et Solidarnosc* Paris: Denoël

——(1991) *L'Espace du racisme* Paris: Seuil (in English *The Arena of Racism* London: Sage)

——(1993) *Racisme et modernité* Paris: La Découverte

——(ed.) (1994) *Racisme et xénophobie en Europe* Paris: La Découverte

——(2000) 'Contextualizing French Multiculturalism and Racism' *Theory, Culture and Society* 17, 1: 157–62

Wieviorka, M., Bataille, P., Jacquin, D., Martuccelli, D., Peralva, A. and Zawadzki, P. (1992) *La France Raciste* Paris: Le Seuil

Williamson, J. (1984) *New People: Mulattoes and Miscegenation in the United States* New York: New York University Press

Willis, P. (1977) *Learning to Labour* Farnborough: Saxon House

Willis, P. and Trondman, M. (2000) 'Manifesto for Ethnography' *Ethnography* 1, 1: 5–16

Wilson, W.J. (1974) 'The New Black Sociology: Reflections on the "Insiders" and "Outsiders" Controversy' in J.E. Blackwell and M. Janowitz (eds) *Black Sociologists: Historical and Contemporary Perspectives* Chicago, IL: University of Chicago Press

——(1996) *When Work Disappears* New York: Knopf

Winant, H. (1994) 'Racial Formation and Hegemony: Global and Local Developments' in A. Rattansi and S. Westwood (eds) *Racism, Modernity and Identity on the Western Front* Cambridge: Polity

Withold de Wenden, C. (1992) 'Les Associations 'beur' et immigrées, leurs leaders, leurs stratégies' *Regards sur l'actualité* La Documentation Française, p. 178

Withold de Wenden, C. and Body-Gendrot, S. (forthcoming) *La Sensibilisation et la formation envers les discriminations dans la fonction publique: le cas de la police* Paris: GELD

Withold de Wenden, C. and Leveau, R. (2000) *La Beurgeoisie* Paris: ED CNRS

Witte, H. d. (1999) '"Alledaags" racisme in Belgie' ['Everyday' Racism in Belgium] *Migrantenstudies* 15, 1: 2–27

Wodak, R. and van Dijk, T.A. (eds) (2000) *Racism at the Top. Parliamentary Discourses on Ethnic Issues in Six European States* Klagenfurt/Celovec, Austria: Drava

Wolf, D.L. (ed.) (1996) *Feminist Dilemmas in Fieldwork* Boulder, CO: Westview Press

Wong, P., Lai, F., Lin, T. and Nagasawa, R. (1998) 'Asian Americans as a Model Minority' *Sociological Perspectives* 41, 1: 95–118

Wood, B. (1995) *Women's Work, Men's Work: The Informal Slave Economies of Lowcountry Georgia* Athens: University of Georgia Press

Woodward, C.V. (1966) *The Strange Career of Jim Crow* New York: Oxford University Press

Wrench, J. (1996) *Preventing Racism at the Workplace. A Report on 16 European Countries* Dublin: European Foundation for the Improvement of Living and Working Conditions

Young, Jr., A. (1999) 'Navigating Race: Getting Ahead in the Lives of "Rags to Riches" Young Black Men' in M. Lamont (ed.) *The Cultural Territories of Race* Chicago, IL: University of Chicago Press

Zerbisias, A. (1990) 'CBC to Re-enact Manitoba Murder' p. B1 in the *Toronto Star*

Index